A NATURAL HISTORY OF THE STUDIO

A NATURAL HISTORY OF THE STUDIO

WILLIAM KENTRIDGE

Slade Lectures at Oxford University

2024

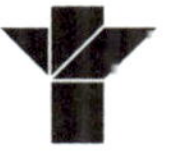

First published in trade paperback in Great Britain in 2026 by
Grove Press UK, an imprint of Grove Atlantic

10 9 8 7 6 5 4 3 2 1

A CIP catalogue record for this book is available from the British Library.

Trade paperback ISBN: 978 1 80471 125 5
E-book ISBN: 978 1 80471 126 2

Printed in Slovenia, by DZS Grafik

Grove Press UK
Ormond House
26–27 Boswell Street
London
WC1N 3JZ

www.atlantic-books.co.uk

Product safety EU representative: Authorised Rep Compliance Ltd., Ground Floor,
71 Lower Baggot Street, Dublin, D02 P593, Ireland. www.arccompliance.com

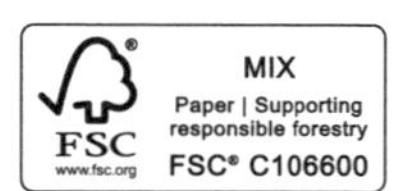

FOREWORD

How do you dance a Rorschach test? A striking – though in this case typical – question posed by William Kentridge at one point during his fifth "Slade Lecture."

The Slade Lectures at the University of Oxford, an annual lecture series devoted to art and art history, have been an institution ever since John Ruskin's first series in 1870. In 2022, the baton was passed on to Kentridge, but the global COVID pandemic forced the rescheduling of the event to January and February 2024. His first lecture was on the 17th of January, and the sixth and final one on the 21st of February.

Kentridge named the series as a whole "A Natural History of the Studio," a title which demonstrates a keen sense of irony. "Natural history" has a grandiose, authoritative ring to it, which is at odds with the small and private idea of the studio – a personal clutter, breeding ground, sanctuary.

Born in Johannesburg, South Africa, in 1955, Kentridge grew up in a nonreligious Jewish family, although, as he writes, "it wasn't that Judaism or Jewishness was expunged. I had a secular Jewish childhood – holidays celebrated, a Bris, a Bar Mitzvah." His parents were "committed liberals," both lawyers (his father had studied law at Oxford after World War II) who devoted themselves to helping victims of the apartheid regime. So from a young age, Kentridge was instilled with a political awareness that was naturally linked to the importance of fighting injustice – something that was not self-evident in young white South Africans of that time – but from the very outset, he was drawn to the arts, to the world of imagination. After completing a degree in Politics and African History he decided to study fine arts. In his final Slade lecture, "A defence of optimism," Kentridge talks affectionately about his elderly father, who is still sceptical of what his now world-famous son does for a living.

At a young age, Kentridge began exploring the world of film and theatre – as a student member of various theatre companies, he considered becoming an actor. His budding artistic activities already included painting, too. Everything fell into place when he discovered the possibilities of charcoal. With charcoal and paper at the core, there was suddenly a space, a voice of his own – unexpected possibilities and unprecedented freedoms. Charcoal allowed you not just to draw, but also to rub out what you'd made, to add to it, to simulate movement, to transform, without completely erasing the previous image, just as histories cannot completely be erased and forgotten. In short, charcoal lent itself perfectly to highlighting the "making process," a key aspect of Kentridge's practice.

The stop-motion films, and ink and charcoal animations that gained him worldwide recognition in the mid-nineties, construct the mental, bleak landscape of apartheid South Africa. Nothing but the black and grey tones of the charcoal, except for some bright blue highlights here and there. His working and thinking processes are visible, nothing looks "finished."

Myriad books have been written about the meaning and allure of Kentridge's enigmatic, engaged and dynamic work, and he has given countless interviews. However, in these six Slade lectures, the artist lightheartedly, meanderingly unfolds an intimate poetics linked to South Africa, to Johannesburg, to political interests, to personal histories, and above all, to the intimate space that is the studio. He speaks animatedly about the importance of the making process and materiality. It is striking that the final result – the spectacle that we as the audience get to admire in various metropolises and leading venues – is often dealt with in just one or two sentences. It is the process which is sacred, *that* is where the pleasure lies.

Or, as Kentridge puts it in his second lecture, "Lapis lazuli": "The faster-than-one-can-write, or think, following the processes of our unconscious brain, gathering the fragments, then sending them out through the muscles of the chest, the throat, the larynx, the tongue and the lips into the world." In these lectures, Kentridge emphasizes the importance of the body, and of the studio as sanctuary. Themes emerge during the act of creating, they don't precede it. At first, this may seem strange in an artist known for his consistently surprising, exuberant, and at the same time politically charged and provocative work. But then again, it isn't that strange: the initial chaos – often nothing but the mash of a few vague ideas – from which a work grows (a drawing, a sculpture, a play, an installation, a film, an opera), is rooted in a political awareness which is already inherently present. Kentridge's interest in our forgotten, scorned fellow humans and his curiosity about histories and global interconnections are already inextricably linked to him and his way of thinking; he doesn't need to drag them in thematically or in forced ways. That is why he is able to write: "[T]he subject of the film is secondary. The outside world dissolves into the materials of the studio. How dark should the ink be? What is the kind of brush? How precise, or how loose should the work be? The fact of making it, the heat and energy of anticipation of making it, having in that an optimism."

The subject is secondary, however remarkable that may sound if we consider, for instance, his impressive *Black Box/Chambre Noire* (2005), about the Herero people in South West Africa (present-day Namibia) who were exterminated by the German colonial power in 1904. No, it's not art for art's sake. It's about a form of optimism (or, a longing) which is "inherent in working in the studio." As Kentridge puts it: "An optimism present in the very act of making a work. An optimism of agency in the arm moving across the paper (the notebooks in which I write).

Whether the drawing is a jar of peonies or a bleak landscape, the very act of making something rather than leaving the paper blank implies (amongst many other things to be sure) a confidence in some future. The drawing finished – of looking at something now there that before was only potential (even if the viewer is only the artist himself)."

No artist can manage without a studio. It is where the world, in Kentridge's words, becomes "construction rather than discovery." It is not just where works are made, but also where meaning emerges. It is where time can expand, can contract, can be held, can be made material. It is where the self can split, "one self walking around the room trying to will a thought or series of thoughts into coherence, whilst another voice, another self, admonishes them for the inadequacy of their efforts." It is where the artist becomes "both patient and analyst." In short, "a safe space for stupidity" and accordingly, a metaphor for the enigma of our creativity, which is a state of mind.

The studio is a place where the question "How do you dance a Rorschach test?" does not sound strange or stupid; where, on the contrary, it is a natural result of improvisation, of interaction, of levity and humour, of adding to and colouring in. The question symbolizes Kentridge's groundbreaking, absurd, and tragic constructions, about a person who has no choice but to be his own patient and analyst.

Together, these six lectures sketch a portrait of "the artist as daredevil," who has less faith in ideas than in improvisation, who cherishes the unexpected connection that emerges when you work with others. After all, our ideas may be necessary, but they are also staggeringly limited, whereas our capriciousness has no bounds.

"When I was three years old, I wanted to be an elephant. I failed at that. So, I was reduced to being an artist," Kentridge remarks in his wonderful film *Self-Portrait as a Coffee-Pot* (2022), which is really a cinematic rendition of the Slade lectures. It is not entirely coincidental that both the lecture series and the film are inextricably linked to the gloomy and unnatural years in which the world was in lockdown due to COVID-19.

In both cases, we are privileged to see and experience up close what that is, exactly: a person who plays against all the odds.

We, too, are that person – or we should want to be.

– Alfred Schaffer

researchers [...] cal Research Council (SAMRC) raising concerns that scientific studies into the efficacy of Covid-19 jabs and the transmissibility of the disease could be held back.

In a media statement on Monday, the SAMRC said the department of health had blocked access to data on [...] electronic vaccina[tion] system to it[s] [...]

[...]entist D[...] "important for rese[arch...] have access to information about who has received the vaccine so that we can link this with the data that we have on breakthrough inf[ectio]ns and deaths. If [...] put [...] data [...] get a picture [...] [va]ccines work, [...] [real]ly important [...]

routine access to home affa[irs] data on jab[s] for resear[ch] [...]

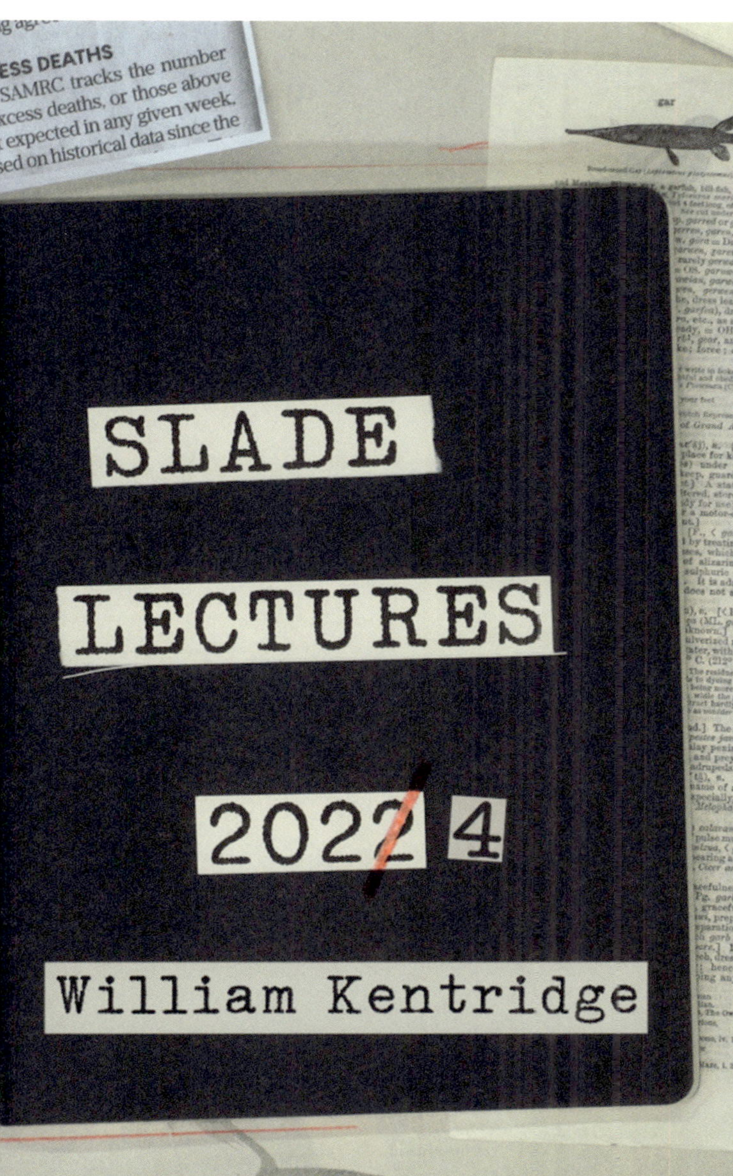

SLADE
LECTURES
2022/4
William Kentridge

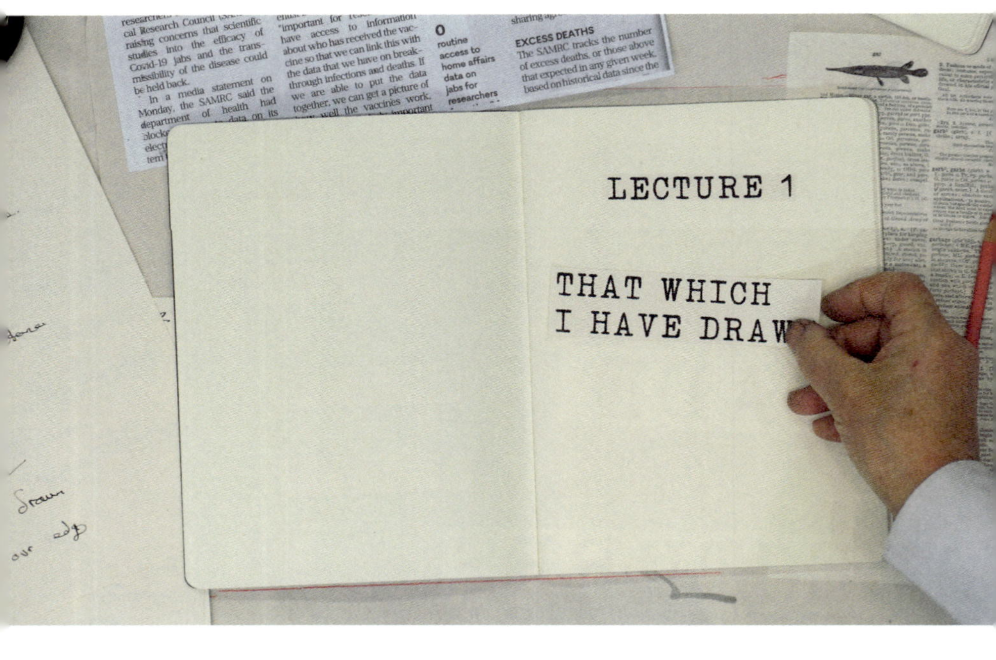

LECTURE 1

THAT WHICH
I HAVE DRAW

THAT WHICH I HAVE DRAWN

The heaviest book on the shelves of my childhood home was the *Shorter Oxford English Dictionary*, a thousand-page, six-kilogram behemoth. Its authority was not just in its weight, but also its stern dark blue covers. *The Oxford Companion to English Literature*, *The Oxford Companion to Music*, were smaller volumes that stood next to it, also in their dark livery.

The authority was this: If this book was the shorter dictionary, how hopelessly authoritative and authoritarian must be the longer dictionary (*The Oxford English Dictionary on Historical Principles*)?

Apparently, it is conventional wisdom to break down a ganglion (a swelling of the wrist) with a hard thwack of the family bible. We had no such bible, but I could imagine the damage done, healing or otherwise, with a blow from our dictionary.

Years later I started drawing on the pages of encyclopedias and dictionaries. There were many copies of the *Shorter Oxford English Dictionary* on the shelves of secondhand bookshops – why go to the library when all the words are in your pocket on your phone? I think part of the pleasure of drawing on these pages (apart from the tooth of the paper, the grid of the text) was resisting the weight of these words – a new thinking inscribed over the old.

Oxford University has always held a powerful aura for me. My father studied jurisprudence there after the Second World War. My sister also "read" English at Lady Margaret Hall; my daughter did a master's degree at St Anthony's. The family stories, the images of the ancient colleges, were irresistible.

While South Africa is no longer a British colony, there remains a strong element of provincial awe for the metropolitan centre, for Oxford as the Ur-university. As if we should always be trying to catch up (the way a child thinks eventually they will catch up to the age of an older sibling). A hopeless task. The University of the Witwatersrand in Johannesburg, where I did an undergraduate degree in Politics and African History, is just one hundred years old. All Souls College, to which I was attached in 2024 when delivering these lectures, was founded in 1438 (to pray for the sons of Englishmen killed in the Battle of Agincourt). How could we compete with this? Or with the procession of the Mallard, an All Souls ritual that takes place once every hundred years?

The connections to Oxford were not just my father's stories of his time in college (there is a hazy mix of his stories and the late afternoon punting on the river, a college tea, that fill so many English novels). There is also the Rhodes Scholarship (a scholarship endowed by an imperial mining magnate for South African students to study at Oxford), a very direct South African connection to the university. As an undergraduate I applied for this scholarship, unsuccessfully. One of a series of saving failures that led me or reduced me to being an artist.

And so the overdetermined pleasure of being let loose in the college hallways as an artist, certainly not as a scholar, to give these lectures. Fifty years later, getting into Oxford through the back door.

To begin

In preparation for these lectures, I made a list of projects, drawings, films, installations and performances I could use as the
spine of these talks – each lecture having a project, to be used
both as a reference to what I was talking about, and also as raw
material with which to think. Thinking in cardboard, or breath,
or ink, or charcoal, or gesture. I wrote down all the projects I've
done over the last ten years.

But then the list expanded from a list of specific films and
installations and theatre productions to a larger list of all the
things I had drawn in my forty-seven years in the studio.

I have drawn:
AN ACACIA TREE,
A PAPINO,
TWO LOVERS,
A PINSTRIPED SUIT,
A MAN IN A PINSTRIPED SUIT,
A COFFEE-POT,
ANOTHER COFFEE-POT,
THIRTY-EIGHT RHINOCERI.

A list many pages long.

A self-portrait in the third person

One can make a self-portrait out of these objects, these drawings,
everything that emerges in pencil or charcoal; or rather one
can't escape these being a self-portrait of the *longue durée*, in the
way the books you have read also become one's biography; the

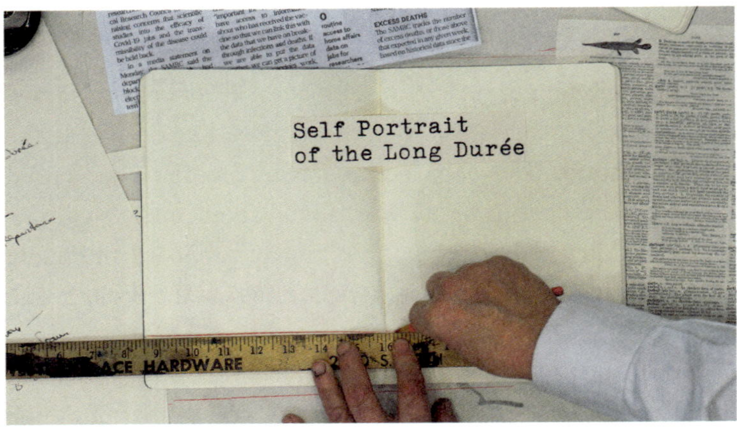

shelves with particular, familiar volumes being another kind of likeness. One is aware of the shelves filled with the books one has read, the books one always means to read, and the ever-larger collection of books one knows one will never read, but one still wants on the shelves. There is the visual memory of the shelves of books, but also an intimation of the weight, the heft of all the words in them.

I am sceptical of Kindle-reading, or reading on screens, and writing, too. The changeability of the screens makes me mistrust them. I mistrust the slipperiness of the screen, because the slipperiness of a screen becomes a slippage of memory. Marginal notes don't find a purchase, the way they do in a book. A phrase a third of the way down the left-hand page, three-fifths of the way through the book – these disappear on the screen. I also mistrust what I write on a screen. I write these notes with a fountain pen. It is more difficult to escape your own stupidity or confront it. (Much of this series of lectures will be trying to find a defence of this evident stupidity.)

More about the fountain pen: it pushes thinking farther up the arm, not just your knuckles working on a keyboard; at least an elbow, a change of pressure that comes from the shoulder.

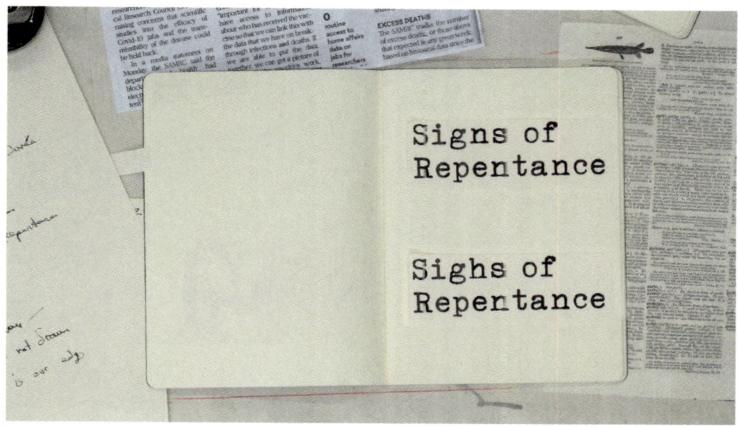

The possibility of uncertain thought, where the speed of the pen outruns the fine control in the effort to write as fast as one thinks, and one gains a productive illegibility. Did I write, SIGHS OF REPENTANCE or SIGNS OF REPENTANCE? MAYHEM AND SLAUGHTER may also be MAYHEM AND LAUGHTER.

But if one can make a biography out of what one has drawn, one can also make a negative biography, a description of the self by everything that is outside it, by that which has not been drawn.

That which I have drawn:
AN ANGEL WRITING,
A CROWD IN A LANDSCAPE,
A COW IN THE WAVES,
A TAPE RECORDER,
THE UNION BUILDINGS IN PRETORIA,
ANOTHER RHINOCEROS,
A *CHAISE LONGUE*,
A SIDE OF BEEF,
MARCUS AURELIUS AND A GARIBALDI,
THE FALLS OF AN AFRICAN RIVER.

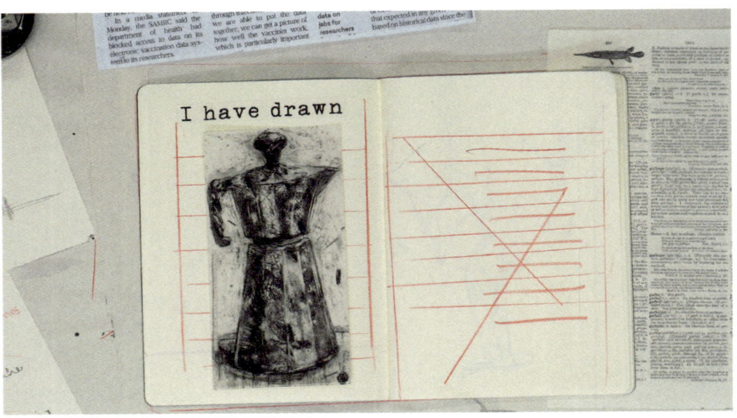

I have drawn

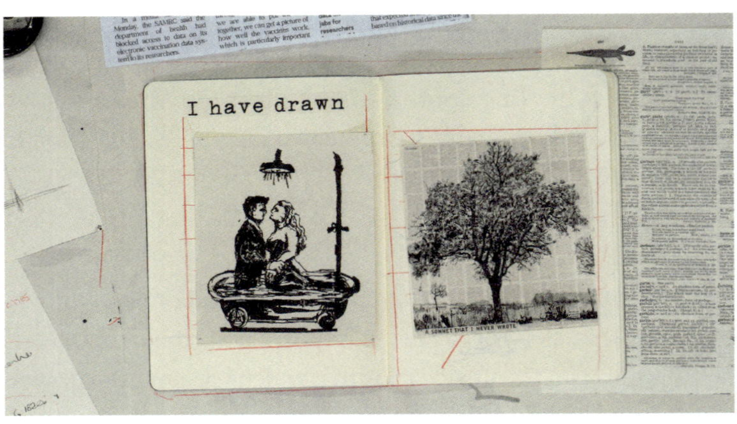

I have drawn
A SONNET THAT I NEVER WROTE.

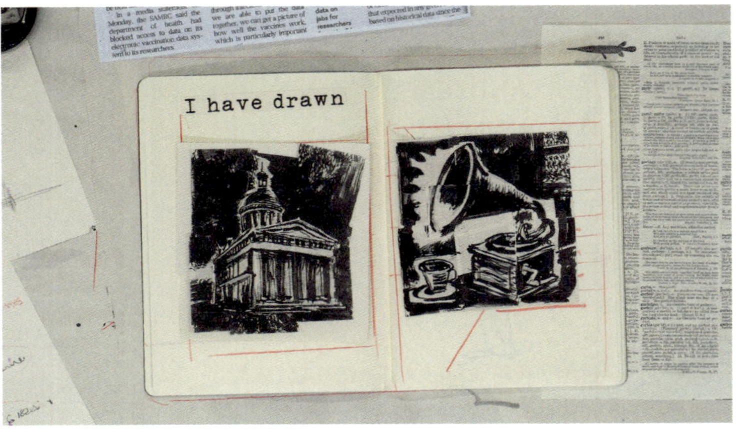

I have drawn

THAT WHICH I HAVE DRAWN

That which I have not drawn:
THE QUEEN OF ENGLAND,
A PHOTOSTAT MACHINE,
A BEEF WELLINGTON,
DON BRADMAN,
A FULL ENGLISH BREAKFAST,
A SPANISH GALLEON,
A WEIMARANER,
AN ELECTRIC TOASTER,
THE MOONS OF SATURN.

I've never drawn a hippopotamus – in fact I realise I have.
I've never drawn sunrise over Cairo.

But I have drawn:
AN IRIS,
A MAN ON A BICYCLE,
A TELEPHONE EXCHANGE,
A BOWL OF PEONIES,
A MINE HEADGEAR,
A ROMAN QUINQUEREME,
A TOAST RACK,
A WILDEBEEST,
AN AMPERSAND,
THE WORLD ON ITS HIND LEGS,
MY WIFE IN THE BATH,
GOETHE IN ITALY.

I have not drawn:
WAGNER . . . IN FACT, I HAVE DRAWN WAGNER,
A COACH-AND-FOUR,
THE YORKSHIRE MOORS,
EMMA,

What is of us, and what is not? Where to find our edge? This is another theme of these talks: What is me and what is the world beyond me? And particularly, what are the negotiations that happen at this border, the meeting point where the world comes towards us, and we go out to meet it?

In this regard, we can think of a drawing as a membrane, a vibrating tympanum. On one side, the world comes onto the membrane. I draw a tree. The world comes towards us with this tree. And at the same time, we project onto it not just all the trees inside us, but all the associations that the image of a tree throws up: memories of specific trees, the mulberry tree in my childhood garden, the two white stinkwoods planted in expectation of the hammock that would one day hang between them. And other less immediate associations: shade, fallen leaves, strange fruit hanging, three trees on a hilltop.

The shade of a family tree

Let us look at a tree: an oak, say (though I have not drawn an oak tree, I have drawn many oak leaves) – a very English tree for someone coming from Johannesburg, where our indigenous trees are generally short and spiky. The green of a great oak tree. These trees are enticing, unbelievably enticing, the green of deciduous trees, of European deciduous trees.

I realise that since this lecture was written I have drawn oak trees. The Quercus alba that is the tree of Orpheus (this for a production of Monteverdi's *Orfeo*), but also English oak trees in Johannesburg – all of which are dying because of an infestation of shot-borer beetle. One by one the great trees are killed, the suburban greenness collapsing.

When I was seven or eight, we went on a family picnic for my sister's birthday to a pleasure resort outside Johannesburg, Henley-on-Klip – a rare short stretch of river with willow trees, reeds, the rowing boat, an afternoon messing about in a boat. There were boiled eggs. There was salt in twists of wax paper. My father's sleeves rolled up at the oars of the rowing boat. My mother spitting cherry pips with me and my sister.

The deep reverberating pleasure (a memory sixty years old) was not just the water, the dappled light, the cosy domesticity of the family, of the rowing boat, but also a sense of rightness. This was how it was meant to be.

My grandfather on my mother's side had given me a book (*Great Landscapes*) in which there was an image of a painting by John Constable. Huge shady trees, a river, dappled light. This is where we were, in this painting of Constable, in this English idyll of rivers, trees, shade; in "this other Eden"; "this sceptred isle," "this green and pleasant land." (The chronology is out; the book came after the picnic, but the later book also constructs the memory of the earlier event.)

How did we get there?

Goose

My great-grandfather on my father's side was a *chazzan* in the synagogue (and I presume his father, too). His name was Woolf Kantorovich. He came from Lithuania to South Africa at the turn

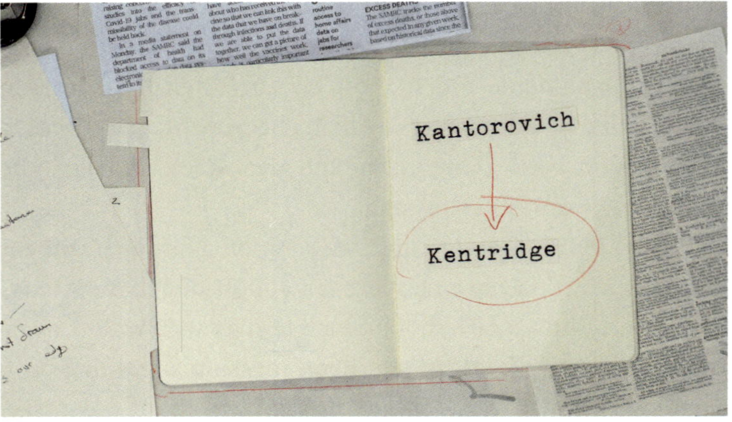

of the twentieth century, around the time of the South African War, fought by the English to gain control of the immensely rich gold fields of Johannesburg. Most Jews in South Africa came from Lithuania, Latvia, Estonia – escaping pogroms and the restrictions on their lives imposed by Czarist Russia, and attracted to South Africa by reports of newfound wealth. They also hoped to find a place where Jews would not be the lowest rung of the social ladder.

In 1908, his son – my grandfather, my father's father – went into politics. And so, to help him, the Reverend Kantorovich from Lithuania changed his name to this very English-sounding "Kentridge." It wasn't that Judaism or Jewishness was expunged. I had a secular Jewish childhood – holidays celebrated, a Bris, a Bar Mitzvah. But it was that I was bifurcated: the Jewishness circling the Englishness, or the Englishness circling the Jewishness.

Some years ago, I read a report of an Elizabethan English cookbook in which it spoke of the melancholy nature of the Jews. This melancholy, the book said, was explained by the Jews' "over-fondness for goose." And I thought, yes, that's me . . . well, duck; there were no geese to be found in South African restaurants.

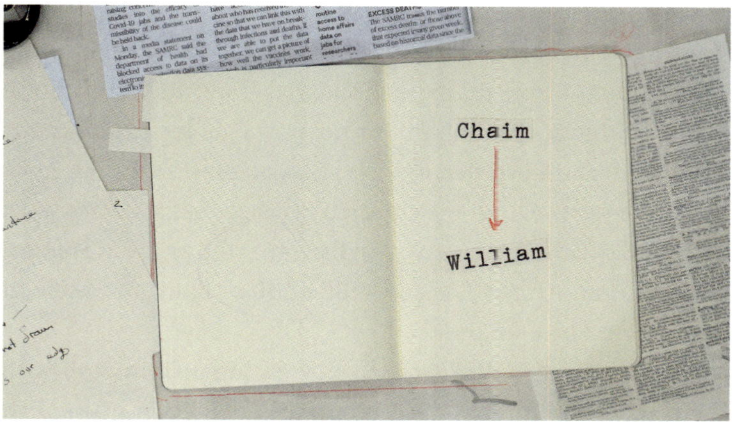

But a duck is almost a goose. Yes, I always order duck when I'm in a restaurant. I can go with this description. Now I know why I love goose. But not necessarily why I am melancholic, or even if I am.

Just William

There was no Yiddish in the house of my childhood; no shouting, no raised voices. I floated in Englishness, and largely through books. All the English children's books, but also Dickens, Brontë, and Austen. My father would read us a chapter after supper. Joe Gargery, comparing slices of bread; the rotund voice of Mr Jaggers in *Great Expectations*. My father as Darcy in *Pride and Prejudice*, but also as Gollum in *The Hobbit*. At that time there was no television in South Africa. The Nationalist government thought television an incitement to sedition. It might show black people that the rest of the world was not the same as apartheid South Africa.

Many years later, I did the same reading with my children. But what with books on tape, with television, with many other distractions, I eventually realised that they were letting me read to humour me, to humour my nostalgic recreation of my childhood, and I acceded to their silent request that I not read.

There were also all the children's classics, such as the *Wind in the Willows*. Here we were with Badger at the picnic at Henley-on-Klip in an Arthur Rackham illustration. Ratty and Mole in their rowing boat on the river.

But also in the *William* books by Richmal Crompton with their between-the-wars description and depiction of English country life: the stream, the wood, the vicarage.

I was both in and out of them. I was a William. How different would I have been if I'd still been Haim Józef Kantorovich? Haim, my Hebrew name.

But what was I to do with the vicarage, or the barn, or even those streams? There were no Bar Mitzvahs in these books. No one hid the Afikomen.

And, of course, no black people. Until the late 1980s, under apartheid, beaches, railway crossings, post offices, post office entrances, and so much of South African land were designated either "whites only" or "non-Europeans" only. The *dramatis personae* of these children's books was strictly whites only. This dislocation was obvious. There were moments of correspondence in my childhood, like that picnic, to that English world I saw, and moments that became larger and larger evidence of dislocation.

I'm interested in landscape, and in talking about being both in it and out of it, in the being distant from it – certainly about the colonial condition of being at the periphery, drawn to the centre, to its distinct and distant promise and allure, and keeping a distance, resisting the centripetal pull, to find a place at the edge of its dream and to hold on to a peripheral thinking.

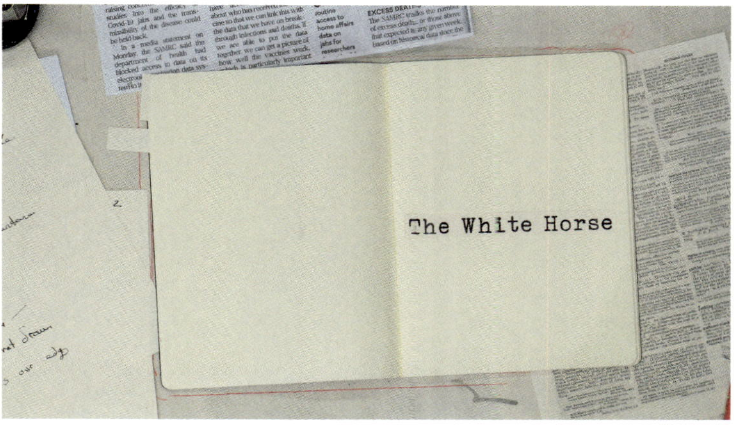

A horse in a boat

In the book of great landscapes, there was an illustration of *The White Horse* by John Constable.

The image was familiar from postcards, purchased at museum shops, pinned first to the bedroom wall and then to the studio walls; familiar from its most fragmented form, from the holiday jigsaw puzzles done on the dining room table, trying to work out which fragment of green correspondec to which tree on the box of the puzzle.

This painting and the others like it, and the birthday picnic at Henley-on-Klip, compress the air around me, fixing me in the middle, under the weight of th:s green richness. But I also step aside from this moment and watch myself in the painting, in the boat on this river.

To pause for a moment at the painting: this was the first of the famous Constable six-footers that won his eventual acceptance into the Royal Academy. The very ordinariness of the image in the picture that Constable had painted had been a block to his professional advancement. He was not painting the sublime.

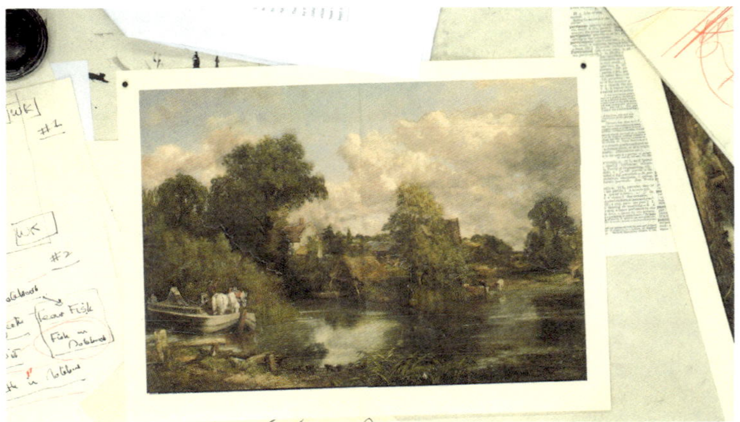

There were no Alps, no chasms, just the countryside around the River Stour. It's not a depiction of classical landscape *à la* Poussin and Claude Lorrain. They're both far away from this.

We see the river, a broken-down boathouse, the roof of a grander house behind the trees, a barge with a horse in it that would tow the barge. A particular breed of horses was needed to pull barges; they had to be strong enough to pull the load, and nimble enough to jump into and out of the barge when the towpath changed to the other side of the river. The painting shows one such traverse, the bargees poling the barge across the river.

The bright white of the horse certainly forms the *punctum* of the image, but as with many of the Constable paintings, the real protagonists are the trees. The clouds are a chorus behind them. The men on the barge, the cows, not even attendant lords in the staged drama – rather punctuation marks on the page.

In recent years, my studio has been filling up with trees.

Not oak or beech, rather trees of the highveld around Johannesburg and of the bushveld slightly farther away. Finding a brush with disorderly bristles to describe the mass of foliage on the tree, allowing the brush, the paper, the ink to resist the Constable lushness.

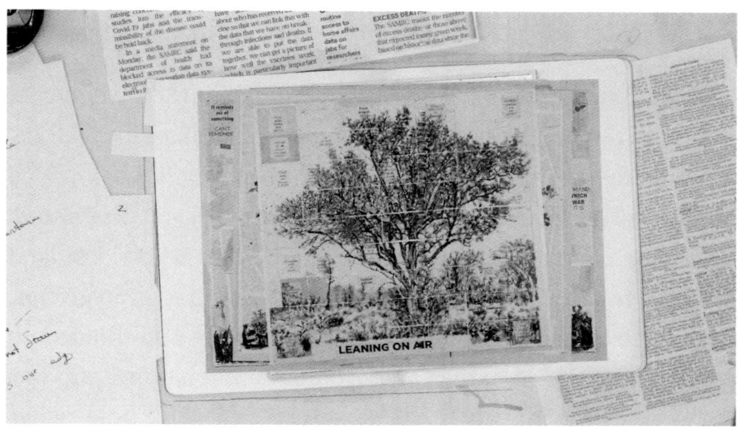

Double Vision

We invite the world in and then transform it with all the techniques and grammar of the studio. The world is reduced to paint. If we look closely, the leaves are just specific brush marks. We see paint, not leaves. But as we step back, we see not just leaves and a tree, not just paint; but we are also aware of our pleasure in this double vision, in our self-deception. We shift between seduction and a self-awareness. We can't resist the seduction. It is not an act of will or a relinquishing of will on our part. We can't stop seeing the leaves.

The seduction of the painting is both with its material – the medium, the brushwork, the texture of paint, the canvas, its depiction – and in the subject: the lush greenery of the tree, the shade, the cool stillness of the water, a seduction increased by its distance from the landscape of Johannesburg, the birthday picnic memorable for the way in which it was a momentary escape to another world.

Digging for gold

Johannesburg is a young city. It was founded in 1886 when gold was discovered. It's just under 140 years old. I have lived all my 70 years there, half the city's life. Johannesburg is a city with a purely geological *raison d'être*: what is in the rocks and the ground. There is no river, no mountain, no trade route, no port. The land has been inhabited for a millennium by different African groups. They were displaced by Afrikaner farmers in the mid-nineteenth century. From 1886 to the Great Depression, Johannesburg was the fastest growing city in the world. Unbelievable gold riches dug out of the ground, first by Cornish miners, then by African miners from South Africa, and particularly from countries around South Africa – Mozambique, a Portuguese colony; Basutoland, now Lesotho, at that time a British protectorate.

The ridges on which the city is built are now verdant: tree-lined streets, full English gardens, fortified enclaves of green and shade, bright blue swimming pools the closest thing to the rivers of Constable. But beyond these gardens the terrain is dry, trees thin; green after summer rains, but parched and bleached for most of the year. The grand houses and gated communities give way to township grids of matchbox houses that have not changed since the days of apartheid, and extensive extending settlements of shacks of corrugated iron and scrap building materials. As if the truth of the city and the country cannot be kept from rising to the surface of the ground.

Sunlight on a leaf

The gardens of the city are constructions – very beautiful constructions, many of them – but we know they are made, not found. This is not how the world is, but how we wish it could be.

The Constable landscape feels found; this is the river; these are the trees. This is how it was. He was painting what he saw. Of course, this too is an illusion: an illusion of the translation of the leaf into paint back to leaf. But it is also a different construction. The paintings are constructed, a collage – a tree moved, enlarged, reduced as the composition requires. It has the appearance of coherence, but it is stuck together from fragments. A horse drawn in March is placed on the towpath eight months later. Sunlight at noon on one tree is placed against the dusk shadows of another.

This practice of collage, of taking fragments from different sources and constructing a new image, is not new (though only with modernism did artists celebrate the practice and make it the subject itself of paintings). Caspar David Friedrich has sketch-books of particular branches, twigs, barks of different trees. The trees in his paintings are all built from these different sketches.

Editing the self

This is a natural history of painting, but also a natural history of the self. We present ourselves to the world as a coherent being. "It's so like him or her," we say of someone whose behaviour or utterances correspond to the person presented to us. But we are aware of the daily work that goes into this presentation. And long-term, how we're constituted by particular memories, hurts, stories, songs. We are always a collage under construction – taking this fragment, editing out another, consciously or unconsciously. A phrase one recognises from a parent suddenly appears to shore up a sentence. Of course, there is always a battle between these fragments: between the need to remember, the need to forget.

This is what happens in the studio. The world comes into the studio as images, photographs on the wall, as newspapers, emails, memories of conversation, books, postcards. There it is fragmented. The fragments are rearranged and sent back out into the world as a drawing, a film. We are aware of the artificiality of the construction even as we are beguiled by it. This is what the studio can show us, a process self-evident in the studio, but which can illuminate unseen processes outside it, a world as construction, rather than as discovery.

An English depression

There is another construction in the Constable. The painting was made in 1819, a year of great depression and distress in the English countryside. The economy in England was in crisis after the Napoleonic Wars. And so, the painting is also a negative portrait of the year. Everything that happened in the countryside is absent in the image. The world Constable is painting is already a nostalgia for him, for the countryside of his childhood, making his own Henley-on-Klip.

1819 was the year that the English government sent out an appeal for people wanting to emigrate and settle in South Africa. Sixty thousand people applied, and five thousand were chosen and subsequently settled on the eastern frontier of the Cape Colony. They were to be a bulwark against the Xhosa clan that resisted the expansion of the colony. The land they were brought to was inhospitable; much of it dry and not suited for farming. Many of the settlers were not farmers. Certainly, the green and pleasant land of *The White Horse* was neither their experience of England – conditions must have been insupportable to push these people to leave familiar terrain – nor was this to be found in the Eastern Cape.

The Settlers arrived to a world of dryness, thorn bushes, and an indigenous population resisting their arrival (seven frontier wars were fought in the decades subsequent to their arrival), but they brought with them a drowning weight of Englishness – no country cottages, but images of them; no ancient universities or public schools, but a desire to create them anew; not by the Settlers, but by the whole imperial machine: Governors-General, military commanders, the missionaries, the Scottish teachers, architects, civic planners.

The world they imagined was the world into which I grew: afternoon teas, days in the sun watching cricket, birthday picnic on the rowing boat. And make no mistake, it was a comfortable world to inhabit: the garden, the house, the servants.

Finding the dapple

The pleasure of the garden is still there. I'm unsure as to the origins of the pleasure of the greenness, the dapple, the coolth, the wetness. Are these learnt pleasures from the books, the stories, a world willed into existence? Or is there a somatic pleasure hardwired into all of us? Is there something in the rods and cones of our eyes that responds to the dimming of harsh sunlight in the shade? Receptors in the skin that crave the cool wetness of the river? Or do these pleasures sit in the chemistry of the brain, traces of expectations grown through stories, books, illustrations?

There is a move towards making gardens nonexotic in Johannesburg, a botanical xenophobia, to uproot and burn alien plants. I understand the artificiality of the green gardens, the dislocation from the terrain they are grown on, the fertilisers, composts, irrigation they depend on. And yet, I can't help feeling that to abandon the shade and uproot a maple to plant a thorn tree has an element of self-mortification, a wearing of a botanical hairshirt.

The landscape drawings I have made over the last decade have been prompted by this discomfort – at first a revenge at the bleakness of the land around Johannesburg, later a pleasure in this different understanding of terrain. The vision of the city when the trees die. Charcoal and ink, monochromatic media have made the landscape. The lush green reeds need oil paint.

When I started as an artist, it was accepted that oil on canvas was the trajectory of all artmaking. Drawing was a preliminary stage, printmaking a side journey. But I could not think in colour. Although I did paint in the early years as an art student, I was always held with the question: How does this painting look?

Although I work with musicians all the time, I am tone-deaf. I can hear how out of tune I am, or other singers are, but it is no help in my voice finding or holding a note. When I listen to a recording of myself, I am shocked at just how bad my voice sounds. In a similar way, I am sensitive to how colours sit next to each other, and have a great love of Matisse and other colourists, but this is no help when I have to mix colours. My hands feel like stumps mixing this mayonnaise. Using primarily the monochrome of charcoal or ink was not a choice, either formal or ethical. It was about the relief of finding charcoal and printmaking; the great pleasure of a medium with which both to make an image and a medium in which to think. The final look of the print or drawing had to take its own chances.

Something about the dryness of the charcoal and the clarity of the ink pushed me from the one kind of landscape to the other, allowing the material, the medium, to do the deciding; to discover at the end not only the image you have made, but also to find out who you are. The landscape stood in for all the other ways this Englishness arrived, the set of references – literary, visual, philosophical, emotional – that had to be overcome.

Gold had been discovered in Johannesburg in 1886. The mines showered their wealth. The English and Afrikaners,

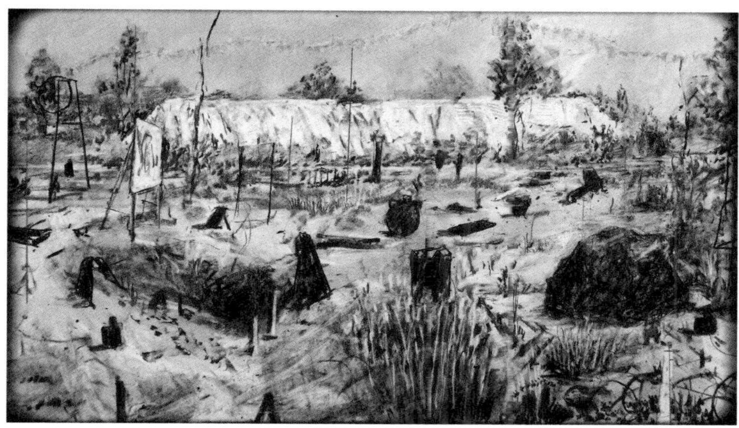

descendants of the Dutch colonists that had controlled the country, fought a war for control of this wealth (the African population, of course, were not consulted on this dispute; nevertheless, they paid a huge price in casualties during the three years of its prosecution). The *rapprochement* between the English and the Afrikaners coincided with the full disenfranchisement and confiscation of African land in 1913.

The Johannesburg Art Gallery was opened in 1915. Lady Phillips, wife of the great Randlord, Sir Lionel Phillips, who wore a ruby that once belonged to Marie Antoinette, wrote to the Randlords, demanding that they support a project of this art gallery, "or their names would live in infamy" for having made their wealth in Johannesburg and hived off to live in grand country houses in England (an accusation that still rings true today). Sir Lionel Phillips donated seven oil paintings and a collection of Dutch lace to the gallery.

The Englishness that accompanied the Settlers was at odds from the beginning with the Englishness I lived inside; a school bound up in the idea of an English public school. We had a cadet corps. We had a marching pipe band. Of course, it was an all-boy, all-white school.

My first animations were a resistance to the boredom of those hours, sunlight coming through the school windows as a double maths period continued, drawing stick figures on successive pages in the margins of school textbooks, then thumbing through the pages.

The things that still hold me today, in the animated drawings I've made on and off for thirty-six years, are essentially the same as the magic that helped me then: a magic of transformation. A palpably still drawing, a dot on a page starting to move. The drawing, the thumb, the eye, all conspiring against and for you. You have made these marks, these marginalia, and in a moment, they are so much more than you have made and so much more than the dots and stick figures. The world is both fact – the particular page and its drawing – and it is process: the page one moment, and then its transformation into movement.

Sappho's toe

Johannesburg Art Gallery was the art gallery of my childhood, the Ur-art gallery. I was always fascinated by the sculpture of Sappho with her lyre, by the sculptor Bourdelle, with her big toe polished by the hands that passed. While some things stay the same – the smell of polish on the parquet flooring, the brass hinges and clasps on the windows and their shutters, the vaulted ceiling of the Phillips Gallery, the Rodin marble bust of Miss Fairfax, it is now a museum fallen on hard times. Neglect, theft of artworks; but also the rain finding its way in through the copper roofs, a dispirited and demoralised curatorial team. When I came to draw this art gallery in 2019, it was both as a memory – its cool emptiness – but also to pin down both the state of the city and my place in it.

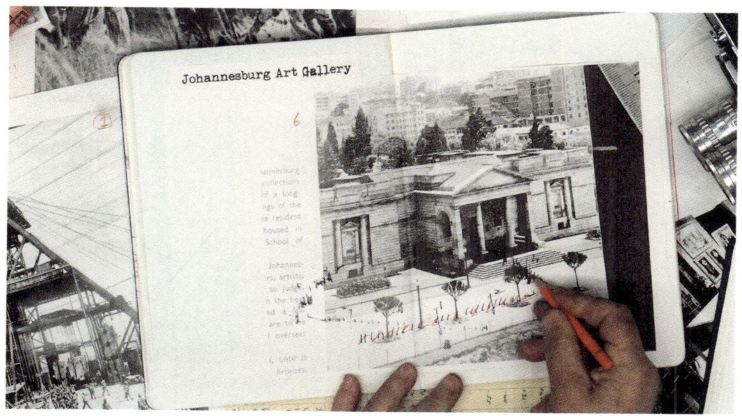

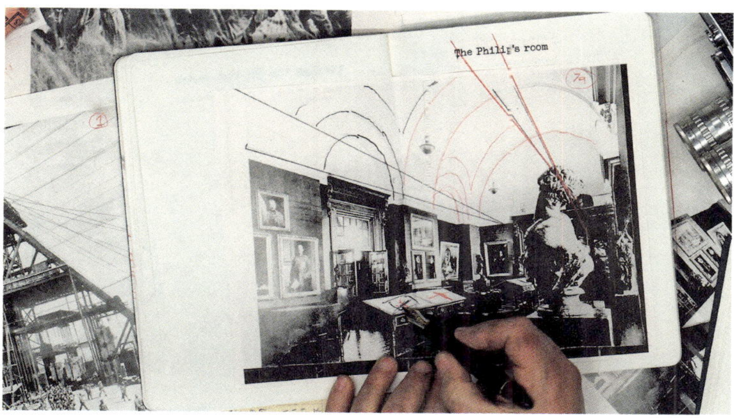

There are other decays and changes in the city. The huge man-made forest in the northern suburbs of the city is now under siege by shot-borer beetles. What city will be revealed when this canopy of green is gone? The hills of the city disappear, too. Mine dumps – the hills of the city – were reprocessed to extract the last of the gold trapped in the leftovers of the mine. I'm not interested in celebrating the decline of the gallery or the illness of the trees, but to understand the verities of the city, which seems so fragile over such an unstable construction.

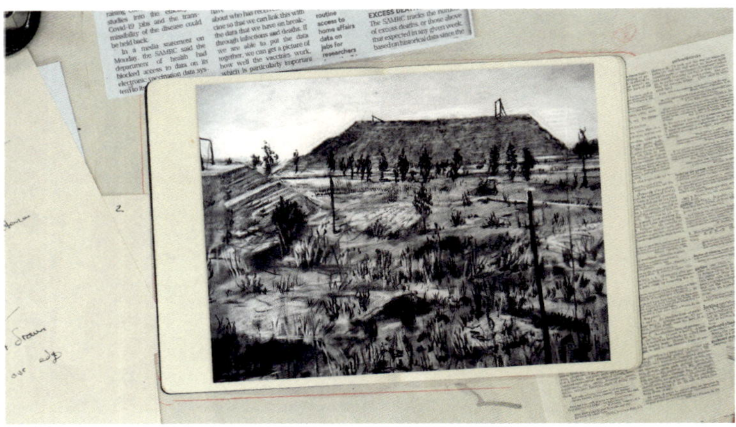

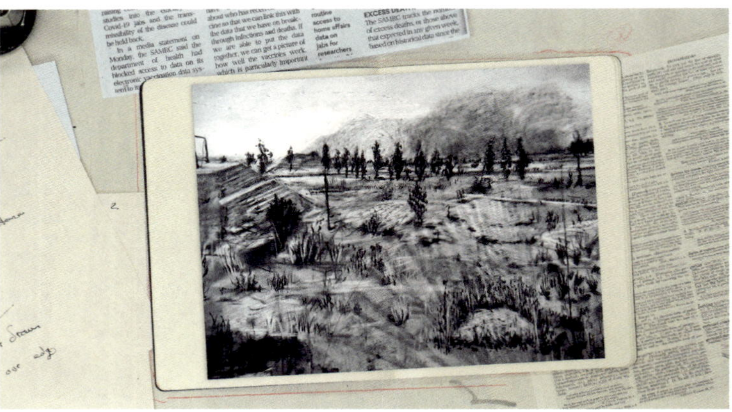

Over the century of gold mining in Johannesburg, the shafts have sunk deeper and deeper, passages dug out between the shafts, following the narrow seam of gold, a ribbon trapped by rock. On the surface there was the grid of the city roads; underground, a shadow city, both the structure and the mines themselves invisible. A city of stopes, of air shafts, of storage concourses the size of the City Hall.

Many of the miners who came to work on the mines came from Mozambique. For decades there was a train that ran from Lourenço Marques, now Maputo, to Johannesburg. It was

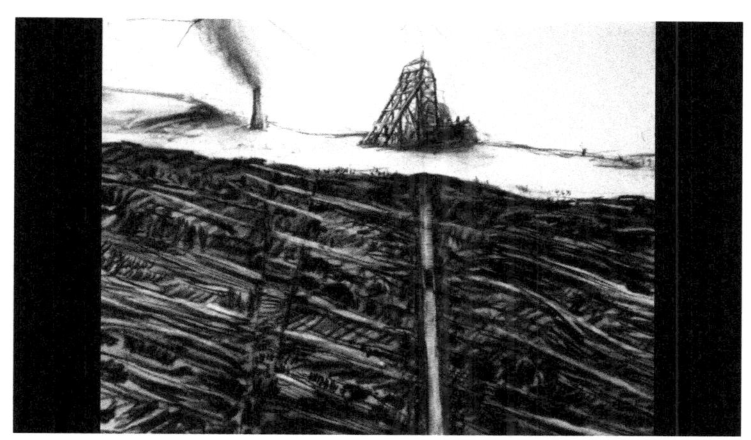

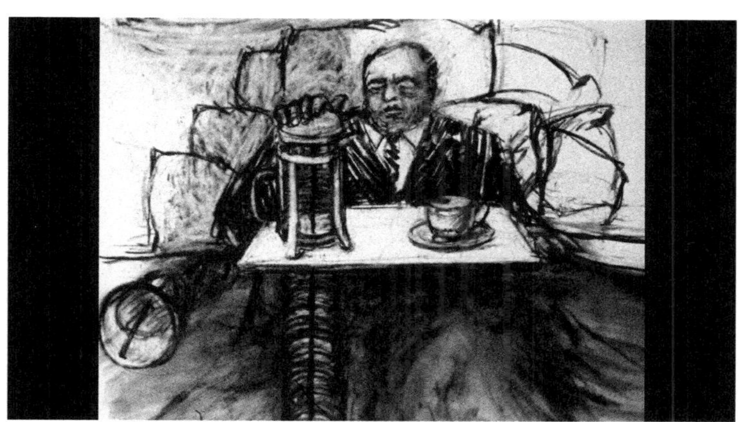

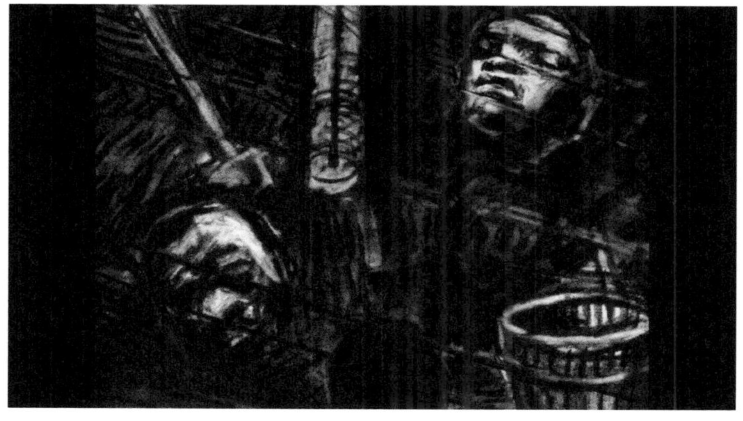

arranged that the train would arrive late at night. A tunnel out of the station was constructed, so that even the arrival of the miners would be discreet, to not disturb the sensibilities of the white citizens of the city using the station.

Thick time

In 1989, I started using a technique of charcoal animation. A drawing was made, photographed, the drawing altered by erasure or addition, and more charcoal marks added. It was photographed again, realtered and rephotographed – a walk between the camera and the drawing on the wall, repeated thousands of times. Fifteen hundred photographs, or fifteen hundred frames, is one minute of projected film.

Since then, I've made ten others of these charcoal animations for projection. The first one was made at the time of the release of Nelson Mandela. The series of films are not a diary nor a polemic, but are made from a mixture of personal impulses, a sideways look at questions in the air. They're made without script or storyboard, starting from an image – the Johannesburg Art Gallery, a glimpse at the artisanal miners in the landscape – and proceed from there, finding a form as new drawings are added, the order of different drawings rearranged in editing, other images added. The filmmaking is slow: nine months for a nine-minute film – enough time in this extended interrupted walk in the studio for images and connections to come to the surface and push the film forward.

Time changes in the studio; it expands and contracts – the thirty-six years since I started making animated films compressed into the ninety minutes of film that the series now adds up to. A gesture may take one second to perform; in its expression into

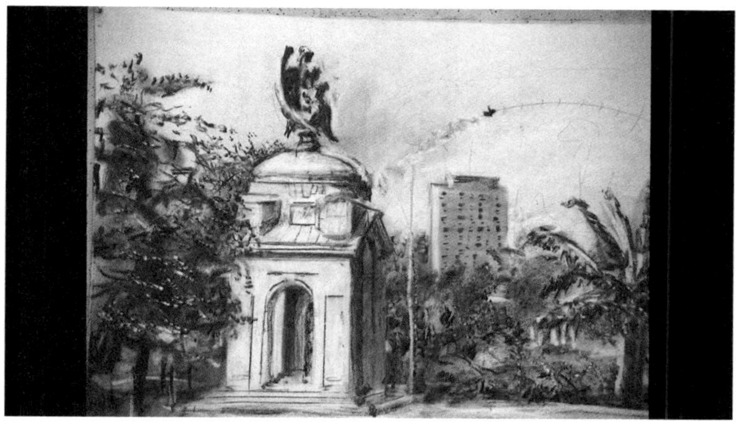

twenty-five successive frames, the drawing altered twenty-five times, it may take two days to draw. Alterations to the drawing are visible. The erasure of the charcoal is imperfect. The breaking down of time into the finite frames can be seen – a trace of time passing.

Time enters the drawing in another way, too. The agency of time changes. If there is this drawing a landscape, say, a Constable landscape, we may look at it for three seconds, or ten seconds, or even a minute. But it is our three, ten seconds; our minute. But once the drawing starts to move – the movement of leaves, a bird flying across the sky – a shift happens. The six seconds of the bird passing belong to the image.

Over the series of eleven films, many birds fly across the landscape. A bird in flight, any child knows, is easy to draw: two pencil or charcoal marks, move the marks along, change the angle of the two marks, the wing, and the bird will fly itself. This is both mimetic – it is rare not to see some bird traversing the highveld sky – but it is also a clock, marking out of time, pulling time into the film.

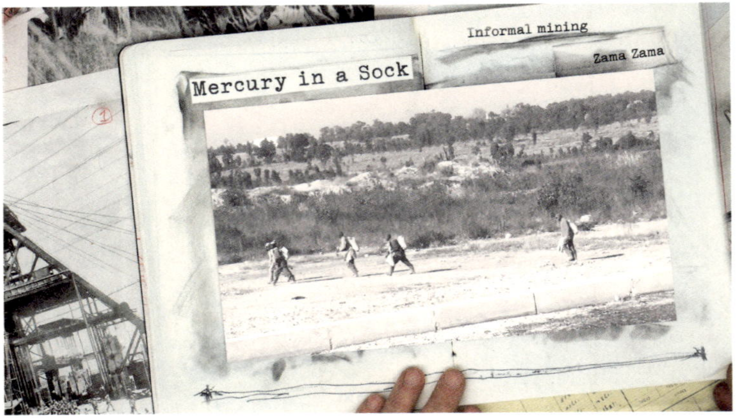

Cactus grab

Over the decades, the seams of gold on which Johannesburg sprung up have been exhausted. Shafts had to continue following the seam of gold. More and more equipment was needed to hollow out the huge quantities of rock to get at the grains of gold in it. This is the formal economy of gold. But now there is another parallel economy. Many thousands of gold gleaners work on the surface. South Africa has more than two million unemployed people. Industries have shrunk. The formal gold mining industry which used to employ three-quarters of a million miners, now uses one-tenth of that total.

These artisanal miners, illegals, or *zama-zamas*, as they're colloquially known, work on the surface digging foxholes, excavating the ground at the edges of abandoned mines, extracting out of the rocks the last gold left behind by the industrial mines. Often using just a hammer and a screwdriver, the rocks are chipped away, then ground between fragments of concrete slabs till the rock is a fine dust, then panned in an enamel dish. Mercury is added and strained through a sock. After a week, a miner may have one gram of this mercury gold amalgam, which is sold to gold dealers at the edge of the formal and informal worlds and then reenters the formal economy.

As with so many other cases, the informal sector subsidises the formal sector. In the formal sector, there are forty-ton Cactus grabs. There are trade unions, there are health programmes, there's housing. The *zama-zamas* have none of this. If they are injured, if they can't work, they starve. They are the easy targets of gangs that increasingly try to control these mining areas. It is the desperation of the underground history rising to the surface.

Main Reef Road

I have two studios. One in the garden of my house – a domestic-sized studio set in the greenness of large shade trees, shrubs and flowers. This is where the animated films are made and these lectures are written. The other studio, which I use for rehears-als of larger groups and for sculptures, is downtown on Main Street, part of Main Reef Road, the road that followed the gold seam from mine to mine. On the way to the studio, I pass the Johannesburg Art Gallery in the middle of the ranks of minibus taxis. On the way back from the studio, I pass on the highway one of the old, now-abandoned mines occupied by twenty or thirty *zama-zamas*, hidden up to the waist in the foxholes in which they dig and excavate the rock cupful by cupful.

Johannesburg as a city is both wonderful and terrible. It has huge poverty and inequality. There is a geographic divide between wealth – protected by high walls, electric fences, private security guards – and extreme poverty. There is violence against foreign citizens and its own. This has not changed in the thirty years since the first democratic election in 1994. (A difference to be sure, is that the black middle class, in terms of numbers, not wealth, is the same size as the white middle class.) But the desperation and poverty is immense.

But there is also a huge energy generated by these very circumstances. A need for artists, dancers, actors to practice their art. There is a huge influx of people from other parts of Africa, mainly to Johannesburg. For many, Johannesburg is still seen as the City of Gold. The mix of formal and informal economy seems a premonition of what is coming to large areas of the world. It is still a place of uncertain endings. For all the cautious pessimism that pervades the city, there are enough cracks and margins for the optimistic energy of making and collaboration to flourish.

This energy is there in the work of the studio – in the tension between the Constable painting and the dry highveld landscape, between the heft of the dictionary and the relief of dodging its fall, between the dense foliage and the bristle of the brush.

These reflections about my childhood, the landscape, the city, the gold mining, move through my head from memory to dream, to conscious reflection, carrying the walk around the studio from camera to drawing, from a photo pinned to the wall of the studio to the sofa, where the afternoon siesta lets the images and thoughts rearrange themselves.

They emerge as the elements of a film to be made, but they run parallel to even more incoherent promptings – this image, not that; this transformation, this cut between images; this sound, not that sound – that constitute the thinking of the drawings or the film. The Constable is the drawing I have not made. But the drawings and film that emerge are not its opposite, nor its flayed skeleton, but rather a fragment projected by its illuminating shadow.

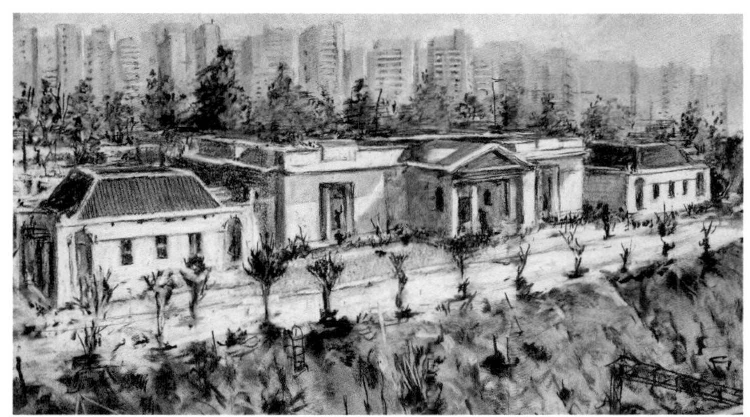

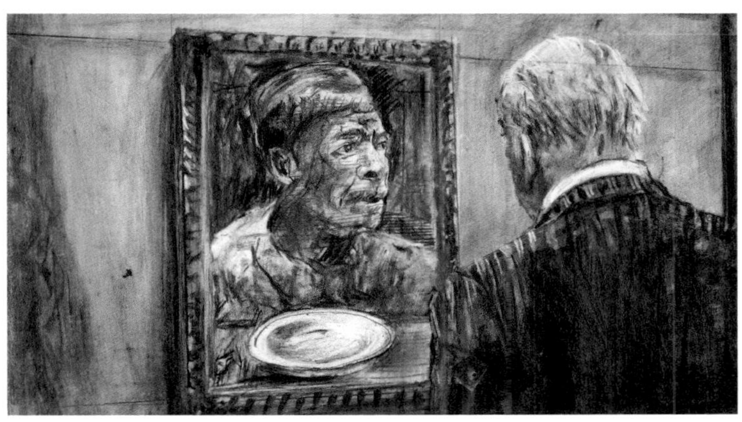

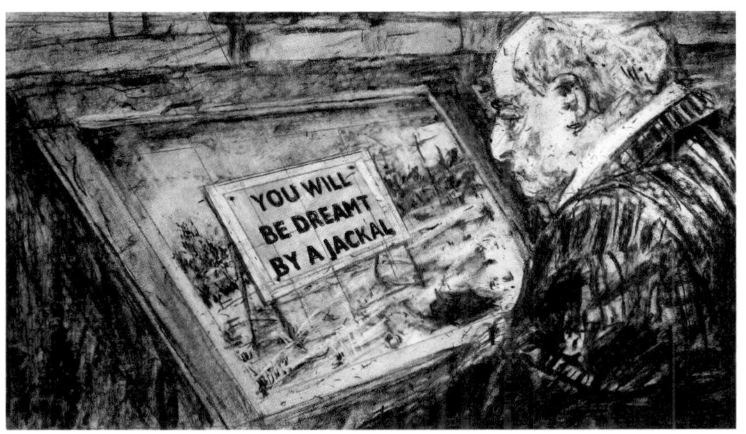
YOU WILL
BE DREAMT
BY A JACKAL

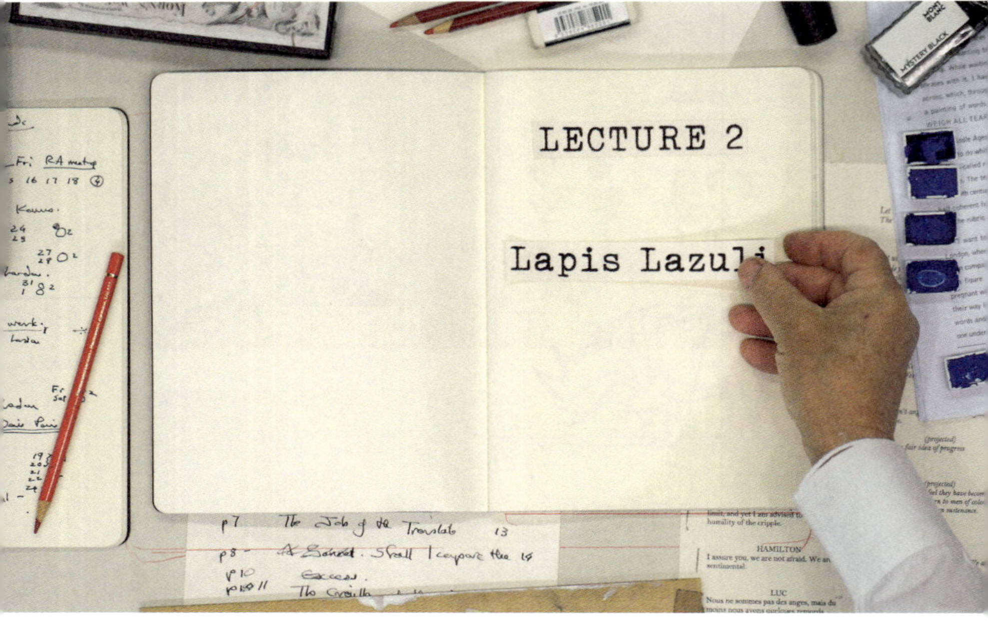

LECTURE 2

Lapis Lazuli

LAPIS LAZULI

Some years ago, two friends gave me a block of watercolour, pure lapis lazuli from Afghanistan. Lapis lazuli is a precious pigment used sparingly in Renaissance painting, now more generally replaced by French ultramarine. But there is an intense blueness in lapis, a colour coming off the paper towards you that is unmatched by any synthetic colour. In projections and photography and printing, this blue always loses its power.

I don't use colour in my drawings. But I painted some squares and circles to see the colour I was given. I was caught, wanting to devour the blue and not knowing how to bring it into anything I was drawing. While waiting to solve what I should do with the blue, I started painting texts and phrases with it. I have a notebook in which I write down phrases or sentences I have come across, which, through their idiosyncrasy, or particularities, feel they need to be held, put into a painting of words to be used later.

GOD'S OPINION IS UNKNOWN, a Setswana proverb.
WEIGH ALL TEARS, a line from a poem by Czesław Miłosz.
YOU WILL BE DREAMT BY A JACKAL.

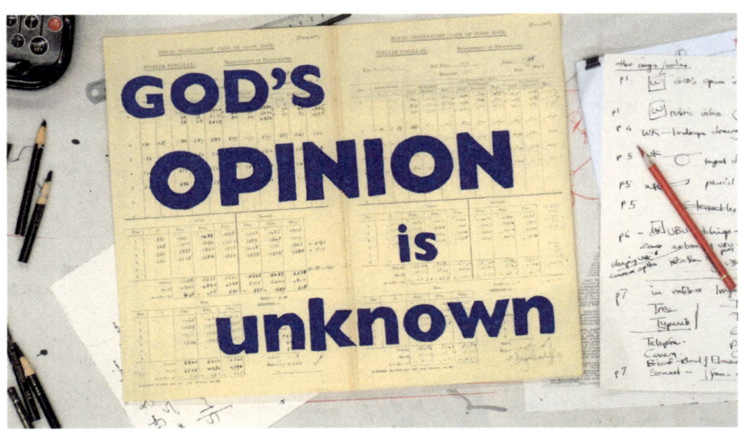
GOD'S
OPINION
is
unknown

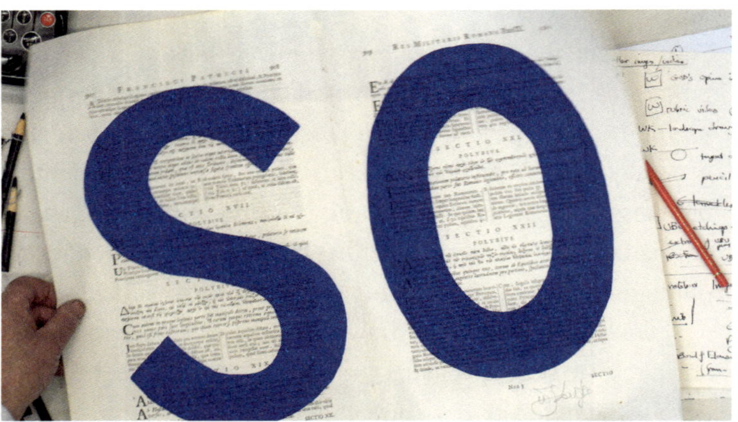
SO

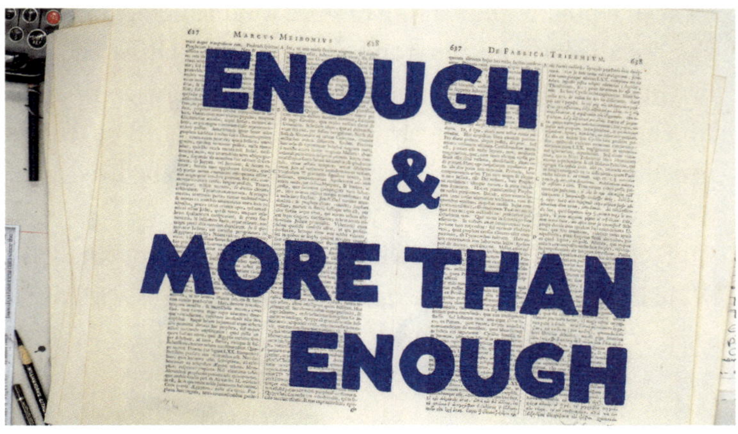
ENOUGH
&
MORE THAN
ENOUGH

In the Middle Ages, books of prayer would have both the words of the prayer and instructions on what to do while praying (a kind of stage instruction). These were painted or printed in red ink, in so-called rubrics. I think of my blue texts as rubrics, something at the edge of discursive language. The texts are generally painted on the pages of old books: religious texts from the eighteenth century, or a record of stargazing from Cape Town in the nineteenth century. A half-coherent fragment, a half-coherent thought, on top of a considered older thinking.

Phrases like:
THE OLD GODS HAVE RETIRED
YESTERDAY'S GOOD IDEA
STRUGGLE FOR A GOOD HEART
A BOX OF SHAME
HISTORY ON ONE LEG
FIND THE LESS GOOD IDEA
RECREATIONAL DANGER
A SAFE SPACE FOR STUPIDITY
DEFENSIVE SLEEPING
THE PLEASURES OF SELF-DECEPTION
ENOUGH AND MORE THAN ENOJGH

I am interested in coherence and incoherence. The limitations of coherence, and the productive possibilities of incoherence. The irresistible pressure to find coherence and avoid the anxiety of incoherence. I am caught between needing a manageable progression of thought and argument, and a wish to allow the fragments to fall where they may. To demonstrate literally the panic inside our rational movement through the world.

Circling the studio

But I want to retreat, to go backwards. The start of this lecture was written in my flat in London, where my wife and I were isolated in COVID quarantine. The studio in the flat is a small room compared to the garden studio in Johannesburg: forty-two paces to circle the studio if one walks in a figure eight. On my table were my notebooks, waiting for words; a full fountain pen, pregnant with all possibilities. But the chair resisted me. I walked around the studio, gathering the words and thoughts in this walking (2,400 steps, according to my phone) – all the small tasks one undertakes to avoid sitting down.

There is a kind of Ur-language. Testing some phrases in my head: "Some years ago, a friend gave me a block of lapis lazuli . . ." "Lapis lazuli is the brightest . . ." "I have never seen a blue as bright as . . ." Phrases or sentences, but more than that, a sensing in the muscles. Somehow in the pectoral muscles, in the tastebuds, a move and a tensing, trying to pull the different thoughts together. Holding on to a thought the way one tries to hold on to a dream as you wake. The thought was there, a clarity. Ah – now it is gone. *Talk about the lapis blue, then about the periaqueductal grey.* As I pace the desk, I write "lapis blue – periaqueductal grey." One part of my head repeats, *start with the lapis.* The other part is off on its own journey: "Mr. Leopold Bloom ate with relish the inner organs of beasts and fowls." Where did *Ulysses* come from, out of the blue? A glance at the table, notebook still untouched.

My thinking is stopped by watching myself walking, and writing. To will a coherence for thought. The unmoving me at the centre of the room instructs the other self, circling like a circus horse trotting around the ring at the end of a rope. *Talk about the words,* I instruct myself.

Translation. Tell them about translation in the studio, about the Markov blanket, about images, from ink to sound, sound to ink to colour, about Kurt Schwitters' Ursonate. *Check the date of* Ursonate *and* Ulysses. I run out of thought. *Now start.* I don't.

Maresfield Gardens in Hampstead. The great secular rabbi Sigmund Freud. No, no. "You are just avoiding the book and the pen." Jewishness in Englishness was the previous lecture.

Did I just say that?

I write down "procrastination." I write down "productive procrastination." Then it finally begins, the first words on paper addressing, in this case, words.

This split of the self, one self walking around the room trying to will a thought or series of thoughts into coherence, whilst another voice, another self, admonishes them for the inadequacy of their efforts, is a common sensation, particularly in the studio.

There is the artist as worker, charcoal drawing, close to the paper. And then as the artist steps back a pace or two to see how the drawing looks, a second self emerges, the critic, who sees at once the weaknesses or mistakes of the work on the wall and sends the first self back to the drawing with a series of instructions (move the horizon down, the cloud is too dark) or admonishes, "How can you still get it so wrong after so many years?"

Language, or language in the studio, is the subject of this second essay. Language – of course, using language to discuss the studio; but also, the processes of the studio: to think about language, the translation from word to lapis lazuli; about the colour, but the colour also changing one's sense of the words. The studio is a place of making, but also a place of making meaning. It is a space and a technique of translation. It starts with blankness, with incoherence, the blank sheet of paper, the words on the paper, hoping they will lead to a coherence, or at least to a provocative incoherence. If the drawing is the finished sentence or the paragraph, then the process of making the drawing can reveal the invisible process behind the spoken or written word. The faster-than-one-can-write, or think, following the processes of our unconscious brain, gathering the fragments, then sending them out through the muscles of the chest, the throat, the larynx, the tongue and the lips into the world. The words come before realising what we are going to say. "Did I just say that? Not me. I would never say such foolishness. If I was in charge of my words, they would be so much more persuasive."

Periaqueductal grey

This is all slowed down in the studio. The drawing is the thinking before the thought is conscious. The walk around the studio is the preamble even to this.

There is a dispute in neurology as to where the font of consciousness lies. Conventional wisdom has it proceed from perception outwards, the gathering of information about the world, which transforms eventually into awareness of the self, seeing many birds in order to understand bird-ness. But there is another theory that feels much closer to me. Consciousness, this line of argument goes, starts not from the frontal lobes, the most sophisticated part of our mind, but from the periaqueductal grey, a pea-sized piece of grey matter at the brain stem, the most primitive part of our brain, a highly sensitive piece of the body. One side registers pain; the other pleasure. This is the periaqueductal grey. It moves towards and away from the world; towards warmth if we feel our temperature drop; away from the burning heat, if you're too close to the fire.

This is miles away from rational decision-making. This is the body thinking. There's an impulse, which will find its meaning later. First, a phrase and later an analysis of what it might mean. Consciousness comes from emotion, desire or repulsion. First, a drawing, and only afterwards a questioning: What does this drawing say? An impulse to make that is prior to the "what" that is made; what the subject is. The pull of the studio is central; the "what" is much less so.

It could be a text, a tree, a drawing of a coffeepot. They are all translations of a much more primitive desire to send something out into the world. This is both me and not me. Something I have made, but which is also more than me. I leave, the drawing remains – a shadow one can leave behind, or a snail trail of the passage of one's life. This is knowing our edge but working to reach through it.

We construct a Markov blanket, that membrane that defines where we end and the rest of the world begins, the edge of what we can protect against entropy. It is the job of the artist to resist entropy. This metaphoric blanket is not the outside world, but it is sensible to it, and sensitive to it, a membrane of negotiation between that which comes towards us and how we meet it. This blanket is a borderline for all life, for an amoeba, a jellyfish, a human, each resisting their private entropy. Something between us and the world.

In the studio, a drawing will stand in for this membrane; something marking the border between us and the world. This is of course a great simplification of neurology. One must understand the artist as scavenger, half-digesting other people's thoughts, taking scraps into himself. What is important here is the nourishment provided, the productivity of these metaphors, not their scientific correctness. In this case, I am held by the image of that unreachable centre in our brain, thought circling it. And of the Markov blanket, not as a statistical proposition

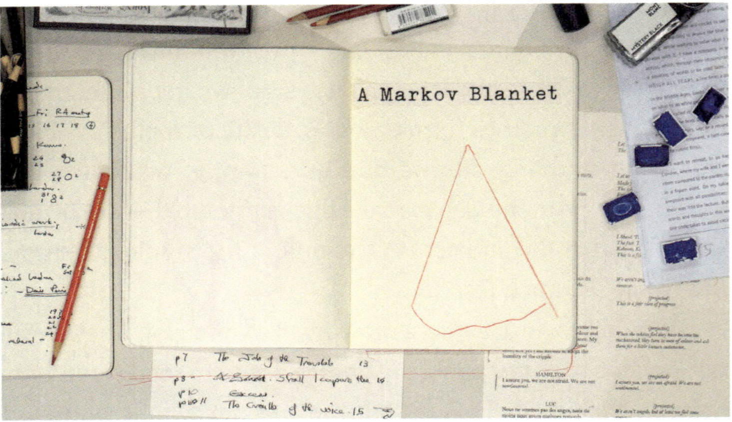

(which correctly speaking it is), but as a felt blanket draped over our shoulders, under which all these thoughts and impulses can churn unseen.

Tummelplatz

There is a blindness under the blanket, a stupidity. Let it be said, the studio is a safe space for stupidity. A space where impulses can be given the benefit of the doubt. Freud referred to the psychoanalytic space between the analyst and his patient as a *Tummelplatz* – a place of tumbling or jousting, a terrain for allowing anything to be said, understanding that there may be a sense to unearth in the flow of images and thoughts that emerge in a stream of consciousness, allowing the unconscious to bubble to the surface. The studio is a *Tummelplatz*, the artist both patient and analyst; the sheet of paper the terrain on which this jousting takes place. Follow the line, follow the lie, follow the image, and discover who you are.

The translations are numerous – swipe across the paper – a horizon line. This is both an impulse, a sweep of the arm, and the thought dividing the paper, sky and earth, the start of

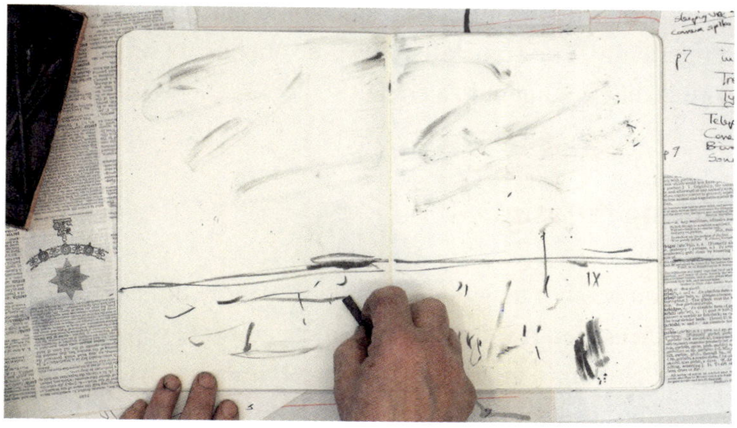

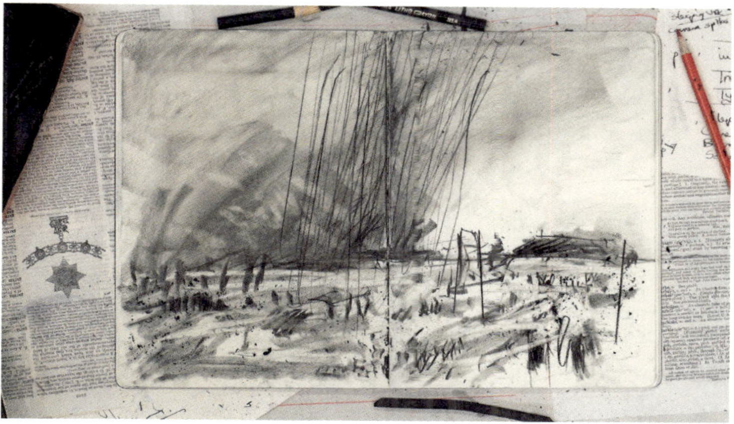

the map. Here is the world, here is the continent, the field in which I place myself (understanding that, in the end, each drawing is a fragment of a self-portrait). So, the translation from impulse to image. This is what it makes me think of: a horizon, so a landscape, the vertical charcoal marks become interventions in the landscape, short lines become the winter stubble of grass after a veld fire to the south of Johannesburg. Looking at the drawing, 10 percent is the optics of seeing the marks, the lines, the grey smudge of the charcoal; 90 percent is predictive, associative, memory.

The drawing touches the original, the veld outside, but only tangentially. The translation always touches its origin, or its source, like a tangent to a circle.

Moving the saint

But even when translation seems closer, more direct, there is a transformation. A mimesis – the most accurate copying of the real original into an artificial form certainly has its pleasures. A trompe l'oeil drawing of an object, painted with such fidelity that your hand reaches out to touch it. A pencil crayon traced onto a drawing so that from a distance you can't tell which is the pencil and which is its copy. All these have their pleasures – a pleasure of knowing, yet still believing. The transformation is at the heart of it. Knowing the falseness of what you're seeing but feeling the tug of its physicalness. Finding the pleasure in the self-deception.

"Translation" in one of its earliest usages refers to the moving of a saint's relics, literally moving these relics from a small, unimportant chapel to a grander setting, commensurate with the relics now belonging to a saint who has been canonised, and her or his miracles accepted. I imagine a grand procession with a band playing, religious banners preceding and following the box, which contains the saint's knuckles or foot. We think of translation as an act of moving something from one language into another.

An idea found in one language moves to another – the panther in Rilke's poem translated from his German cage to an English zoo, knowing that the panther will be transformed by this translation, a single German panther becoming a dozen different translations. The saint's bones multiply and change. Or, as Walter Benjamin reminds us, English bread is not the same as French pain. Baguette is not the same as German *Schwarzbrot*.

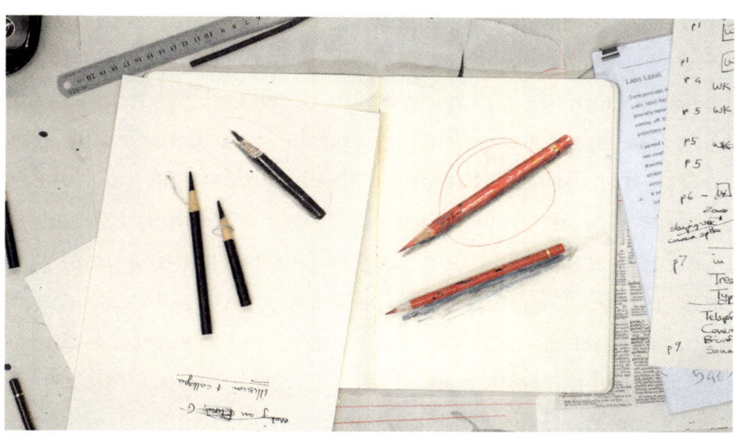

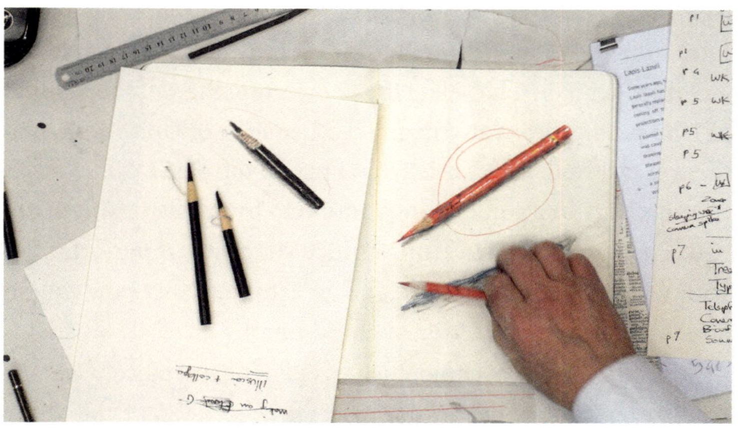

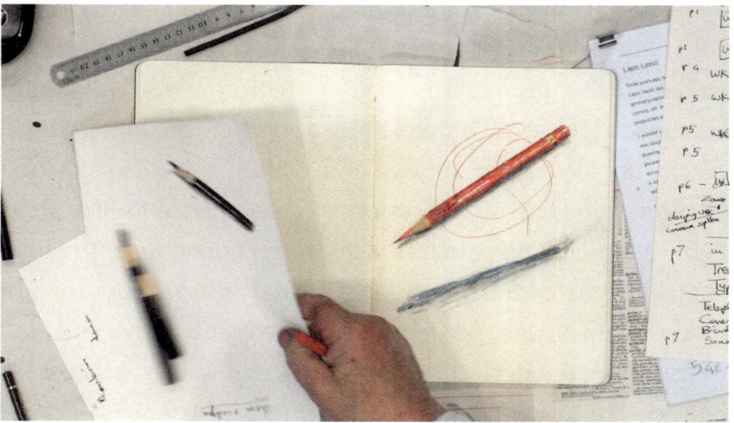

I am not so interested in what we lose in translation, but in what we gain in its impossibility, in the gaps between the original and its translation; the gaps between the translated logs that let a fire burn. The fire is always the logs and the space between the logs.

The translation in the studio also includes many migrations, a carrying of an image from one form to another, a relic of a drawing placed on another sheet of paper. A starting point may be an image – Alfred Jarry's Ubu, a sixteen-year-old's caricature of his teacher as a self-pitying tyrant. I made several etchings first around the centenary of the first performance of the play *Ubu Roi* in 1896. Jarry had a clear image for Ubu: a large gown, a peaked hood, a spiral drawn on the considerable belly. I used Jarry's formulation for Ubu in the different scenes shown in the etchings. Ubu on a bicycle, Ubu showering, the self-flagellation of Ubu (scenes from an imagined other story of Ubu). And then there is a second "Ubu," a self that I put on top of it. I worked with thumbprints in a soft etching ground to make the fleshier alter ego. The completed suite of etchings suggested a performance with white chalk projections, and an actor or dancer moving in tandem with the projections behind them.

These etchings became the basis of a theatre piece, *Ubu and the Truth Commission*. In the performance we kept the white line drawing, like Jarry's drawing, as projected animation, but substituted a live performer for the thumbprint figure in the etchings. The production used animation and archival film material to look at the human rights abuses during the apartheid era, as revealed in the sittings of the Truth and Reconciliation Commission. This Commission was established to hear from both victims and perpetrators of state-sanctioned violence under apartheid. Its central premise was that in exchange for full disclosure of crimes, perpetrators could receive amnesty: a kind of pact with the devil in which knowledge was exchanged for justice – the kind of deal that Ubu would have wholeheartedly

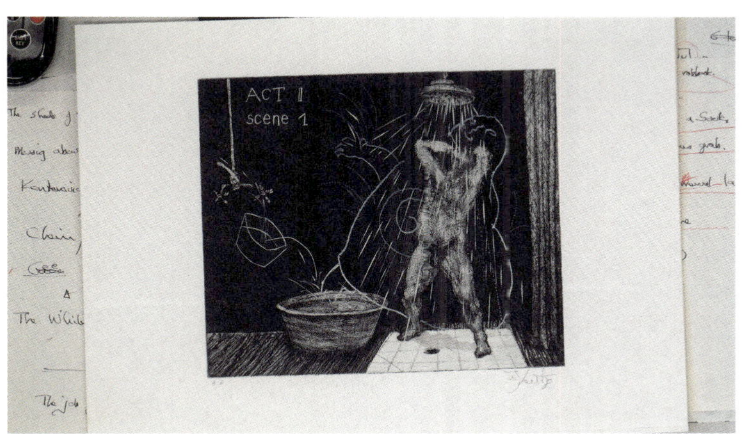
ACT II
scene 1

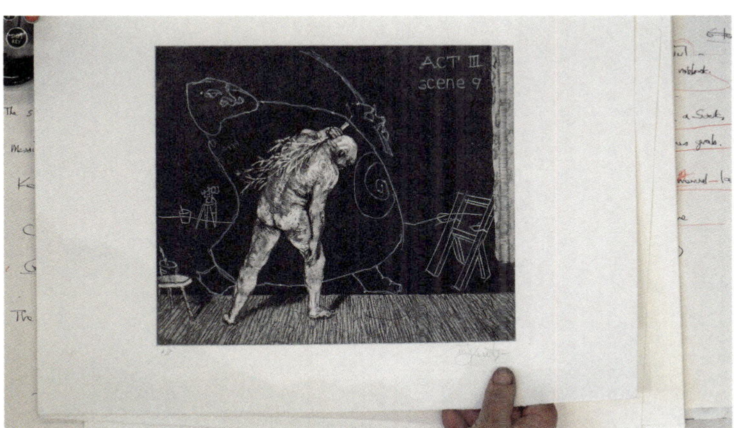
ACT III
scene 9

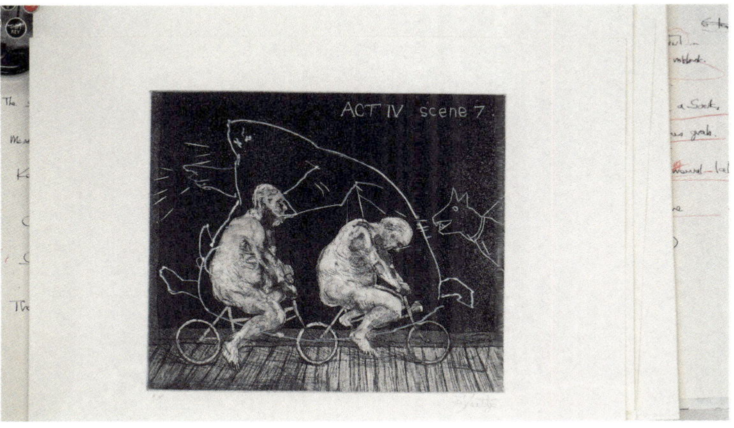
ACT IV scene 7.

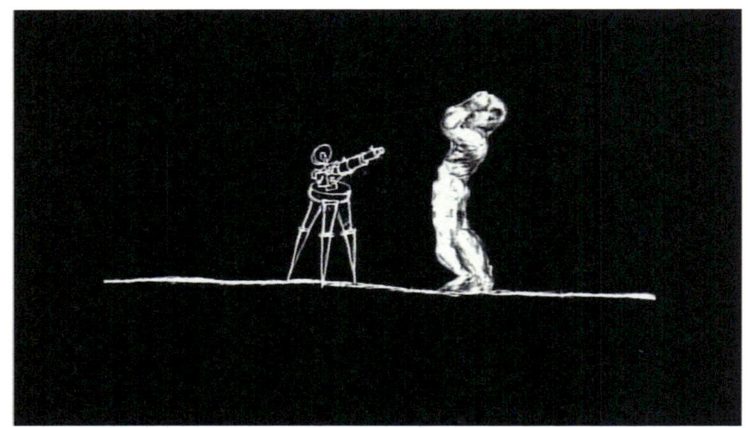

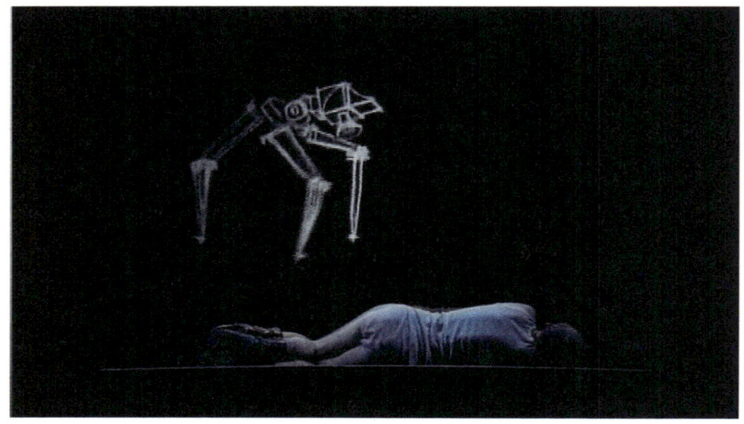

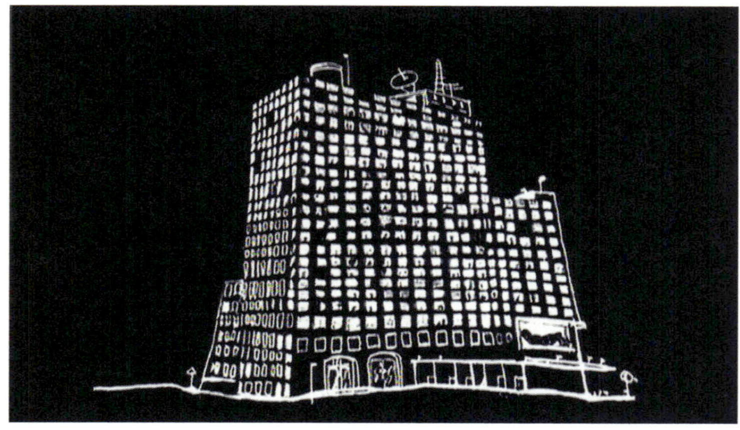

approved of. The text used a combination of verbatim transcripts from witnesses and a new text close to Jarry's style and tone.

The etchings were there in the background. The play touched them only tangentially but essentially. The play was indebted to the original images, but then went its own way. The hope was that the rough animation, provoked by Jarry's image and language, would give a new way of seeing the archival material: film footage of student protests, of police beating students, of police shooting at schoolchildren. Material that we have become blind to, having seen so much on television and in documentary films. In return, the hope was that this archival material would give a greater weight to the comic grotesque of Jarry's Ubu.

Later, elements of the animation used in the production became a film in its own right (*Ubu Tells the Truth*). The animation and archival material coming from the play, but again, given a new form independent of the performance.

Self-portrait in the third person

To complete the circle of migration, there was a further set of drawings that came from the play and the earlier etchings. They were not self-portraits, rather drawings of the self in performance; a self-portrait in the third person. These drawings were a translation in scale – a ten-inch etching becoming a six-foot drawing, thumbprints replaced with footprints, slaps by the hand, a bicycle rolled over the paper, making the drawing a record of the damage done to the paper. I photographed and filmed myself in the studio, lying on a table as an ungainly odalisque, naked riding a bicycle. It was a self in the *Tummelplatz*. It was "he," not me. *I would never perform, show myself off that way at all. Do not ask me to take responsibility for his actions. But you are here,* says the other self. *Take responsibility for who you are.*

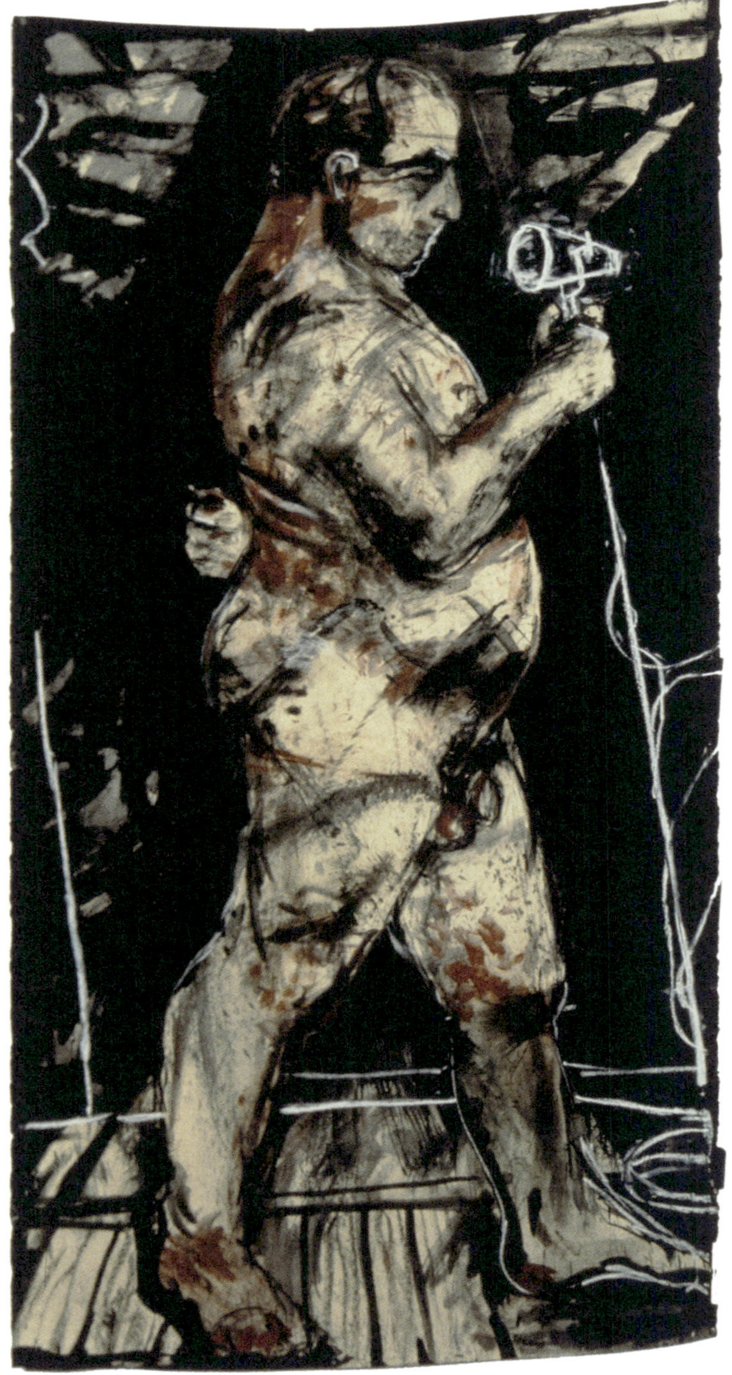

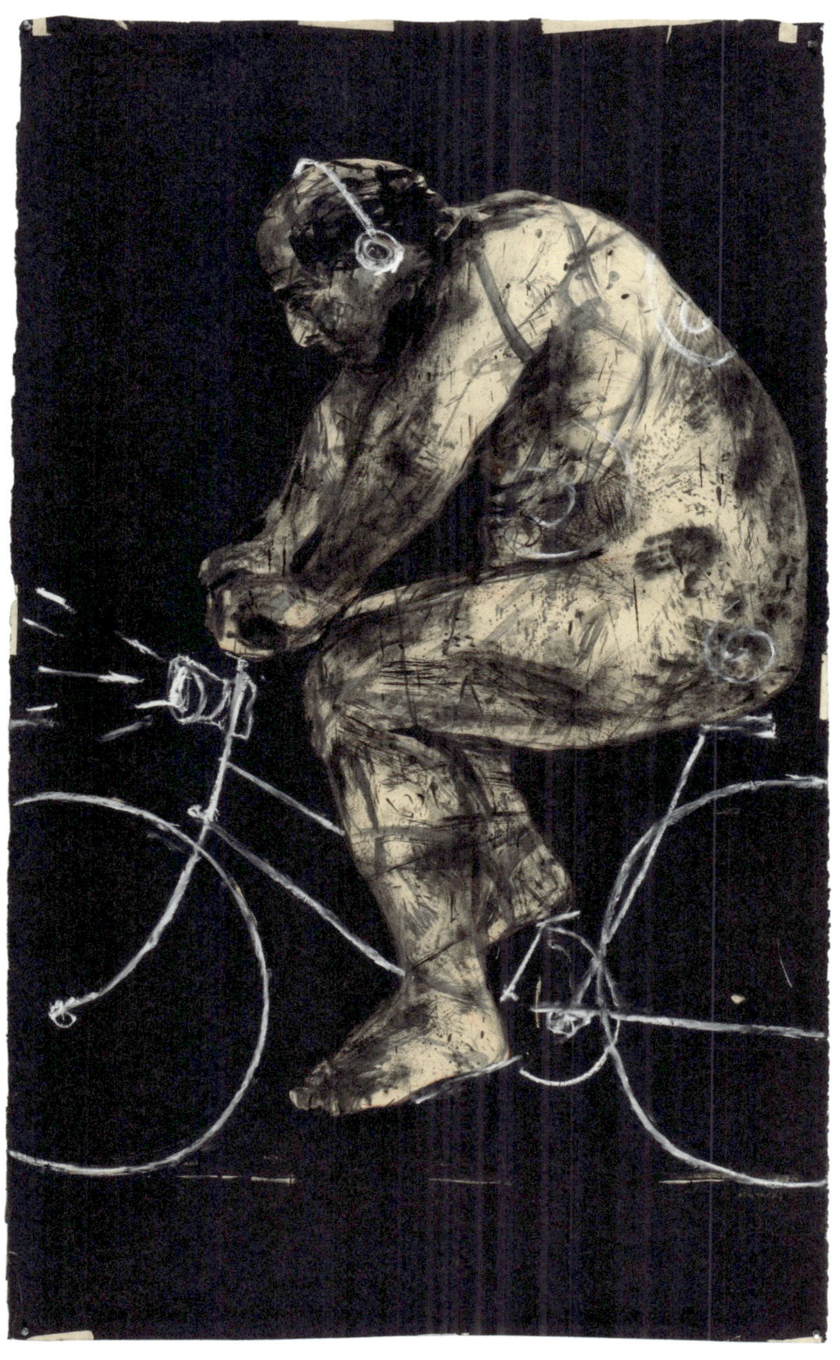

There is a connection, faint but there, between this doubling of the self – artist as maker and artist as observer – that feels like the tug between a first language and that which it is translated into. This tug, this unstable connection, is where we find ourselves in the studio; a clash sometimes gentle, sometimes less so, between the rational and the part of us that rejects this way of thinking.

So, what is this translation?

The work of translation:
WK 2: Only when there is a gap can we think – thank
      heavens for mistranslation.
WK 1: A typewriter must remain a typewriter.
WK 2: A typewriter is also a bird.
WK 1: A tree remains a tree.
WK 2: A tree is also a book, a table, a fire, ash.
WK 1: We need to keep the meaning.
WK 2: We need to remember that a language is as a
      dialect with an army and navy.
WK 1: The poem must stay the poem.
WK 2: We need to find an unclarity, to turn things on
      their heads, to allow a reversal, a somersault, to let
      a word become a colour, a shadow, a sculpture.

This is talking about language. But the studio work jumps from language to non-language, from lapis lazuli to a phrase, from a word to a colour – not to try to find an exact equivalent, but to hunt for the spark that flashes from these connections. A spark that arcs across from the separation, when the vertical marks on the paper are both grass and charcoal, when the green is both oil paint and the leaf. It is always about recognition, rather than knowing. A second degree of knowledge, closer to the periaqueductal grey than to the frontal lobe.

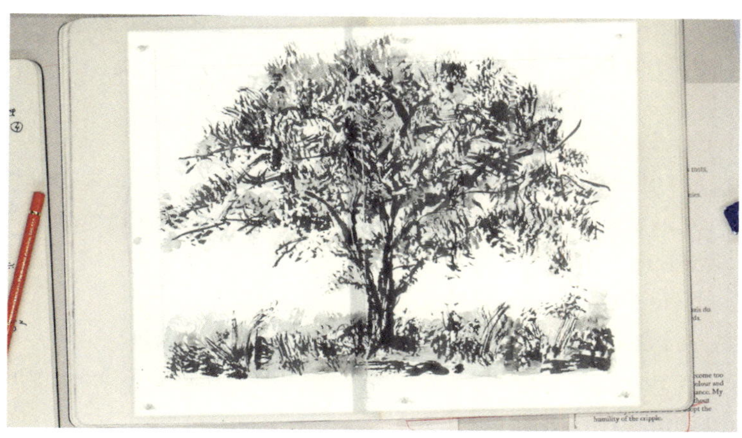

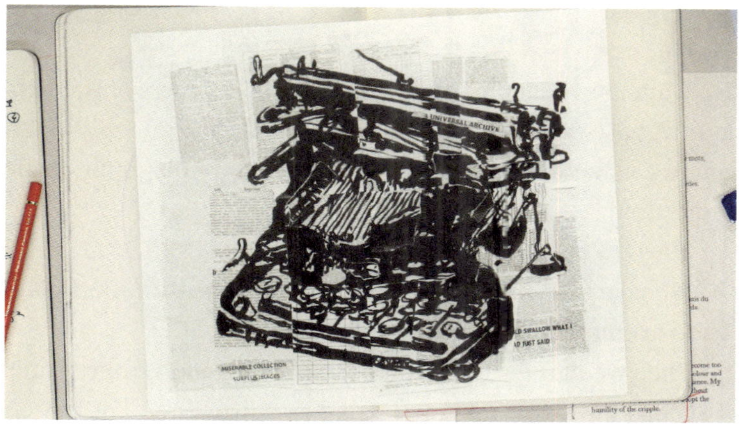

The challenge of these lectures is to try to bring half-coherent ideas to the rational linearity of a lecture. To undo the processes of the studio, knowing that a description of the chaos is always so much clearer than the chaos itself.

The order of things:

An impulse – a memory of a childhood stick figure in a school textbook; the desire for the engine to pick up speed, for the pages to turn; abandoning the subject of the impulse but following the logic of the machine set in motion; learning the rules of what one is doing.

We gather different elements:
Pages of a dictionary (not a narrative, but not random: a coherence in the book that the book knows, even if the pages are out of order).

The idea of a flipbook.

A box of watercolour paints and coloured pencils.

A poem, a sonnet to set the pages in motion, to learn the grammar of this undertaking.

How to make it work:
How intense must the colour be? One or two layers of watercolour? A base watercolour with a coloured crayon on top? Which colours make the transition from paper to photograph or the projection?

How many frames for each page?

We take the line: "Shall I compare thee to a summer's day? Thou art more lovely and more temperate."

Then we start the translation, the disintegration in the studio.

I read the text. That's eight seconds, thirty-three words: four words per second.

We paint the pages of the dictionary, so the words of the poem become the coloured pages.

Four words per second is about six frames per word, or three frames of each page filmed twice.

And what for the air between the words, or the breath between the lines?

Do we keep these pages unpainted?

The specifics of the poem – a sonnet of Shakespeare – dissolve into questions of making. How quickly should the pages turn? Should the twenty-five frames per second of the film be

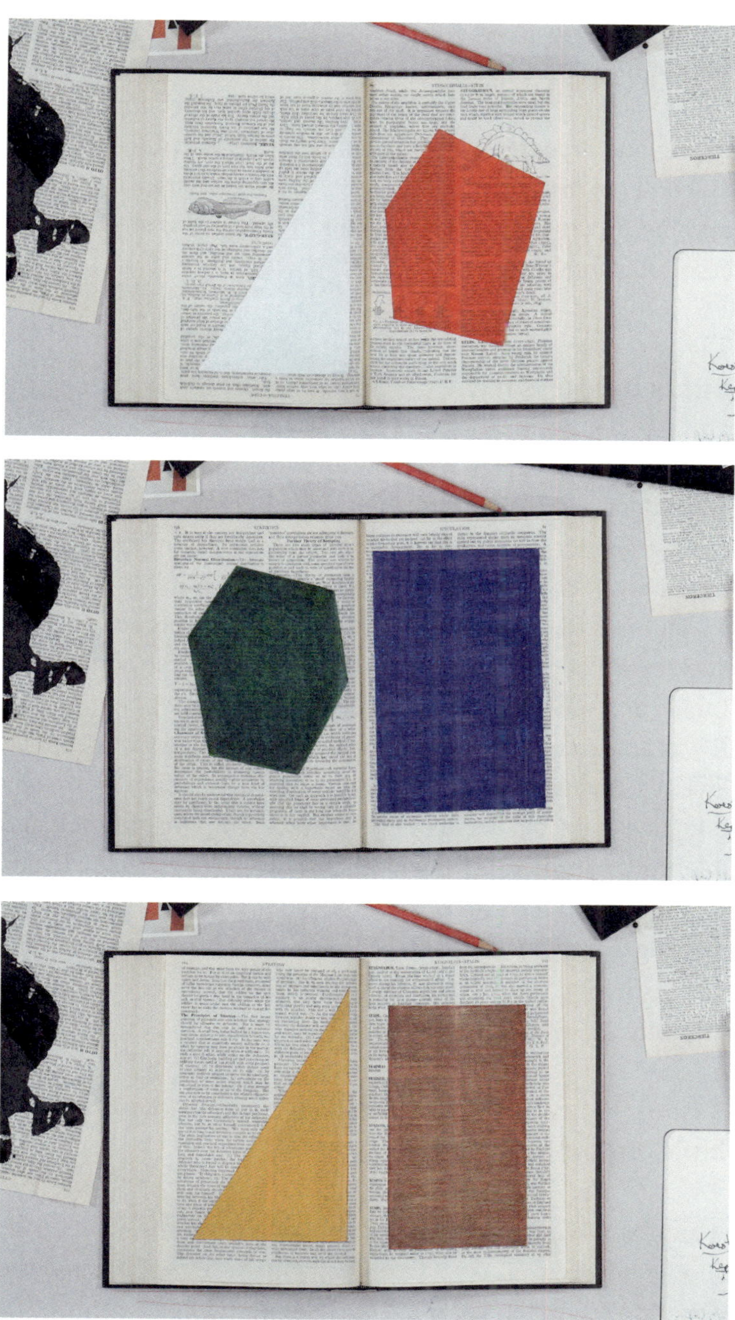

twenty-five pages of each page filmed twice, or thrice? How intense must the colour be, one layer of watercolour or two?

These are the questions in the studio, a learning done by testing and repetition. The meaning of the poem recedes into the corner of the studio. All energy goes into this transformation, into the process of transformation, the pleasure of one thing becoming another.

But is it necessary?

My father has always been sceptical of this kind of work, putting projections inside an opera, doing a Büchner play with puppets, adding colours to a sonnet. "I'm not saying it's impossible," he would say, "I'm just wondering why it's necessary." A question, which I'm still, at the age of seventy, trying to answer. It is not necessary. The poem on its own is fine, perfect. The best answer I could give was that it was essential because it was not necessary. It was an excess, a drowning excess some would claim, but an excess. There is a split here. On the one hand, I am aware of a rational person talking about an exploration, a justification and interpretation after the event, the chaotic excess rolled up inside coherence. On the other hand, the other artist not talking, but reacting to the impulse to make the sonnet film. It's an infantile, unquestioning urge. Let us leap and then look, a desire for an impurity, an overabundance.

Holding on to the grain

A similar project: twenty-four Schubert songs, the *Winterreise*, and twenty-four films to accompany them. How far could the films stray from the text of the songs and still find a connection to them? In many of the films which are made for the cycle the distance between the image and the words seems so great that they only touch at one point. The film is as a tangent to the circle of the song.

I grew up hearing the *Winterreise* sung by Dietrich Fischer-Dieskau. My father would listen to these recordings lying on the sofa after lunch on the weekends. (My mother would leave the room. She had a precept: after fifty, no German lieder. No Puccini.) Dietrich Fischer-Dieskau acccmpanied by Gerald Moore, a symbolic postwar rapprochement between Britain and Germany. Even though he enunciates each word of the song perfectly, I had no German. So, the sense of the songs was not in the text. I did not understand the text, but could hear from the impulse, from the emotion, from the volume, from the emphasis, that there was a meaning inside the song. The words were there, but they were not the meaning. There was a quality of a meaning just out of reach. Even later, with many songs sung in English, the effect is the same. I'd either not recognise the words, or I'd hear the words and register them in one part of my brain, and then they would fly off, but the song would remain. Roland Barthes writes of the grain of the song, a vocal quality that contains the essence of a song, rather than just making the words clear. He was a great champion of Panzera, the prewar baritone who sang *Winterreise* on old 78 RPM records, with all their hiss and crackles. Barthes was very critical of Dietrich Fischer-Dieskau and his clarity (though this may also have been a dislike for the clarity of 33 RPM long-playing records and a nostalgia for the older 78 RPM sound).

Some of the twenty-four films of the *Winterreise* are made expressly for the songs, but in many cases, it was a found connection between some of the songs and sections of films I had made many years before. There is something in the rolling rhythm of the songs pushing the walker forward on his winter journey that also propel the animation of the films, that pull the films through the gates of the projector.

I'm interested in excess. My father would listen to the *Wintereisse* with his eyes closed, a pure listening. In the recital hall the impurity of the listening is always clear. One watches the pianist's fingers. How close to the piano will the singer go? It looks as if he might climb right into the piano. What does he do with his hands? Will the page-turner miss his moment? Did I remember to take the fish pie out of the freezer? An excess through which one wades to find the music, or through which the music finds us. But even on the sofa, eyes shut, I'm sure other thoughts would have moved across the music. Memories, anxieties (in a postprandial state, even dreams). Purity is always wishful thinking. Hope to still the chattering in one's head – impossible. We have to celebrate the anti-Zen in us.

In the song, comprehension lies both in the words and beyond them; in the near breath, in posture, in gesture, in emphasis, in volume. And so with speech. Anne, my wife, begs me not to try to speak French. I change, she claims. I swell up. I become grandiose. *Je gonfle*, filled with big French vowels: the *ai*, the *oeu*, the *ou*. In German, she says, I sound like a rabbi. I don't dislike either of these disguises, but make sure not to parade them before her.

Dietrich Fischer-Dieskau was one introduction to language beyond the edge of comprehension. I was of course also surrounded by languages heard but not understood. The African languages which enveloped me, not just in childhood, but still today in Johannesburg: the isiZulu, isiXhosa, Sesotho, Sepedi, Setswana of all the Africans, both in the house and around, while I was stuck in an English monolingualism, understanding that translation would always be an essential condition for me.

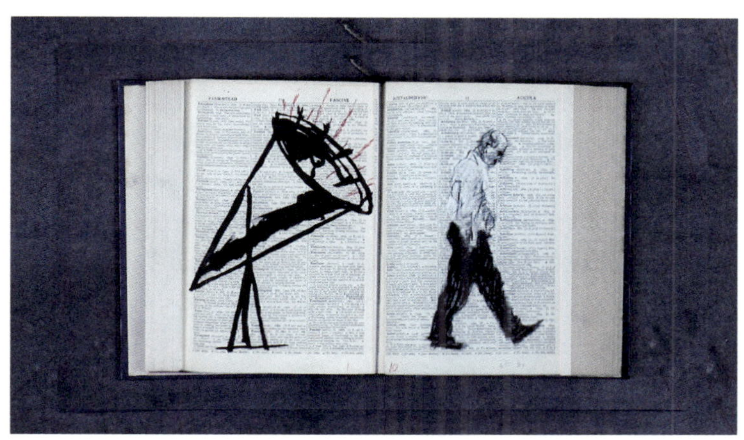

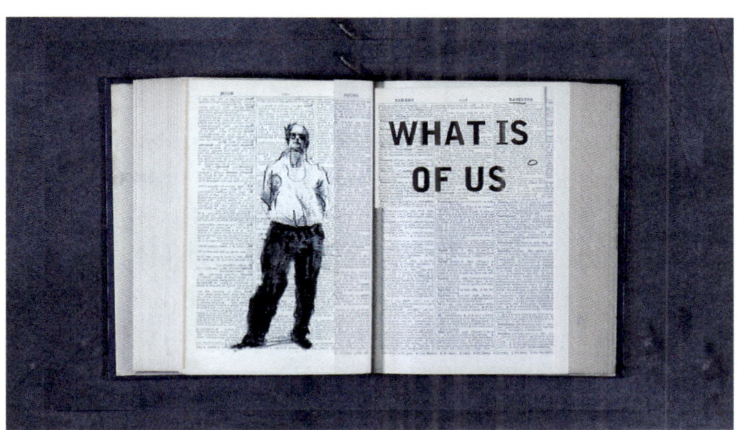

WHAT IS
OF US

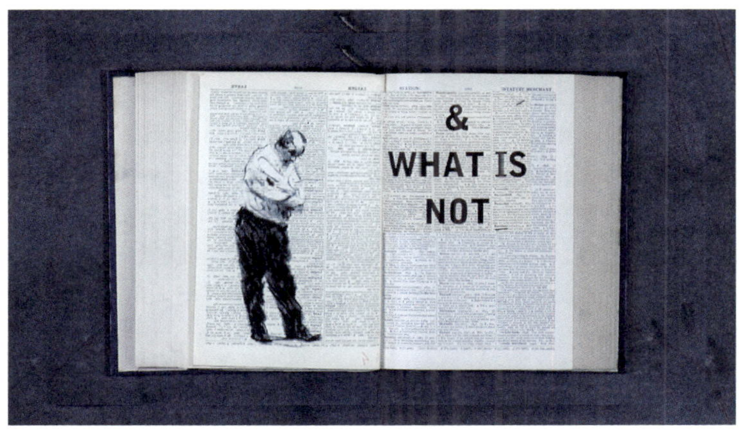

&
WHAT IS
NOT

The white spaces

On Friday nights I would attend shul services with my grandfather. The incomprehensible patterns of the Hebrew letters in the prayer book, opaque when rattled off at an impossible rate. I would float along with the service, recognising the songs, familiar with the pauses when the congregation would turn towards the ark and mouth the words to themselves. And then, to make the unmoving clock turn, I would read the prayers in English, comprehensible and incomprehensible. One statement of praise after another. How could God ever bear it, my adolescent thoughts would run, this toadying? What universal ego can put up with this nonstop adulation? Such the thoughts that went in parallel to the incantation of the prayers.

I now have a sense of the understanding. The words are the logs, but the heart of the prayer is the gap between the logs. Everything, not just the words. And to have the fire, we need both the logs and the gaps between the logs. There is a branch of Hasidic Judaism that claims that the words are there, and God understands them, but devotion comes from the white spaces between the words. And so, one discovers who one is, rather than decides. Goose and the gaps. This is who I am.

But if words are so light, so ephemeral, how does one tie them down, give them a weight, which we know they should have?

Svetlana Alexievich, the Russian writer who crafts her books from transcripts of interviews, describes an extreme situation where there is nothing to be gained from ambiguity, from sophistry, from rhetoric. This is from her book on the Soviet war in Afghanistan in the 1980s: "The young boy took a long time to die. As he did so his eyes looked around him like a bird. And he said the words of things he could see: sky, mountain, tree . . ." Language at its most essential. The words echo as a chastisement of language that takes off on its own. We want to tie the words to the world, but of course, we cannot.

The weight of a word

How does one give weight to something as light as a word, as a shadow, as a series of signs, of words or phrases? A silhouette or shadow of an object – a phone, a megaphone, an ampersand, becomes a torn paper shape. This can be cut out of cardboard, already some weight gained. Held together with masking tape or glue, the cardboard can thicken, can gain a certain fatness. Then, if it is covered in wax, it can be moulded and cast in bronze, patinated black, and brought back to its original silhouette.

These glyphs are hand-sized, the weight of a fist-sized stone. Gravity pulls them down. The glyphs were made to give a substance to the silhouette shapes, to take something essentially two dimensional – a letter, a shadow, the ink drawing or the paper cutout – and give it heft, to give a shadow its due. Put these together, and there emerges almost a phrase or a rubric in bronze, not a clear meaning, but a push towards an illegible comprehensibility. A riddle which has no answer, but which intrigues us precisely because it has no clear solution.

If the ink drawing or even the paper has the ephemerality of a digital text, has only the weight of a pulsing cursor, the bronze has the hard-won sense of letterpress, of words put together metal letter by metal letter, or having the heavy thwack of the manual typewriter. If the digital carries the malleability, the fickleness of our scattered thinking, the typewriter is its rebuke. These are your words, you can't escape them, even if you put a line of X's through the words you need to change, the first thought is there, and shows its changes. The thinking and the process of thinking is there. There is a commitment to the decisiveness, to the striking of the keys, an ethics of the typewriter.

Svetlana Alexievich writes about war and the way the extreme situation reduces language to its most direct, its most indisputable. But war also has the opposite effect, of revealing a language removed from the world. One thinks of the grand words of all

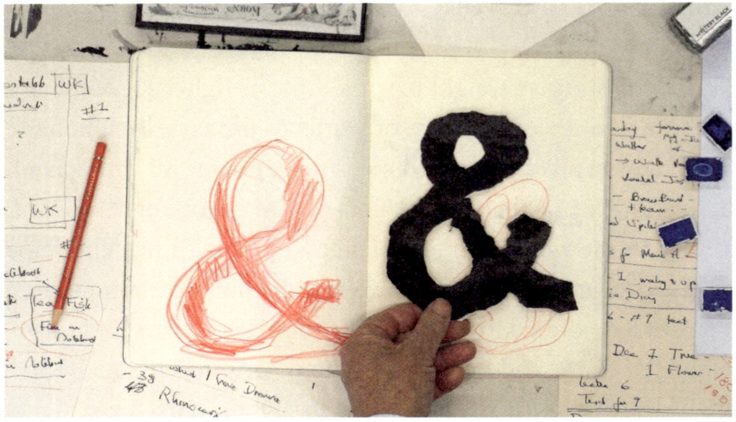

the agreements and treaties of the great powers which become the incomprehensible nightmare of mud and death in the First World War. A clear logic, as clear as a train timetable, that leads to such disaster. If this is what a clear logic does, let us find a less clear logic. If this is language, let us find a non-language.

This was the fundamental principle of the Dadaists in Zurich in 1916, and their legacy since then. Language was a focus of this demonstration of less good logic. An exuberant absurdity where all was possible, where the rallying cry was, "Let us try, for once, not to be right." The performances, simultaneous poems, came out of the need to destabilise the word, to operate within a destabilised world. To uncertain the word. To show the uncertainty of the thoughts. To take the uncertainty – inside us all, everyone is fighting a huge battle – and put it onstage. As they wrote, "Even God is depressed and can only pick at his food."

A walk around the studio is the preamble to drawing, a space and time when one is in the chaos of thinking. These lectures are trying to find the point of contact between this invisible origin of image and words, and the words as they are finally put down. The lapis lazuli text – both the words and the colour – and the tang of the riddle that does not have an answer. The writing over the certainty of centuries of letterpress printing, using a charcoal smudge to disturb this clarity. I think of Schwitters' *Ursonate* as a trompe l'oeil, not of an object, but of the process coming out from the periaqueductal grey, of trying to tie us to the word and the world, of holding tight, knowing we cannot pin down a sense in the world, but living as if we could.

Ubu and the Truth Commission
1997
Theatre production with actors, puppets, and animation:
William Kentridge and Handspring Puppet Company
Writer: Jane Taylor

Winterreise
2014
Song cycle for voice and piano with projections by William
Kentridge
Composer: Franz Schubert
Piano: Markus Hinterhäuser
Baritone: Matthias Goerne

Ursonate
2017
Sound poem by Kurt Schwitters, performed and with
projections by William Kentridge

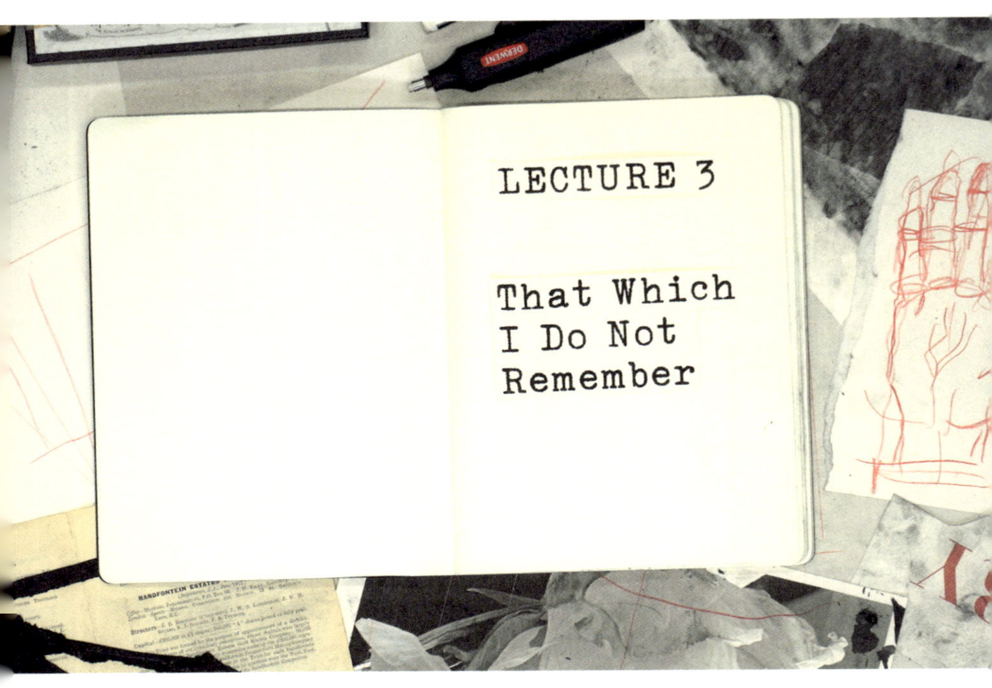
LECTURE 3

That Which
I Do Not
Remember

THAT WHICH I DO NOT REMEMBER

I was first taken to Rome when I was six years old. My father had finished the arduous five years of the South African Treason Trial. This trial in which 156 people, including Nelson Mandela, were tried for treason against the South African state, lasted from 1956 to 1961. All defendants eventually were found not guilty. In relief and in triumph, he took the family on our first European holiday. I had a book, *This is Rome: A Child's Guide to the City*. In it there was a drawing of a wolf in a cage, I presume in the Rome Zoo, which I came to combine with the story of Romulus and Remus, and the she-wolf suckling them, and imagined that this wolf in the cage was somehow that original wolf grown old, like the Sibyl who could not die.

Sixty years later, I was invited to work on a project in Rome, a frieze along the banks of the Tiber River. I must have had that wolf somewhere in mind as I had made an animation (for Rilke, in Trieste; an image of a panther pacing in its cage) and had the idea of making a projection of a pacing she-wolf on the walls of the Tiber. This possibility was enough to get me started, to say an enthusiastic "Yes!" to the invitation to make a work on the site.

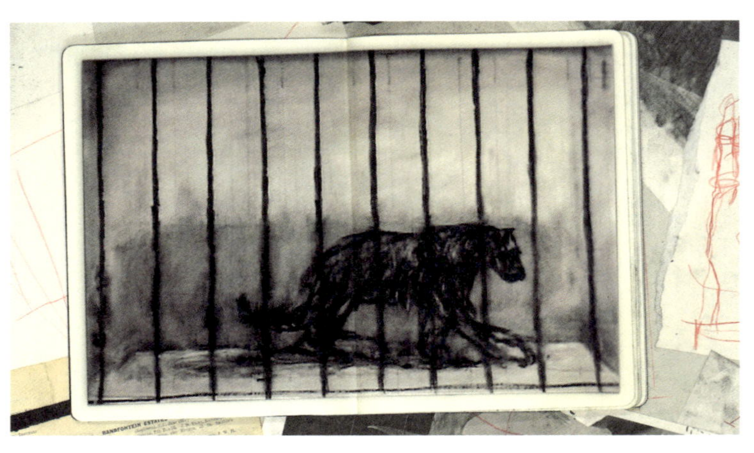

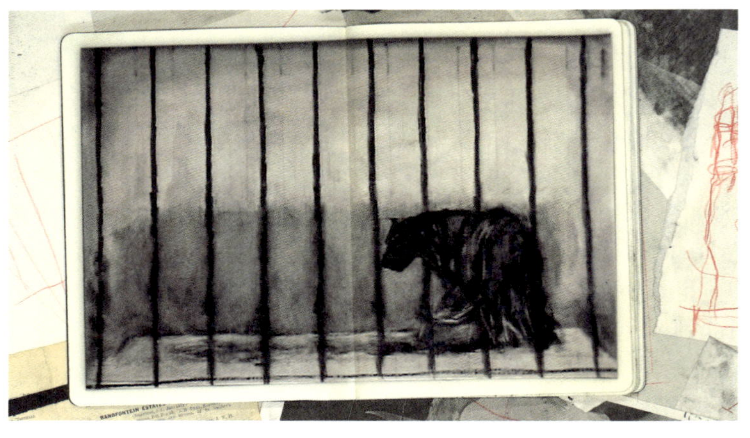

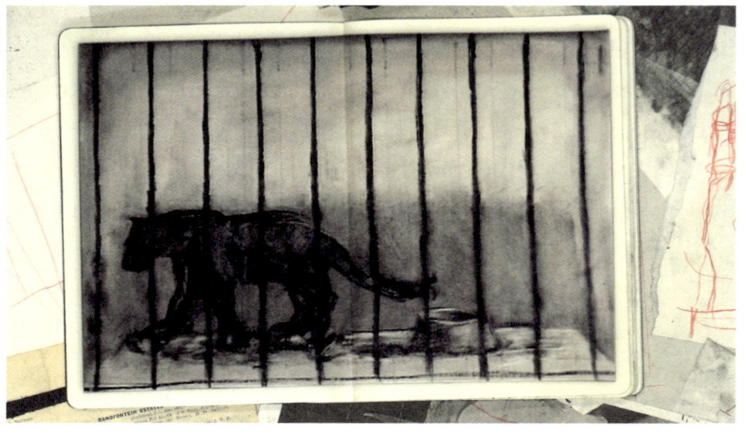

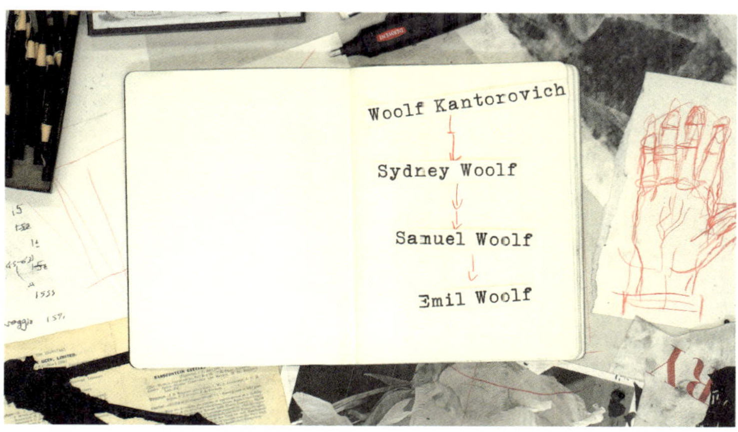

One takes a fragment, and it expands in one's head, and makes its insistence felt. I could see the she-wolf, prowling along the edges of the river, protecting and threatening.

It was also the wolf from Prokofiev's *Peter and the Wolf*, another childhood image in my head of a wolf less benign than the Roman one. But then again, my great-grandfather was Woolf Kantorovich; my father is Sydney Woolf; my son, Samuel Woolf; and my grandson Emil Woolf. It is as the psychoanalysts would say, an overdetermination of wolves. Overdetermination is important. Not just one thought but several that come from different directions adding a pressure, giving greater chance to ignite a spark between them. Not just one thought but a plurality of associations. Enough and more than enough. A wolf projected onto the wall.

The section of the Tiber River I was to animate runs from the Ponte Sisto to Ponte Mazzini. For this projection to be possible, we would need massive projectors, generators, the lights of the city to be switched off. The wave of this good idea came crashing down against this wall of practical and logistical impossibilities: forty projectors, forty generators, rerouting Rome's traffic. What was I thinking? A less good idea had to be found.

Again, I want to think about the studio and what emerges from the studio, but also about things outside the studio that are given meaning by the work in the studio. The work done in the studio is the only justification for the ideas presented here. And of course, in this conversation between the outside world and the studio, the biographical is inextricably implicated.

Fettuccine Alfredo

Rome was the first European city I saw. My connection to Rome and Italy was shaped by my father's love and enthusiasm for Italy and all things Italian, in his case formed by his experience in Italy during and after the Second World War. I remember not just the she-wolf from that early visit, but also peach ice cream in Levanto, the terror of having my hand bitten off by the Bocca della Verità, the *carabinieri* hats, riding the donkey in the Pincio Gardens. This was in 1961.

The idea of the frieze on the wall retreated from an extended series of projections of a wolf to the idea of a long *graffito*, a drawn frieze five hundred metres in length. This seemed not impossible.

The project of the frieze was several years in the making. From the first enthusiasm of the video projection tests, to the question of finding the resources to make the frieze; and for eighteen months, the vexed question of getting permissions – the *permessi* – to make the work. "Over my dead body will there be contemporary art in the heart of historic Rome," was the response of one cultural bureaucrat. The issue of turning that "no" into a "yes" could be the subject of a separate essay on post-Machiavellian politics.

The walls of the Tiber are not marble, but travertine stone. A light-coloured stone, but the walls now are charcoal grey,

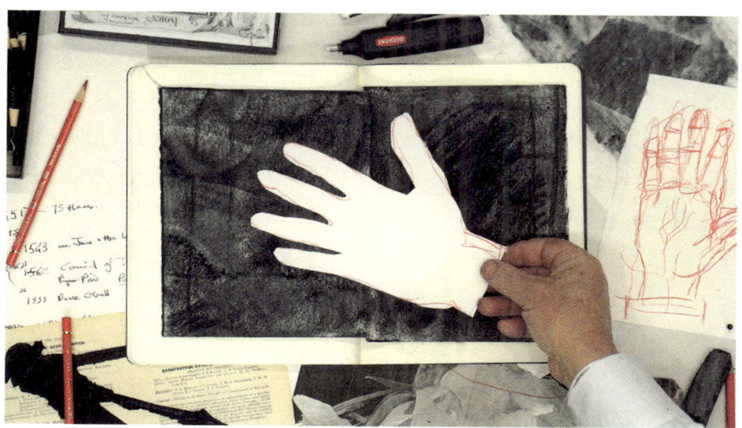

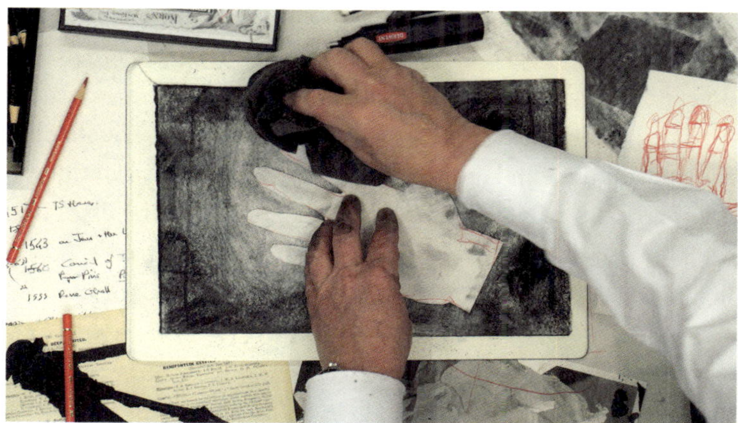

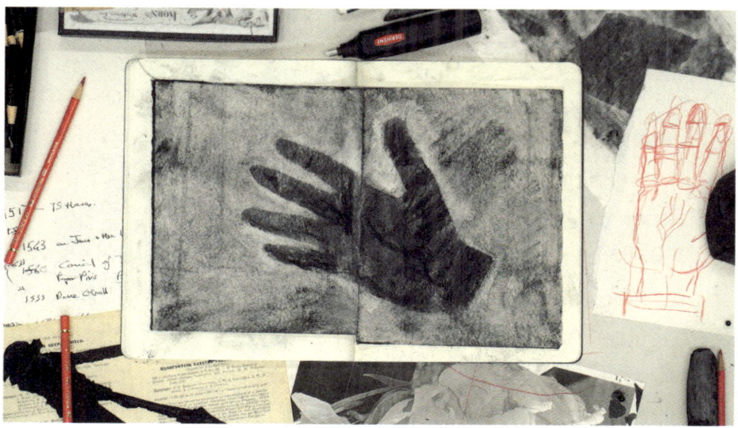

darkened by a mixture of pollution and bacterial growth, mainly the latter. So instead of drawing the figures that would make up the frieze, we would wash away everything that was not the frieze, like a woodcut, or a lino cut, where the active marks, the gouges, are not seen. An image is made from what is untouched.

To describe the order of the events.

Yes or No

I choose an image to draw. First, there is a charcoal drawing, drawn on the pages of an old cash book. The lines and margins of the page on which the drawing was made approximate the lines of the travertine blocks on the wall.

These drawings are then remade in Indian ink. The indeterminate smudges and grey of the charcoal had to be resolved into the sharp YES or NO of the white of the paper and the black ink.

The ink drawing was then traced on a computer, into a mathematical file, a vector file, that could be enlarged or reduced as needed.

This file was then sent to a factory outside Rome, where the vector file was used to make a full-scale plastic stencil of the drawing. A 35cm ink drawing in the studio becomes a 10m plastic stencil.

The plastic stencil was then placed against the stone travertine wall, suspended from the parapet at the top of the wall, at the street level. The stencil was pressed against the wall by people on ladders (using large brooms).

Water from the river was pumped out, heated up, and sprayed at pressure onto the stones around the stencil. It washed off the bacteria and pollution. The area sprayed went from grey to the off-white of the travertine stone. The area under the stencil, protected from the spray, stayed dark. And when the stencil

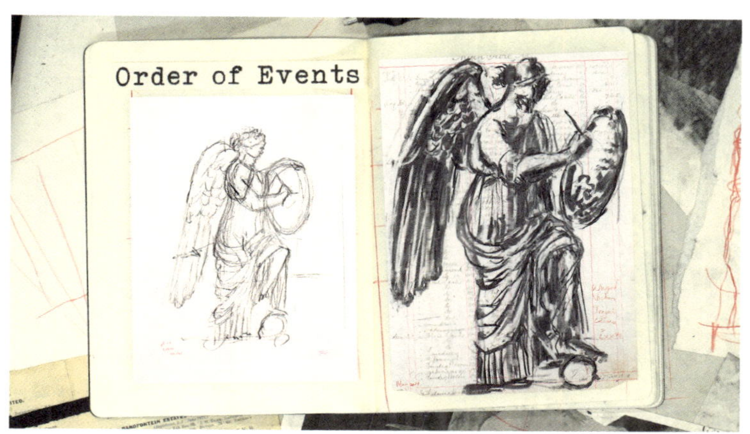
Order of Events

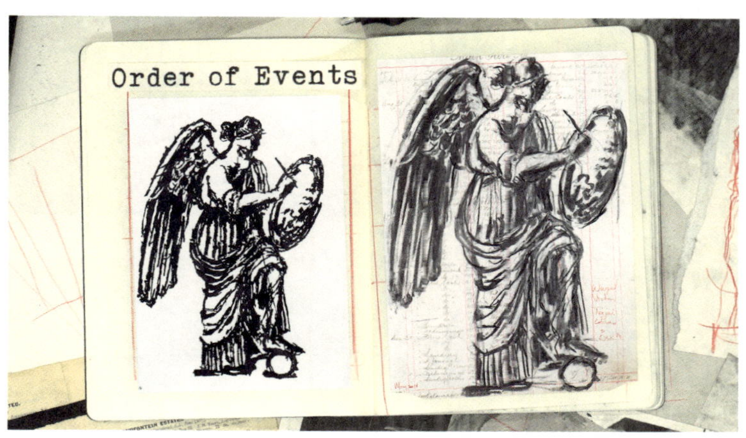
Order of Events

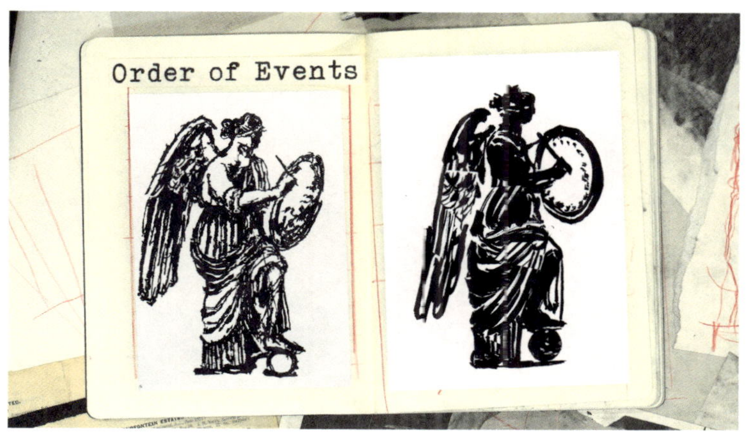
Order of Events

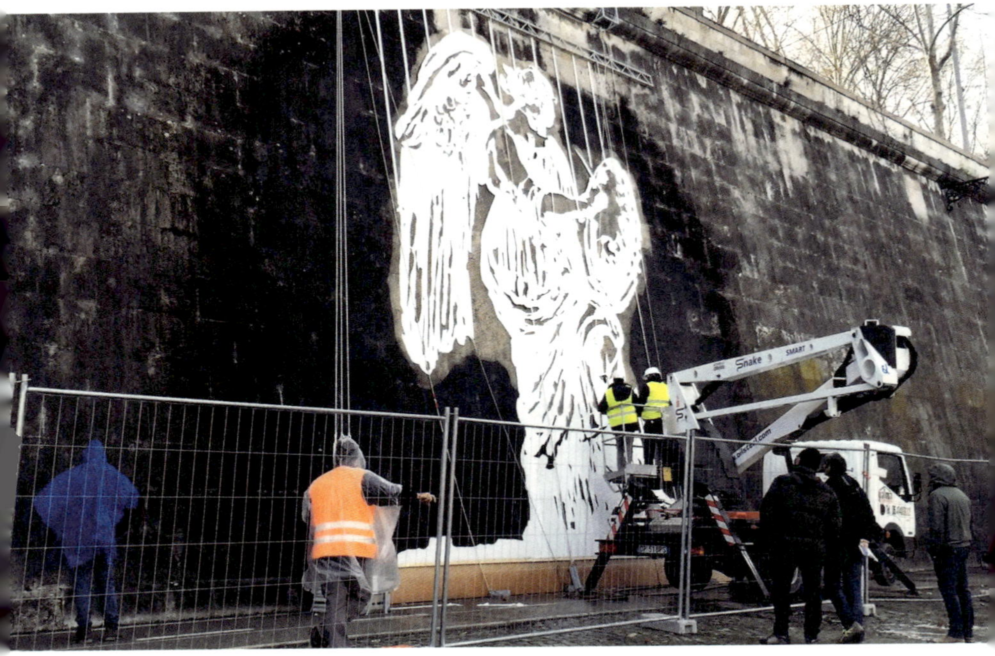

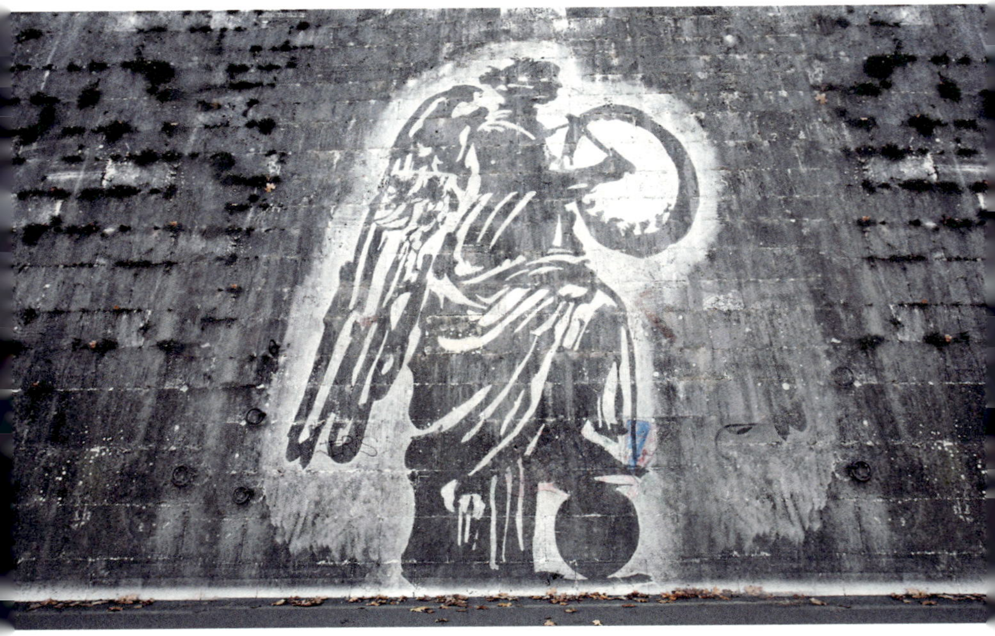

was removed, the dark drawing, the leavings of the spray, was revealed. The temperature, the pressure, and the type of nozzle were all controlled by the Monuments Commission, the city authorities, and the river authorities. Nothing was added to the wall.

This was where the project started: a technique, a site, and the pleasure of the prospect of working in the city. But as to what I would do, I was stuck.

Baedecker's guide

I made some sketches from images of Trajan's Column. I imagined unrolling Trajan's Column along the length of the river. Of course, I made drawings of Romulus and Remus and the she-wolf. But essentially, I was stuck. I could find no more than a tourist guide compendium of images.

There are two things for a project to work: a material through which to think about it, and the theme from outside the studio. I had the medium but not how it would grab the world outside. So, another walk around the studio; looking at books; a guide to Rome from 1907; Gombrich's *Story of Art*; the short novels of Primo Levi.

I read a book of poems about the Jewish ghetto, which is virtually across the river from where the frieze was to be, and some of the history of the Jewish ghetto in Rome. I was amazed. I had always assumed that the ghetto was a pre-modern medieval project, and that by the time of the regrowth of humanism in the Renaissance, it was an anachronism. My shock was in realising that it was only established in 1555 and continued until 1870, only ending after Garibaldi conquered Rome.

On the one side of the river, you had St Peter's Basilica, the Vatican, Raphael, Michelangelo. My grandfather had given me a book of Michelangelo's *Last Judgement* when I was twelve. I still

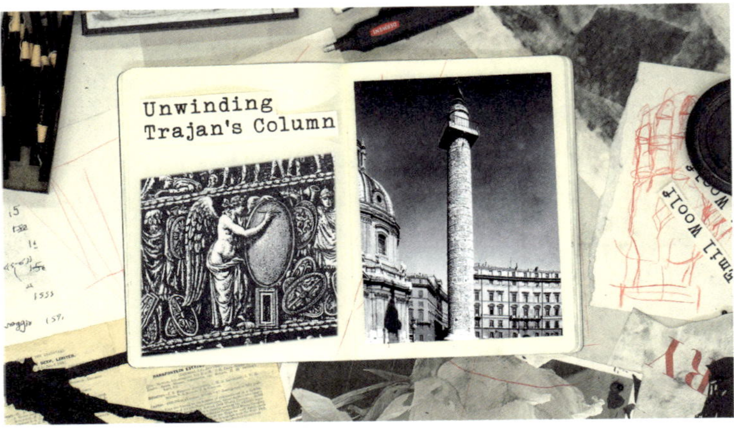

have it on my shelves. All the glories I had studied in art history and visited on trips to Rome. On the other side of the river, the ghetto. If you draw a line from St Peter's to the ghetto, it would almost bisect the frieze. I had never put the two together.

On Jews and their lies

There is a chronological link. The ghetto was established at the same time as St Peter's was built. But I think there is more than a chronological coincidence. To refresh our knowledge of history: Bramante starts building the cathedral in 1506. Michelangelo takes over from Bramante, and the Basilica is eventually finished in 1626. At the time, many, even in Rome itself, saw the church as an unjustifiable piece of Pope Leo's vanity. Part of the financing of the church was through the sale of indulgences, pushed hard by Pope Leo. And Luther's break with the hierarchy of the Catholic Church, his ninety-five theses – "the disputations of Martin Luther on the power and efficacy of indulgences," pinned to the carceral church in Wittenberg – were about the wanton expense of St Peter's Basilica. His conflict with the Church was over these indulgences that peasants and princes in Northern Europe had to buy to fund the building.

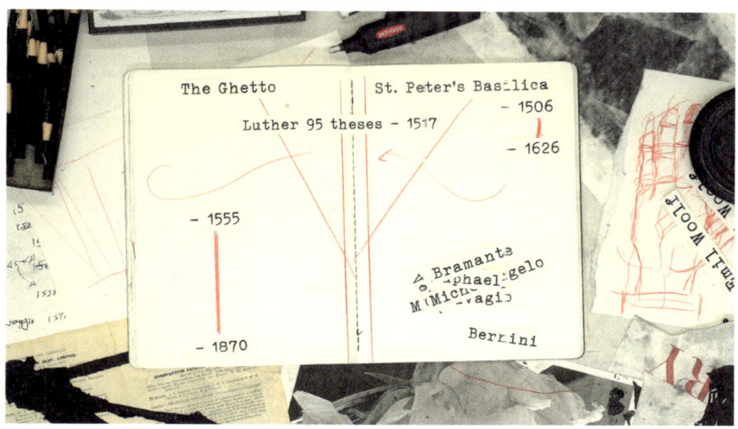

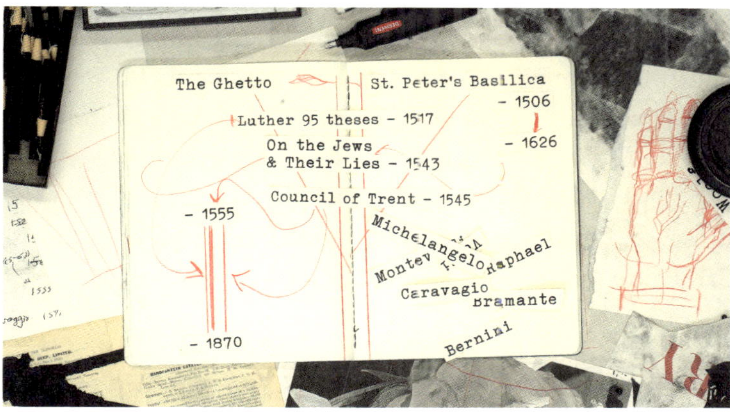

Only much later did Luther write his treatise *On the Jews and Their Lies*. This treatise was written at the same time as the Council of Trent was working on the response of the Catholic Church to the Reformation, to try to reverse the loss of support it had suffered in Northern Europe. And then Pope Paul IV established the ghetto, partly as an answer to Luther's claim that the Church was too soft on the Jews. I'm sure this is a simplification of history, certainly an abbreviation of it. But we know that Pope Paul was tough on everyone, not just the Jews. He founded the Roman Inquisition to search out anyone who deviated from orthodoxy. As he said, "If my father were an heretic, I would gather the wood to burn him."

Coincidence is not an answer

But nonetheless, there is a pressure for connection between the Basilica and the ghetto.

When this connection came to me, I didn't think, "How clever I am at working out this connection." Rather, there was an anger and a shame in myself at not having seen this connection earlier. Again, there are three types of ignorance here. There was a history hidden. Nothing I had been taught or read about the glories of the Renaissance in Rome, during different art history lessons, had ever mentioned the ghetto.

There was a second ignorance on my part, an ignorance in which I am complicit. Even if I knew about the ghetto, it was as a footnote against the monuments, the buildings, the frescoes that so filled me. The context, and even the meanings of the paintings and sculpture, was subsidiary to the pleasure of the presence, the carvings of Saint Teresa, the frown of Moses in San Pietro in Vincoli. It is only half an answer to say that I was an artist looking at artists' work.

A third ignorance was the ignorance of not being able to put the fragments together, even when I knew of the ghetto, and of its humiliations and degradations placed on its inhabitants.

A kick in the rump

This is not in the distant past, but right up to 1870. Even so, I did not see its connection to other histories. I could not see that the glory and the shame were inextricably linked.

The ghetto. I had an idea of a ghetto, a walled-off, restricted part of the city, where Jews could live and work. In Rome, this was at the edges of the river, which would flood every year. The travertine walls on which the frieze was made were built only at the end of the nineteenth century, to protect the city from the annual flood. At night, the gates of the ghetto were locked. There was a series of ritualised humiliations: parading Jews on donkeys during Carnival, the Bishop of Rome giving the chief rabbi a symbolic kick in the rump every year, restrictions of occupations.

I expected this of a ghetto. But to continue until 1870, that was the shock. This was continuing, while Verdi was writing his operas:

Nabucco
Attila
Rigoletto
La traviata
Un ballo in maschera
La forza del destino

The ghetto was there right through the century of enlightenment. I expected this in Eastern Europe, the restrictions in the Pale of Settlement, but not in Rome, *città aperta*. How to reconcile the pleasures of *carciofi alla giudia* – the fried artichokes – and the history, my history, behind them? I was upset that I was not more upset by this almost personal history.

This became the starting point of the project, the finding of the history both triumphant and lamentable.

I think coming from South Africa is important. Our large, painful history is so present that, even now, thirty years after the end of apartheid, the connection of history and shame is self-evident. The ongoing disputes in South Africa over the status of bronze statues and monuments to the leaders of our *ancien régime* are appropriate. Every statue to a hero is a monument to the disaster that left thousands bereft.

Red in the face

In the classical Roman era, a triumph was granted to a general who had won victory in a foreign war. The victorious general would be honoured with a procession showing the spoils of his campaign. The stolen booty, the arms, the banners would be paraded through the streets of Rome, together with the slaves captured, the defeated king or chief in chains.

The general himself, his face painted red, would lead the procession in his chariot. A slave would ride behind him, holding a laurel wreath over the general's head, and from time to time proclaiming to the general, "Look behind you. Remember, you are mortal." Painted banners depicting the battles won would be displayed on the Capitoline Hill, where the procession ended. The procession for the Caesar, of course, was a disaster for those newly enslaved, for the defeated king or general.

The wall between Ponte Sisto and Ponte Mazzini on the Tiber is five hundred metres long. The walls are twelve metres high. If the frieze started one metre above the pavement and ended one metre below the parapet, it would mean the figures, the *dramatis personae* of the frieze would be about ten metres tall. Even with gaps, I would need seventy to eighty figures in the procession. The task of the imagery of the frieze, these eighty figures, became to make a record, one of many possible records, of the unbreakable connection between glorious and shameful histories.

These are thoughts that were clarified during the making of the project. The heart of it is always in the studio.

Speeding up / Holding on to the Renaissance

I've spoken about the shame, historically, and particularly personal, of the embarrassment at my own lack of understanding;

and of needing to keep the history separate, to hold on to the six-year-old's view of the city. But also, the art student's need to hold on to those sculptures, drawings, and frescoes that were so much part of the foundation of how I saw, how I see, and how I work as an artist. A need to hold on to the best ideas of the Renaissance and its consequences; and a need not to see its dark underbelly.

But when I realised this blindness, there was an energy that came with this anger. Anger, let me stress, not at the events of history, at the ghetto, but at myself. This energy fills the studio. It's not an anger anymore. It's an energy of connection, of readiness to work, of wanting the project to get off the ground. This energy speeds up the walk around the studio, the dismantling and reconstruction of images, the shifting of different things pinned to the studio walls or on different pages of the notebook. It allows a connection to jump from one image to another.

I collected images. A team in Rome started scouring archives, medieval manuscripts, taking photographs of the statues in Rome, making photographs of photographs, and putting them into two files of images, which were sent to me in Johannesburg – a file of triumphant images and a file of lamentable images.

This file of images grew. In the end, there were several hundred possible images of triumphs and laments, from which I made a choice for the final seventy or eighty figures in the procession. These images were to be used as raw material to be cut up, to be disembowelled, to be recombined, one image with another.

Taking it apart

Let us look at this question of fragmentation and collage in more detail. We have different scraps of paper which we start arranging. Black torn sheets of paper. Two verticals, a horizontal, an angled line, and suddenly we can't not see the horse. It is not about us generously pretending that there is a horse; we simply cannot resist the way the horse comes towards us. We are in fact seeing three things. A collection of black torn shapes – we know that we are seeing this. We see a horse. And thirdly – and again, to stress this activity evident in the studio, but in fact, what happens outside as well – thirdly, we are aware of being outside of ourselves, of seeing the paper and the image, of seeing our pleasure, which is our pleasure of self-deception. Knowing that these are just sheets of paper, but still unable to stop seeing the horse and all the other horses hidden within the image. The horse of Don Quixote; Goya's horse balancing on a tightrope, the horse elected to the Roman Senate. This is the first kind of collage. In the same way that there is a rearranging of fragments of material to find an image, there is also a working with the larger historical fragments to find a new understanding.

The *Winged Victory* on Trajan's Column is another kind of collage. The figure shown on the column is taken from a classical Greek figure. In fact, it is an image of a woman showing the invention of writing. She is writing on the shield.

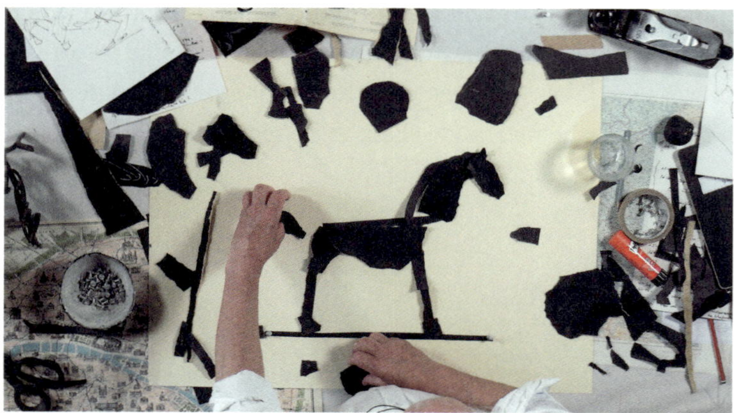

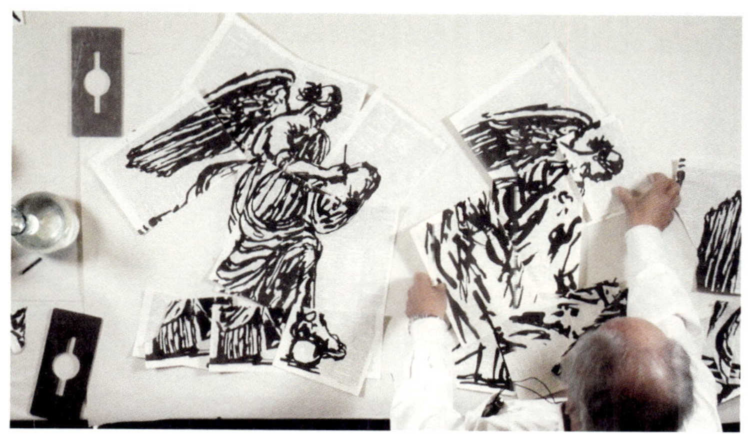

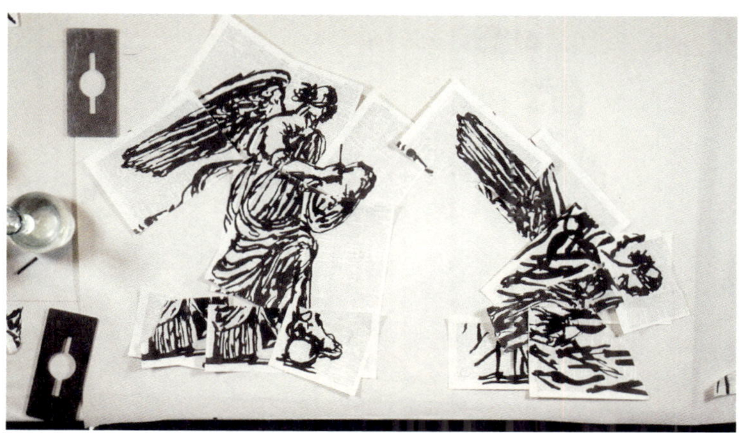

The angel's wings were added to her by the Romans, the two images combined to make a new one. We can take this figure of victory further and break it up again. Cut up the *Winged Victory*, let it collapse on itself, as if we are showing the ravages of time, but in which we show both a torn-up drawing, a collapsed *Winged Victory*, and coming out of that, an image of the folly of grandeur. Even the very emblem of Rome, of the she-wolf and the two boys, is a collage. The emblematic image is a mixture of the Byzantine wolf and a more recently added sculpture of two boys.

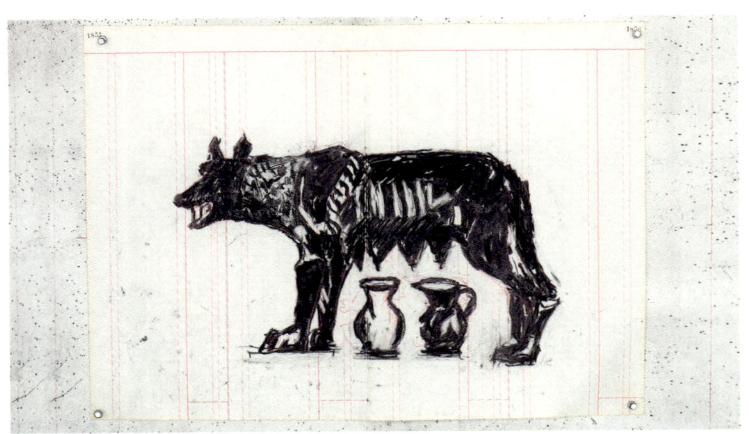

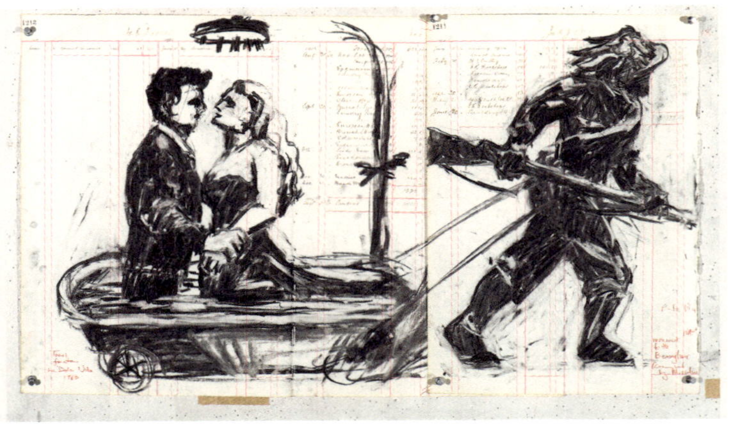

The third collage, of course, is a collage of different larger fragments, where the very disjunction is the heart of the matter, where it is impossible to miss the construction of the image. For example, taking the stone bath from outside the front of the Palazzo Farnese, together with Marcello Mastroianni and Anita Ekberg in the Trevi Fountain from *La Dolce Vita*. We know we are seeing a construction, and we are set a riddle that may or may not have an answer. We are at the edge of meaning. We can feel a pressure towards meaning, without necessarily reaching the goal and relieving ourselves of that pressure.

We may find a meaning or ascribe a meaning, but we are aware that we are doing this, that our biographies and our sets of associations are complicit in the meaning. So, the meaning can, at best, be provisional.

The image on wheels

Everything started to speed up in the studio. There was the need to choose the fragments, to find a balance between image and history. I needed a procession to walk along the wall of the river, like a triumphal or historical procession, like unwinding the frieze on Trajan's Column.

I wanted a mix of surprising, unexpected images, idiosyncratic images, and also images that the citizens of Rome who would either walk or cycle past the frieze would recognise. What was the balance? How many different popes could be in the procession? I could have made the entire frieze just out of images of the popes. There were historical needs. Who were the cast of characters to be included in the procession?

But there were also the studio needs, the formal demands. I needed images of people walking in profile to have a sense of the movement of the procession. This made many of the images sent to me unusable.

There was always a question of how an existing image or historical event would turn into an image on the frieze. What would the drawing be?

O Dio, che dolore

Rome is a wonderful city to work with, as it is so filled with public monuments and its heroes. Many of the groups or figures were

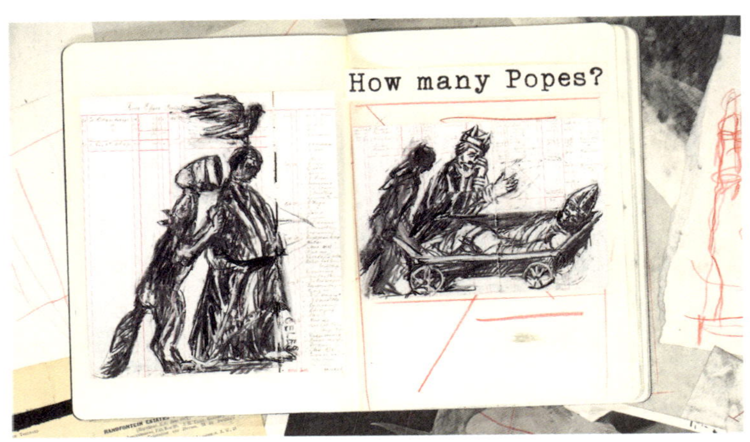

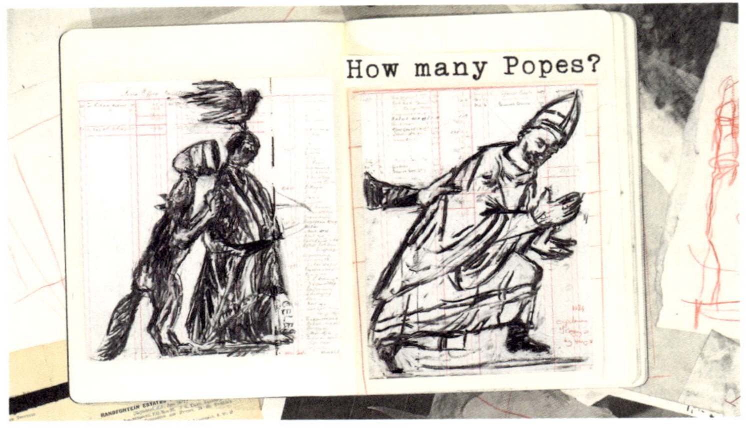

easily recognisable. They were based on familiar Roman public sculptures: Marcus Aurelius, Garibaldi on his horse, Giordano Bruno. There were less familiar images too, taken from medieval manuscripts.

There were many images I wanted to use, but which did not fit into the needs of a frieze. So, Giorgiana Masi, killed by police in the student demonstration on the edge of the Tiber in 1977, and her dying call, *"O Dio, che dolore"* ("Oh God, such pain"), should have had a place on the frieze. But the portrait image that I could find of her was not possible. If I think of it now, it could

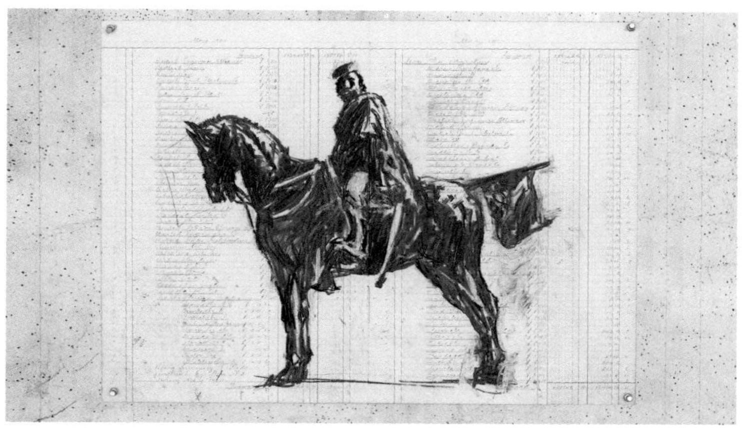

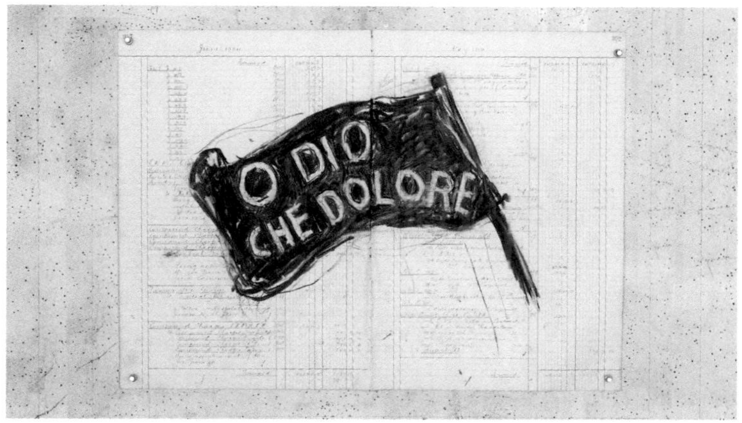

have been a portrait on a flag, carried in the procession, like a religious image of a saint. But at the time, I had no space for that.

There were connections. An image of the dead Remus from a Renaissance engraving, and a newspaper photograph of the dead Pasolini, were put together. There were many horses, from Marcus Aurelius to Anna Garibaldi, to a drunk pony from a sarcophagus showing the triumph of Bacchus, to the humiliation of Jews on a donkey during carnival.

One could do a whole frieze and essay just on the horses and their riders. One could talk about the magnification of a man

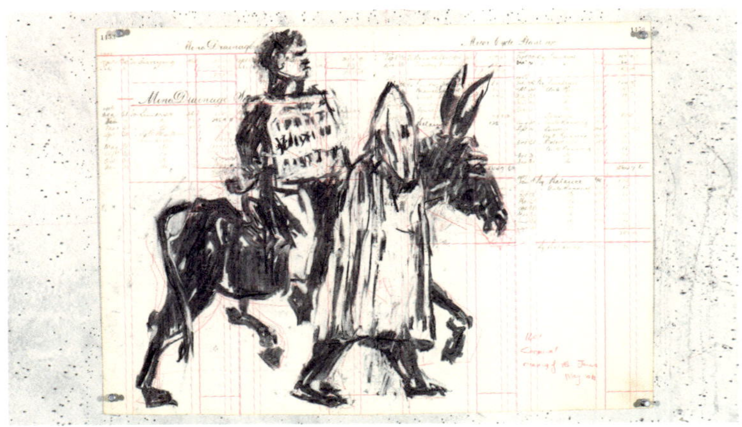

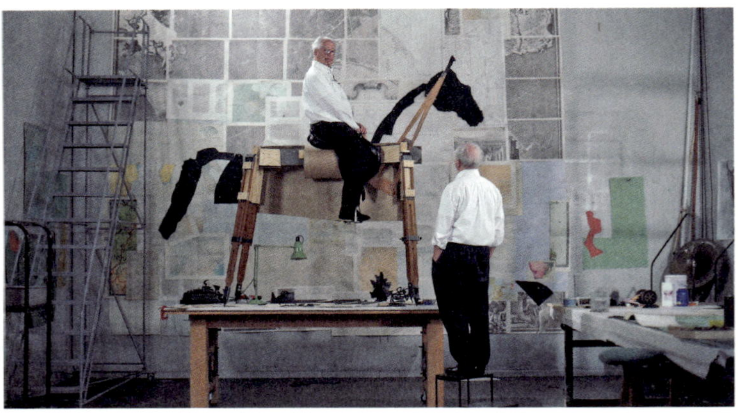

when he sits on a horse. A man or woman on their own seems so puny. A person shrinks when turned into life-sized sculpture. It appears a miniature. Putting the sculpture on a pedestal helps. But put the person on a horse on a pedestal and we have the makings of a hero. The figure takes on some of the attributes of the horse. A straight back, a more confident posture.

Horses and their fragmentation became a central element of the procession. I rearranged different fragments of horses on the table, disassembling the monument, allowing the hand and the paper to do the thinking, arriving at a skeletal horse to end the procession.

Juventus / Roma

Images from the heroic file were juxtaposed with images from the lamentable file. If there was an image I needed, but it was not in profile, I compromised by putting it on a cart, like the gods in a Greek drama that would be pulled onto the stage on a cart, to show their different status from the mortals. And then I would have a person, or a horse pull the cart.

There were far more images than I had space for. In the end, the choice was personal; biography and history mixed. Many glories, many triumphs, were personal ones that I needed in the procession. Bernini's *The Ecstasy of St Teresa*, Michelangelo's *Jeremiah*, Haile Selassie were all there. There were juxtapositions of people escaping from the flood on the Tiber in 1934, together with images of refugees trying to reach Italy from North Africa in 2014. Parallel to this were images of the widows of Rome, mourning during the plague, and widows of Lampedusa, of women mourning men drowned trying to get to Rome.

I allowed myself a personal choice, wanting an image by Masaccio. I chose his painting of St Peter crucified upside down. In this case, it was both a love of Masaccio and wanting to have an image that could come down from the top of the wall. There was also an image of Mussolini, based on a fresco that still exists in Naples, in an abandoned park built for a trade fair in the 1940s. The fair never took place. Bullet holes from partisans, from retreating German soldiers, or perhaps South African soldiers, still pockmark the fresco. I was astonished that there would still be a fresco of Mussolini in a public place in Italy, and that pushed it into the procession.

Initially, when doing the random placing of heroes and villains next to each other in the frieze, I had Mussolini next to St Peter hanging upside down, but then I realised, as I placed the cutout figures next to each other, that this reference to

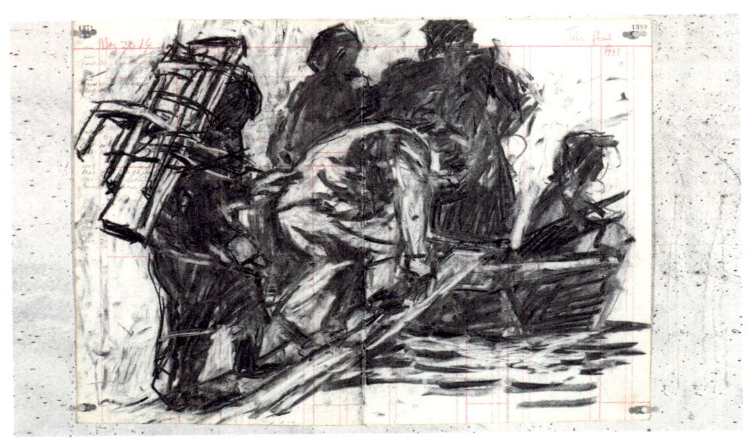

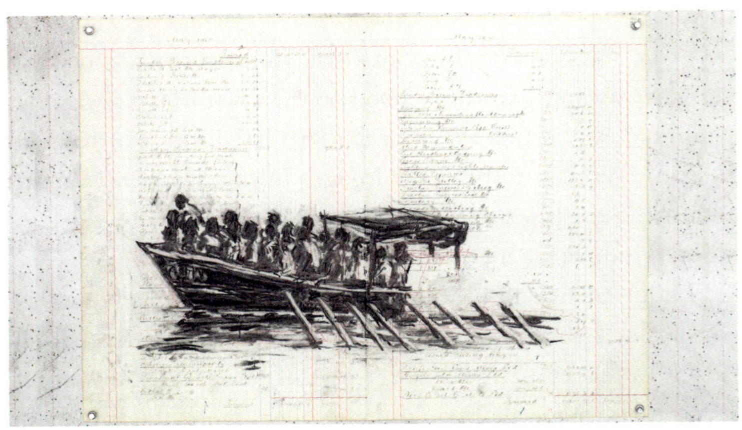

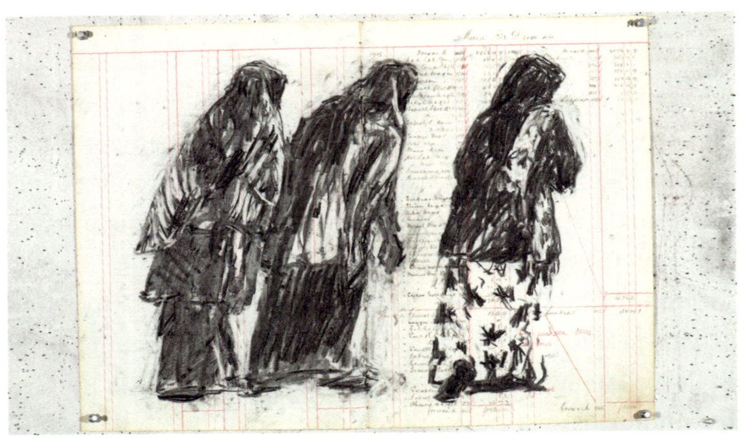

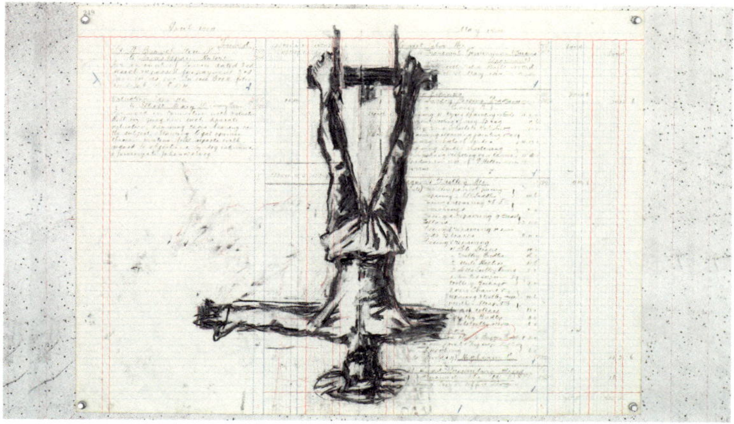

Mussolini hanging upside down from a lamppost in Milan might, by association, turn him into a martyr. So, St Peter and Mussolini were moved farther apart on the studio desk, and on the walls of the Tiber River.

Public associations had to be taken into account. I was told that the positions of the wolf and the desiccated wolf skeleton had to be considered; this, because of the use of the icon by the right-wing Juventus football fans, versus the left-wing Roma supporters. There were many petitions as to who should be in the procession, and who out. Some I acceded to, and many not.

Trusting the hand

But each figure had to earn its place twice, once as a visual image, and again as a mark of an historical moment. There were of course many hundreds of possible images. I made choices. Some I'm sorry about. Some figures I wish I could have fitted in. But in any event, it was only possible to fit in a certain number. This is only one out of many possible groupings of characters and figures; only one out of many possible accounts of history.

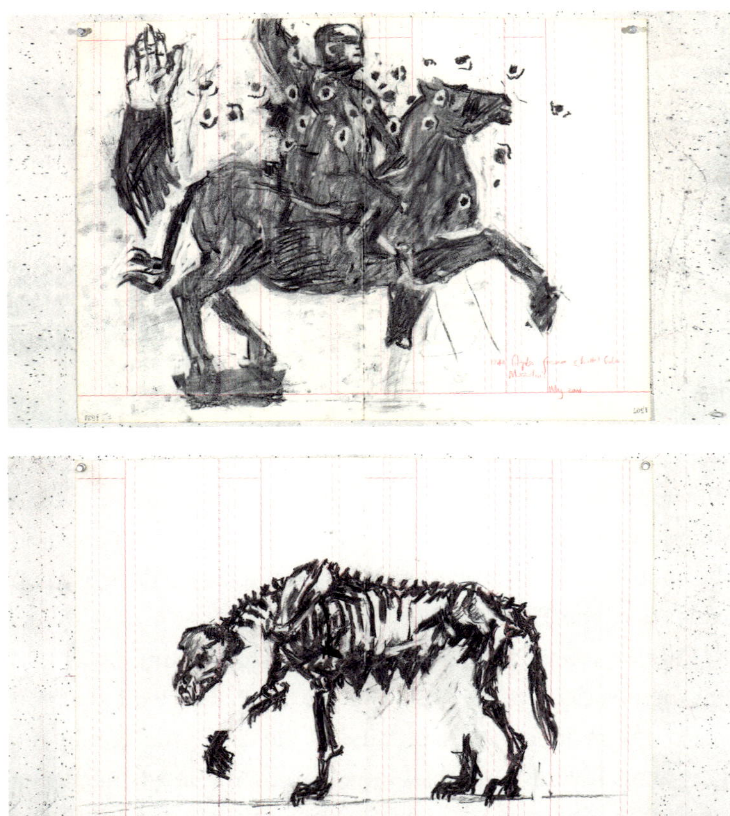

The ordering of the figures is neither random, nor scientifically worked out. The drawings of the figures were spread out in the studio as little black paper cutouts. And moving quickly among the tables, I placed and replaced the drawings, not interrogating each choice, but allowing the movements of the body, of the hand, of the eyes, to find a place for each figure; relying on all the knowledge of the images, of the history they carried, to guide the physical placement. And then of course, I stood back, looked, assessed, and altered what had been done.

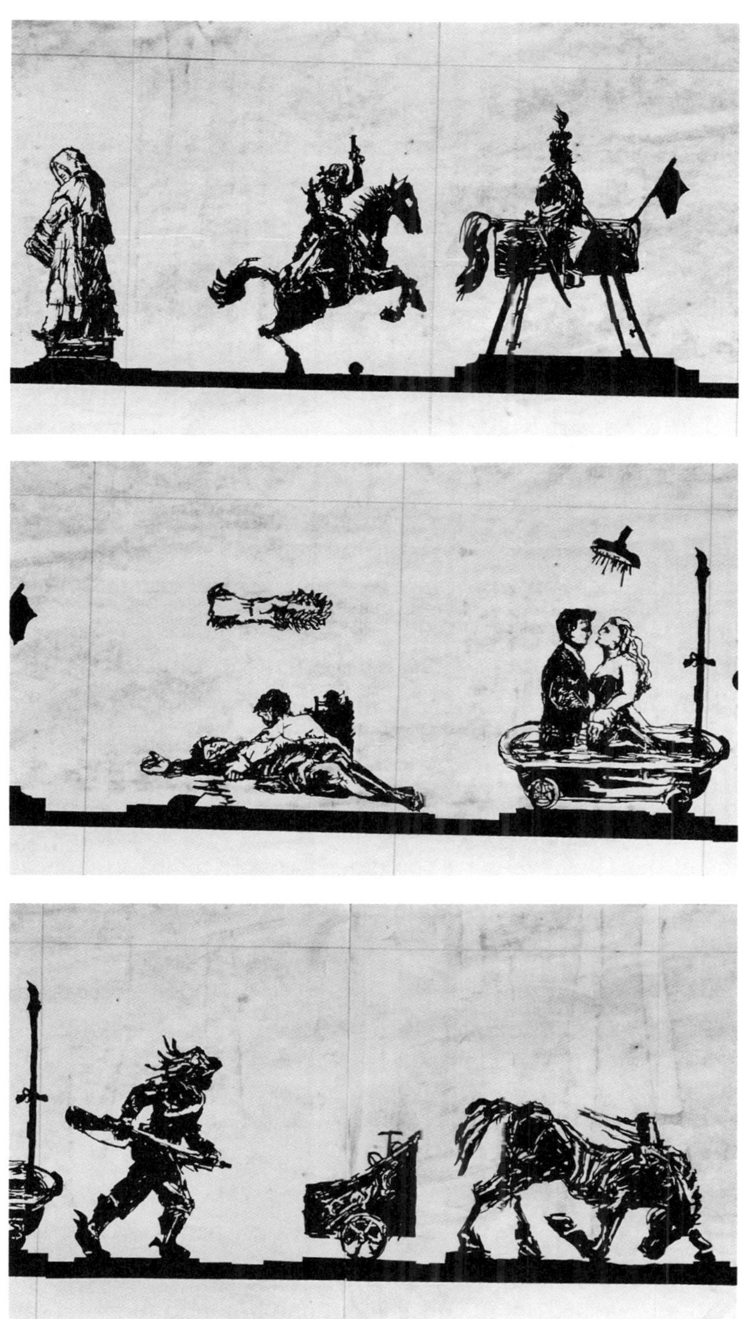

That which I do not remember

The heart of the project was made in my studio in Johannesburg, but of course it had to be achieved in Rome. When almost all the figures had been washed onto the wall in Rome, I saw there was a disjunction between the spacing I had made in the studio in Johannesburg, and a gap of several metres that needed to be filled. It was too late then to make another figure and another complicated stencil. So, I left it as a black square, just tracing an edge to it. I gave it the legend, "That which I do not remember." *Quello che non ricordo.*

This must stand in for all our gaps, and my gaps, of understanding; that which we do not remember because it was hidden from us; or because our heads were too filled with easier, more consoling thoughts; or because we could not summon the energy to find the connections in our histories.

When all the preparations had been made – and the stencils cut in the factory outside of Rome, and the system worked out with scaffolding and broomsticks and hanging trusses – we had four weeks in which to actually erase the frieze onto the walls of the Tiber. This was the period between the ending of the flooding of the Tiber, when we could get access to the pavements at the bottom of the wall, and the birthday of Rome, when it was decreed the frieze should be opened. This was not our timing. This was the timing given to us in the various *permessi* of the twenty-six organisations that control the river and its banks.

Singing across the water

To mark the opening, we made a concert and a parade. The parade and the concert would be watched from across the river, which is to say, we had an audience about one hundred metres away

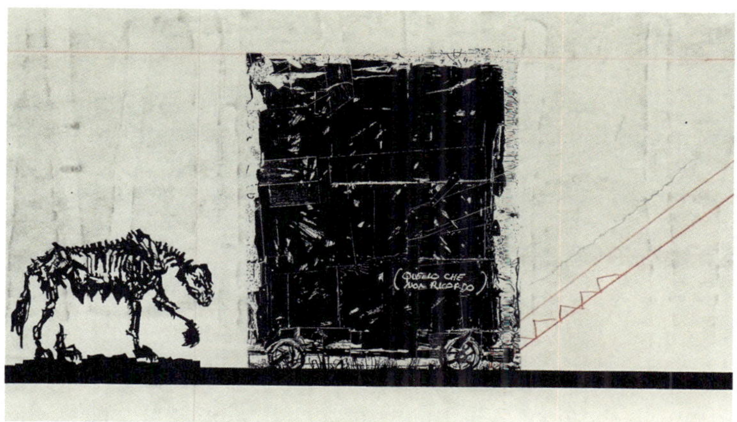

from the performers, but a stage five hundred metres in length.

I invited a South African composer and long-time collaborator to work on the music for this opening parade. He invited another South African composer to work with him. We decided we would have two orchestras, an orchestra of triumph and an orchestra of lament, which would start at opposite ends of the five hundred metres, walk through each other, and disappear past each other.

The initial idea was from the Charles Ives composition *The Three Places in New England,* of two brass bands marching through each other, but it soon changed in its form. The composers worked with the music of Salamone Rossi, a late Renaissance Jewish Italian composer from Mantua, and based their work on a piece of music titled *Al naharot bavel,* which is itself rooted in a text of Exodus, relating to migration and exile.

A twenty-first century procession was obviously also a procession of migrants, of refugees, of the stories that were in the newspapers, and still are, but particularly around 2015, of people from North Africa, trying to make their way across the Mediterranean to the island of Lampedusa, and then onto the Italian mainland.

The music of Salamone Rossi was part of the music. But there was also the music of street musicians, a tarantella; the music played on a *kora* by an African migrant living in Rome and performing on the streets. There were also South African songs.

Spoglie

There was the question of what the people in the procession would be carrying or holding above their heads. In a Roman triumph, the booty, the spoils of a campaign, the *spoglie*, the armour of the defeated enemy would be carried behind the victorious general. We found portraits, Roman portraits, contemporary portraits, and objects to be carried aloft. There were also a series of personal objects. For example, a Vespa scooter, which was from my memory of the sixties of what Rome was: Vespas and Lambrettas; my mother's sewing machine, which was a Necchi; her typewriter, which was an Olivetti. The fifties and sixties were the heydays of Italy's industrial resurgence after the Second World War. We had 150 musicians and volunteers making up the procession. They would carry these cardboard objects. We made or own *spoglie*.

We had the idea of a procession. We knew the music we were playing. It had been rehearsed with the musicians. But the audience was one hundred metres away on the opposite bank of the river from the side of the frieze and of the procession. At that distance a person looks tiny. We had to find a way to enlarge the performers and musicians. This enlargement was done through casting the shadows of the performers, and their musical instruments and *spoglie* onto the wall of the frieze behind them. There was a whole other grammar to learn. And this is what happens in the studio: a first idea and impulse, an image; and then the work of learning what the image tells you.

A note on geometry

There were several lessons to learn.

To set the scene: The pavement below the wall is approximately ten metres wide from the base of the wall to the edge of the river. So, we could place lights every twenty-five metres on the ground, at the edge of the river, pointing at the wall. If you walked through this beam of light, your shadow would be cast on the wall. This was obvious. We had an idea of a shadow procession, of a procession of the shadows cast by people, going across the wall. We had twenty lamps, each of which lit a distance of twenty-five metres.

The first lesson is obvious. If you are close to the wall, the shadow you cast on the wall is more or less your height. When you are right against the wall, your shadow, the part of the wall that your body obscures from the light, is exactly life-size. But as you move away from the wall, towards the light, your shadow grows – this is elementary geometry – so that if you are right up against the light, your body obliterates and covers all the light, and your shadow covers the entire wall.

There was a distance of approximately two and a half metres away from the light in which your shadow would be the ten-metre height of the wall. We traced a line on the pavement, roughly in the "sweet spot," where, if you walked along the line carrying your banner, your shadow would be the full height of the wall. We thought we had solved the projection question. Everybody would walk along that line, and their shadows would fill the wall. We would have a procession of ten-metre-high figures moving across the wall, which would be easily visible. The actual musicians and players and performers look like tiny dots across the hundred-metre width of the river, but their shadows would be very clearly visible at a height of ten metres.

That was the first lesson.

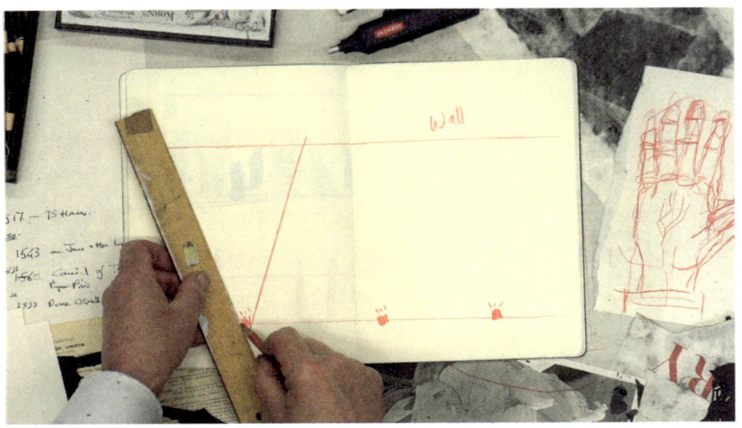

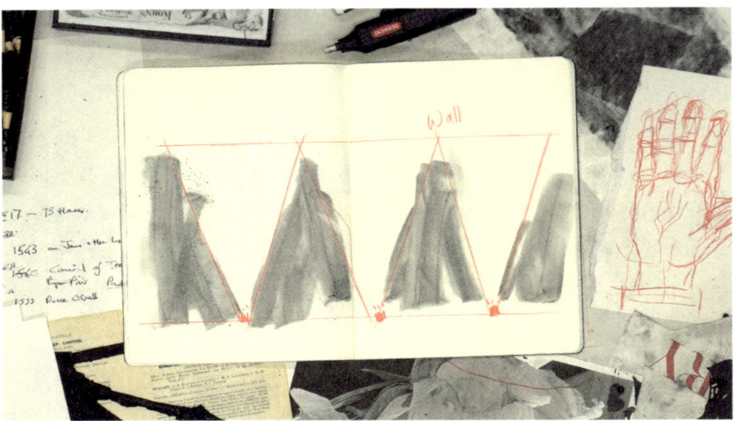

The hard lesson was the second lesson, which in retrospect is also obvious, but which we had not anticipated. We had our performers, in a rehearsal, walk along the line that made the shadows ten metres high. But instead of having a wall of eighty figures, whose shadows filled it, we had about six figures, and huge empty spaces.

If you are only two metres away from the light, in that triangle of light from the projector lamp to the wall, you have approximately four metres to walk before you go out of the cone of light; four metres to enter the cone of light and to exit it. Then you

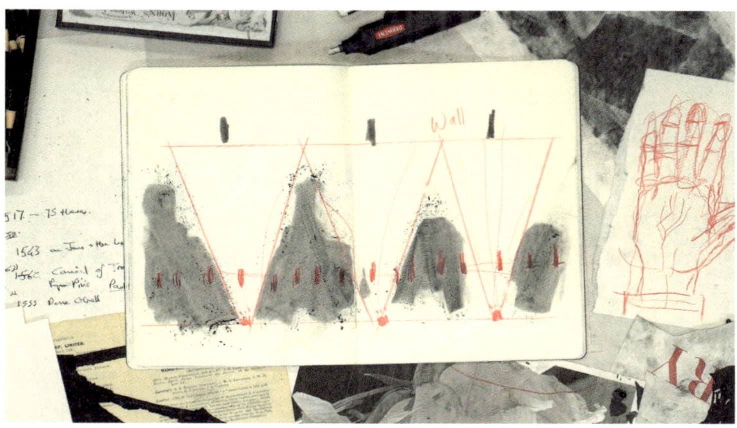

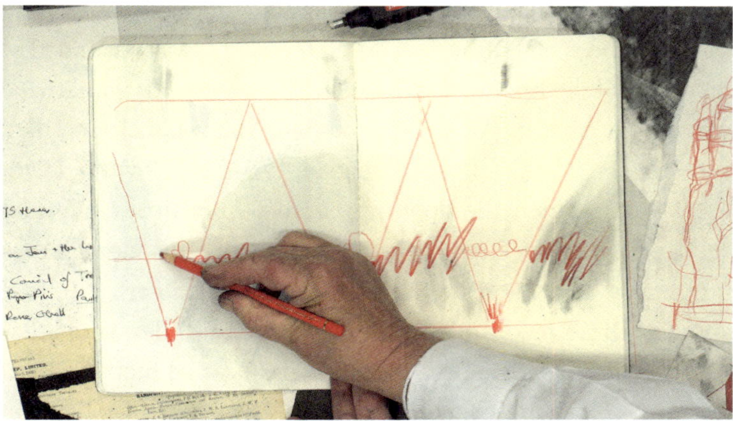

have approximately twenty metres of darkness between the two cones of light as you approach the next light. So, we were stuck. Instead of having eighty figures, we had four or eight figures visible at a time and a crowd invisible in the darkness between the cones of light.

This was the second lesson, from which we had to learn the third lesson, which was how to deal with this gap of darkness between the short areas of light. This was done in rehearsal with the performers. As you entered a cone of light, your speed had to be very slow, very measured, before it exited the cone of light. But once you exited the cone of light, you had to run as fast as you could to be ready to enter the next cone of light – in a sense, slowing down and speeding up time to account for, and to swallow, these dark areas.

Our shadows became an expansion and contraction of time. To play with the dark matter between the lights. The images going from invisibility to clarity. From across the river the shadows of the procession becoming visible when they were in the light and disappearing when entering the shadow spaces in between.

To achieve this, in the rehearsal and in the performances, we had teams of people best described as sheepdogs, shepherding the performers and telling them to slow down as they approached the light and speed up as they exited the light. I was reminded of an image of the first wolf I'd had for the processions – an image of the wolf parading up and down along the walls of the Tiber, nipping at the heels of people, presenting itself, slowing down.

We performed the opening parade three times. We had rehearsed it once. Then the procession was gone and exists as a memory. It becomes erased. It was recorded certainly, and some of these recordings still exist. But one understands that most recordings disappear into hard drives, and then the hard drive develops a glitch, and it is gone. Computer files become corrupted. The life expectancy of a digital file is three years. Unless it is constantly backed up, it will disappear. So, it exists still in fragments on the "cloud" and internet, video recordings I still have, which still have some patency, but which probably will disappear in the next few years.

The record of this procession will disappear far more quickly than any of the other more durable, more solid, physical monuments that fill the city. Perhaps the most durable version of the frieze along the Tiber will be photographs which have been physically printed out on paper. But this too only has the life expectancy of paper, approximately six hundred years.

Rhodes must fall

Monuments are always about the loss of memory. A monument is like a list. We take a list to the supermarket: milk, eggs, potatoes, aluminium foil, fusilli. The list remembers for us, outsourcing our memory. Just as we outsource our laughter, while watching a sitcom with canned laughter. The programme laughs on our behalf. The monument remembers for us.

There is something shameful in our inability to keep memories, to keep history, to keep emotions alive. What to do with old monuments and their shame? The heroes on plinths are always someone else's villain. Rhodes of the Rhodes Scholarship, presiding over Cape Town university, and sitting two stories up in a niche at Rhodes House in Oxford, where these lectures are given. The Cape Town Rhodes has been removed. The Oxford Rhodes remains, behind a wire netting to protect him from the city pigeons. To remove the statues or to leave them? Neither solution feels right. Leaving the statues untouched feels like a failure, their metaphoric authority continuing. But the absence is inadequate, putting history in a cupboard and closing the door. We need a less good solution. Only while the contestation is alive, is the monument adequate to its history.

In praise of the ephemeral

In Roman triumphs, the scenes of the triumphant general's exploits were painted on cloth, and these banners were displayed around the city. They were left hanging open to the weather. In a few weeks and months, the fabric would rot and the paint fade. All that remains are reports of them. Another general would soon have another triumph. New banners would be made.

The drawing of the frieze was achieved by the removal of all that was not the frieze, cleaning the dark bacteria and pollution on the wall that left the images against the cream travertine stone. But the bacteria and pollution return. The wall darkens again. The images get swallowed by the growing charcoal grey. Not all at once. The bacteria and pollution grow at different rates on different sections of the wall. Most images have disappeared entirely, just six years after the frieze was made. Of others, ghost images remain, but not for long.

Provisionality was built into the very medium and process itself. And the very fact of the ephemerality of the work made for a freedom. The collage, the construction of history, was not there forever. It was not the one, definitive history. It was not even going to be there for a decade. The collage was only one of many possible combinations of understanding, one particular history and biography. Others could take its place.

Musil wrote that monuments must try harder to keep their visibility. I think that the disappearance of the *Triumphs and Laments* frieze feels just right. The wall is ready for a new history to be made.

Triumphs and Laments
2016
500 m frieze on the walls of the Tiber River, Rome
Opening performance April 21, 2016: Theatrical event with live shadow play and two processional marching bands performing against the backdrop of the frieze.
Composer: Philip Miller
Musical director: Thuthuka Sibisi

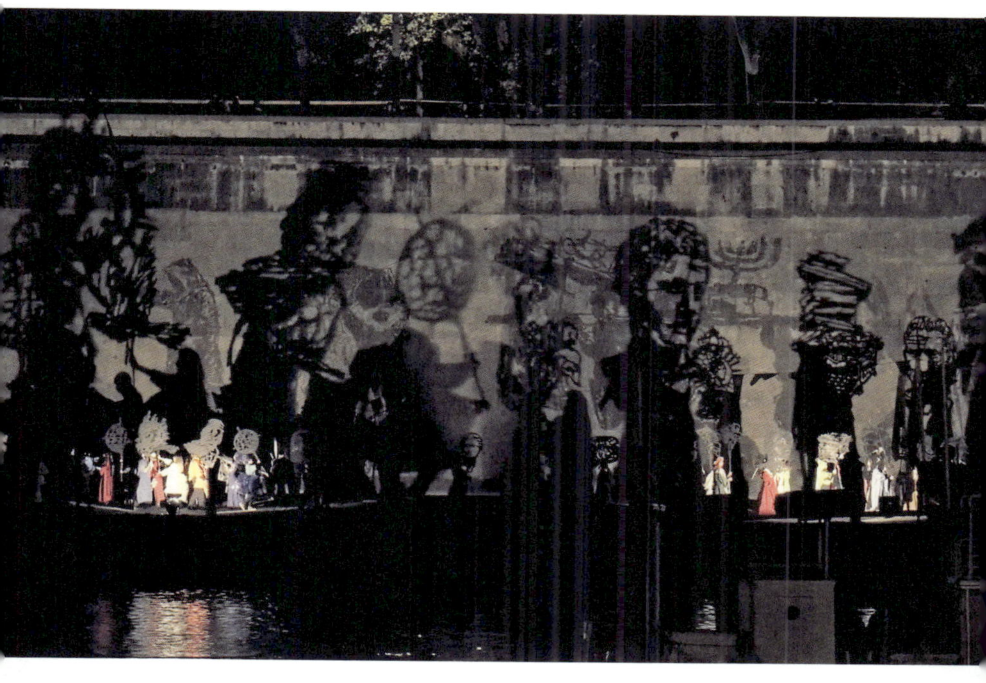

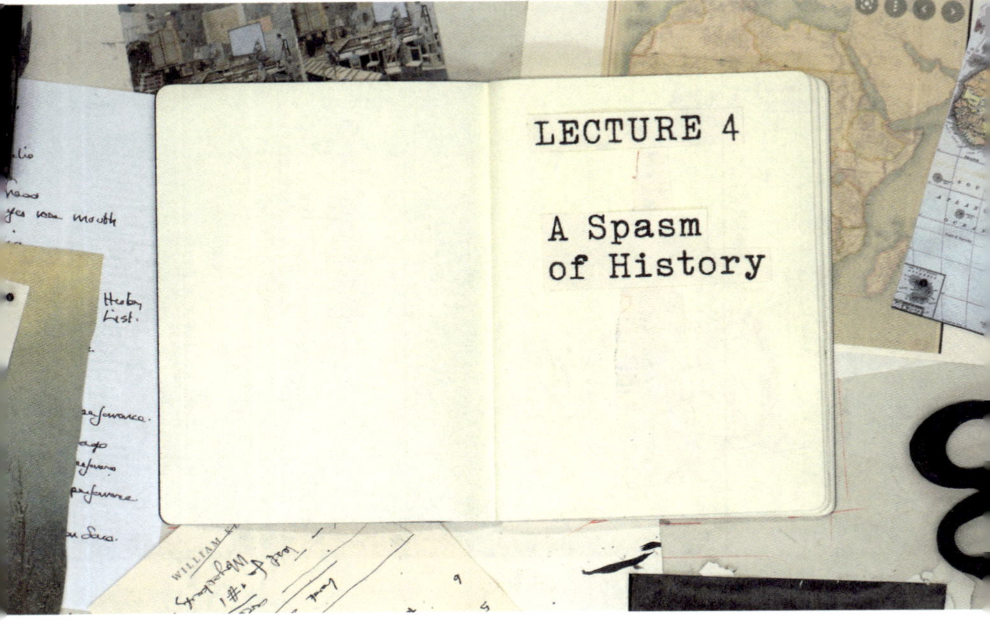

LECTURE 4

A Spasm
of History

A SPASM OF HISTORY

I draw a line down the page of a notebook. I write STUDIO at the top of one column. I write HISTORY at the top of the second column. We set an agenda.

The vertical line feels wrong. I turn it on its side.

STUDIO above the line; HISTORY below the line.

No, reverse this. HISTORY above the line; STUDIO below the line.

The line dividing the centre of the page, so there is space to think.

Then I list the associations as they arise – placing them as fast as I can, the hand slower than the thoughts.

History – what I know. School lessons. What I was taught. What remains of that. What I have forgotten. What I was not taught.

STUDIO – stupidity. Techniques tried and tested.
HISTORY – divide the lines and add IGNORANCE, three types of.

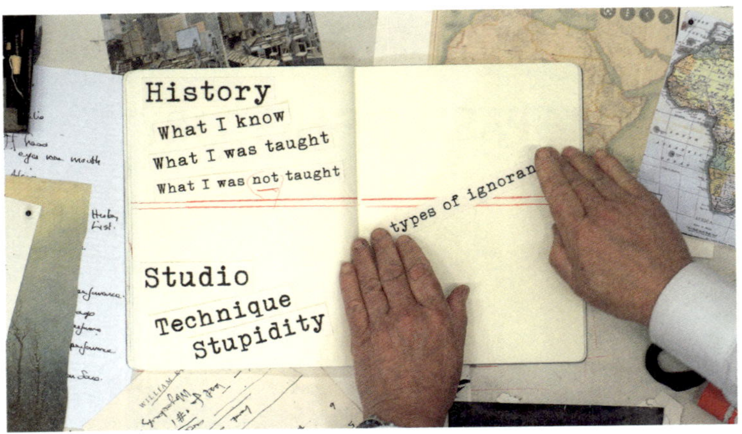

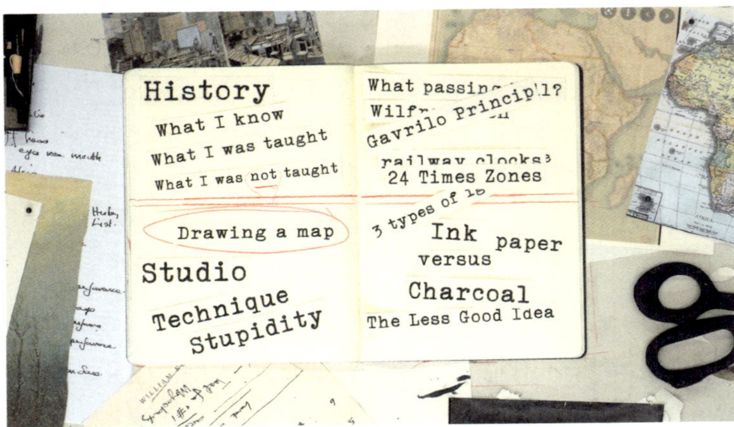

Let the thoughts flow – follow where they lead.

Then: What passing bell for those who die as cattle?

Not Wilfred Owen. Enough and more than enough of Wilfred Owen, Siegfried Sassoon, and Rupert Brooke.

IGNORANCE AS A STARTING POINT.
FINDING A LESS GOOD IDEA. INK VERSUS CHARCOAL.
FINDING THE MEDIUM, FINDING A SUBJECT THAT FEEDS
THE MEDIUM.

On the history line, waiting for a spark, for the shot in Sarajevo, the death of the Archduke and his wife, the unforgettable name of Gavrilo Princip. The railway timetables; the precision of the Prussian railway timetables.

In Switzerland, Einstein coordinating clocks in railway stations. Coordinating the clocks in the world. The division of the world into its twenty-four time zones. These are the thoughts accumulating. All these thoughts need to find their place, nudging this lecture into shape. The drawing of a map.

Here is a starting point. Let us begin. No, not yet, first a different thought. A geography of the screen.

Returning the gaze

Let us start with the face and its eyeline. It is amazing how constant this level of the eyeline is – the relative position of the eyes between the hairline and the chin. Across different facial types, different genders, different representations . . . at any rate, an eyeline. Put the face in a screen, a closeup but also a medium shot or a wide shot, and the eyeline remains remarkably

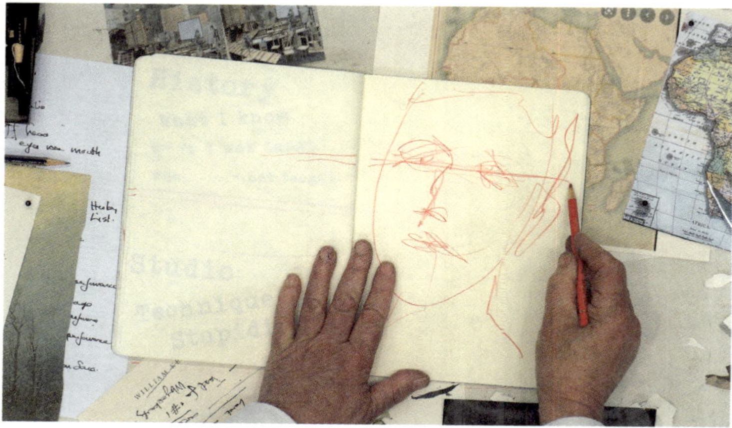

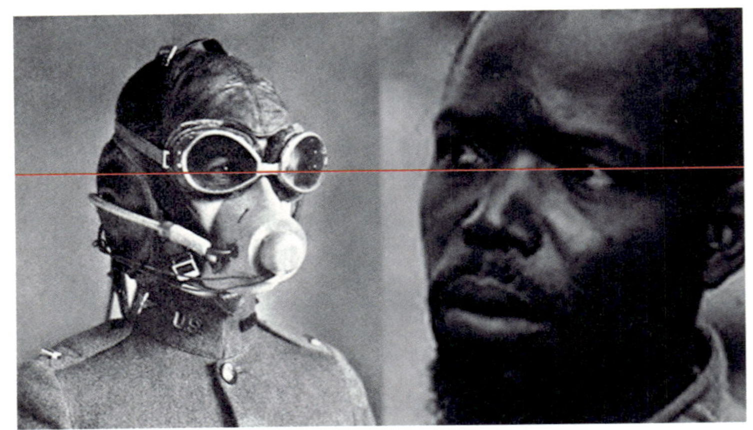

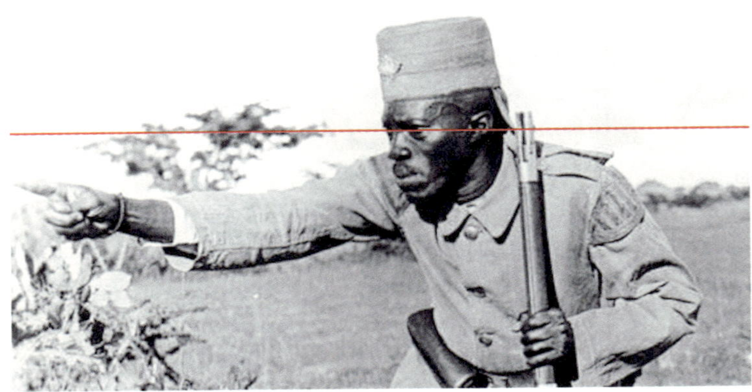

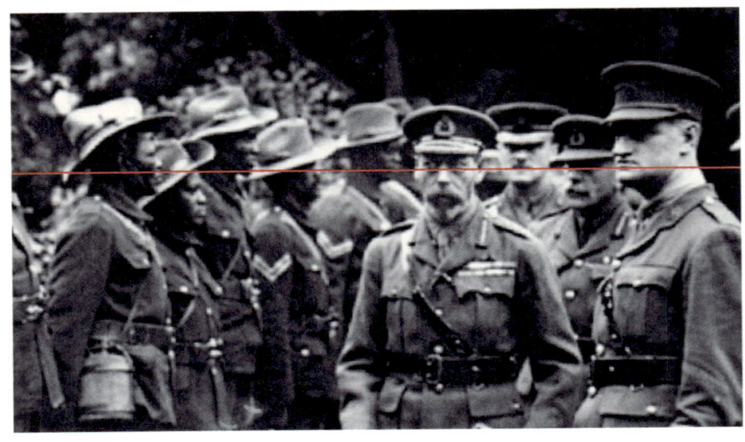

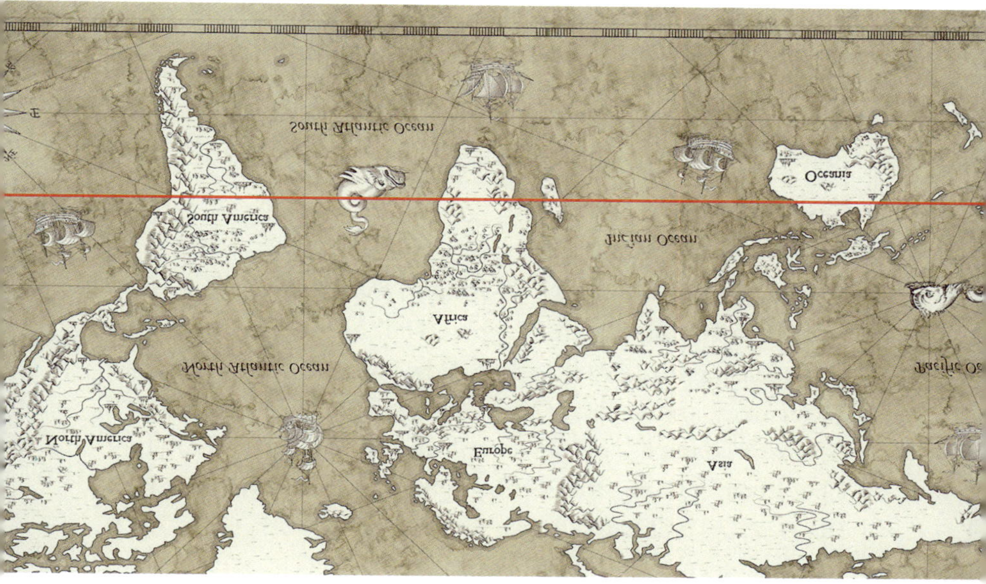

constant. Not by design. The cinematographer is not thinking about composing the shot in accordance with the golden mean, but framing the shot so that it feels right.

So, an eyeline in a face but also across the screen. Our faces looking at the screen; the screen becomes a mirror. The eyeline is the line that looks back at us. The screen looking back at us, the gaze of the screen.

When we have our usual map of the world, the eyes of the world look at us in Africa from Europe. This is neither random, nor a conspiracy. It hovers in the space where understanding lies behind conscious reasoning. If we invert the map, it feels somehow improper, even obscene. Europe at the bottom, bending its head down, looking up our collective southern skirts. But now we have Africa, South Africa, Johannesburg looking back at Europe. Time to rearrange geography, time to cut up the map.

Berlin, 1884: under the patronage of Bismarck, the European powers agreed to the division of the continent of Africa, between

Germany, Britain, France, Portugal, and Spain – dividing the land, the population, the resources. The division of Africa between European powers was complete.

Reverse-engineering

The theatre performance *The Head & The Load* was first performed in London, in the Turbine Hall of the Tate Modern, and subsequently in Amsterdam, New York, the Ruhrtriennale in Germany, and Johannesburg. As the previous lecture had at its centre *Triumphs and Laments*, the project on the walls of the Tiber River in Rome, this lecture will pivot around the work for *The Head & The Load*.

These lectures all look backwards to projects made years before the lectures were written and have a reverse-engineering as the *modus operandi*. There are no secrets to be told, nor revelations to be had in the end, but rather a confidence in and a desire to show the fragmented, inchoate process used to arrive at the finished work (finished only in the sense that this is where the work stopped, not that it could not have continued further, or that more could not have been made and shown); and to test the proposition that the fragmented, reconstructed collage is a way of thinking about the past and making a history.

The walls and tables and shelves of the studio are filled with photographs, narratives, maps, diagrams, hopes and desires and despairs; insights and blindnesses, waiting to be glued to the blank paper pinned to the studio wall; ink, rulers, and pencils sharpened, waiting to draw the lines of connection, to make a drawing and the history of reconfigured fragments.

But first, maybe it is good to emphasise again, I have no list of projects I am waiting to do, a bucket list of grand themes or specific stories. There is no list of proposed projects, not a list which has on it *Fidelio*, the *Ring Cycle*, a memoir, or worse, a novel; no burning desire for a project on fate, or on desire, or on remembrance. Where there should be this list, there is I would say a blankness, a nullity, or if one was generous, an openness. Several of these themes have been in projects made, but never as a starting point. There's always been an external prompt, a goad, a stick with a point at the end pushing me onto the stage, where I quickly assemble allies and collaborators to both respond and to keep it at a safe distance and discover what we make.

"Reveille"

In the case of *The Head & The Load*, there were several starting points: an invitation to make a performance in the Park Avenue Armory in New York. The Park Avenue Armory is a drill hall built in the nineteenth century for the New York National Guard regiment. It is a huge shed, eighty metres long, forty metres wide. This was the beginning – a scale, the size of the project.

But with the physical space comes a set of connected associations. A second prompt: the military associations of a drill hall. A march rhythm begins in my head, bugle calls to be heard, orders and commands. But it is mainly a physical pressure to think in scale, an anti-proscenium.

In the previous lecture, I talked about the five-hundred-metre frieze on the banks of the Tiber River and the processional performance we made for the opening of the frieze. Here was a chance to develop the ideas of that performance, to make another procession with musicians, singers, shadows – I reassured my collaborators. These were the video editors, designers, composers. I showed them the eighty-metre hall and reminded them that we had made a performance more than five hundred metres long, so these eighty metres could be considered a miniature. This too is part of the work of the studio: performances of confidence to hide a consuming uncertainty.

I reassured myself with the list; again, a list of possibilities.

A LONG STAGE, EIGHTY METRES WIDE.
A PROCESSION.
EXPANDING THE IDEA OF WHAT WE HAD LEARNT
IN ROME.

In Rome, the procession and concert were a footnote, a sort of late addendum to the project of the frieze. Here the procession would be the whole project. At any rate, people carrying objects, their shadows thrown onto the backdrop of the theatre, moving slowly across the stage. But a procession of what? Of marching soldiers, musicians, a marching band? Somewhere in the auditorium, a bugle playing "Reveille" or the "Last Post." List-making is a reassuring way for me to work. A neurotic, repeating his symptoms, as if repeating a problem is a way of solving it. Sometimes it is.

A premonition

A third starting point, another overdetermination of the project, enough and more than enough to get going, was a production of Alban Berg's opera *Wozzeck*, made for the Salzburg Festival. Work for the opera began in my studio a year before starting on what was to become *The Head & The Load*.

The Last Days of Mankind by Karl Kraus, the great satirical novel of the First World War, gave the impetus to the *Wozzeck* production. As with the Büchner play on which *Wozzeck* is based, it invokes the passionate absurd to reveal social contradictions and cruelties. Although Büchner's play of a private in the Prussian army was written in 1836, Berg wrote his opera just after the First World War. We staged our production as a premonition of World War I. Some of the Kraus texts leapfrogged over the *Wozzeck* production and made their way into the libretto of *The Head & The Load*.

Anti-Waste

All the theatre productions I work on are developed in my studio in Johannesburg, even if the final performance, in this case *Wozzeck*, would be performed by singers in Salzburg, with an Austrian chorus and many European singers. In the studio we work on a German opera, but it is inflected and infected with the Johannesburg collaborators – dancers and actors who will join me in working out the possibilities in different scenes. How to make a polka of gas-masked, damaged soldiers with chairs as partners? This we did in a Johannesburg workshop, preparing *Wozzeck*, a 1920s opera to be performed in Austria.

But at the end of the workshop, there was a sense of so many extraordinary moments that emerged in the workshop that would be lost, that would find no place in the libretto and music of the opera. What a waste, the performances emerging from the actors and dancers and singers, who were part of the *Wozzeck* workshop, but would not perform in Salzburg. So, we add this to the list of impulses behind the work.

We have the long stage of the Armory. We have the First World War. We have the passionate absurd. We have the presence of African dancers, actors, voices.

A final prod, a gift. A question from the 14–18 NOW festival in Britain – a phone call: Did I have anything that might fit their brief of a connection to World War I?

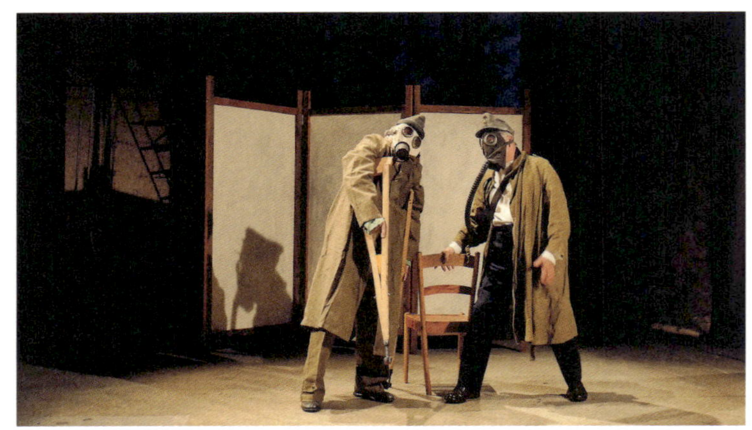

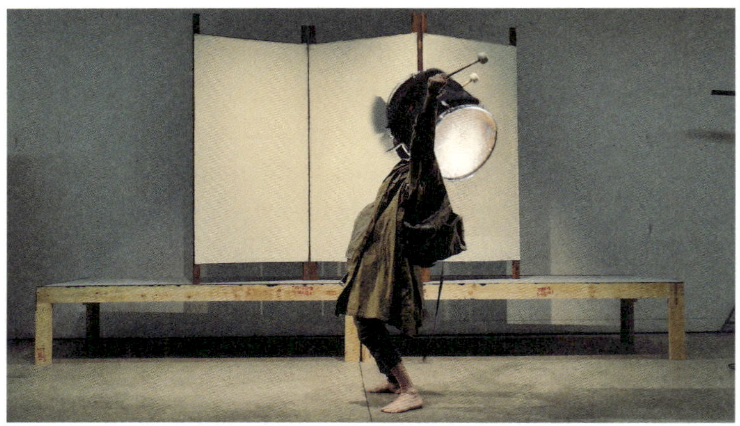

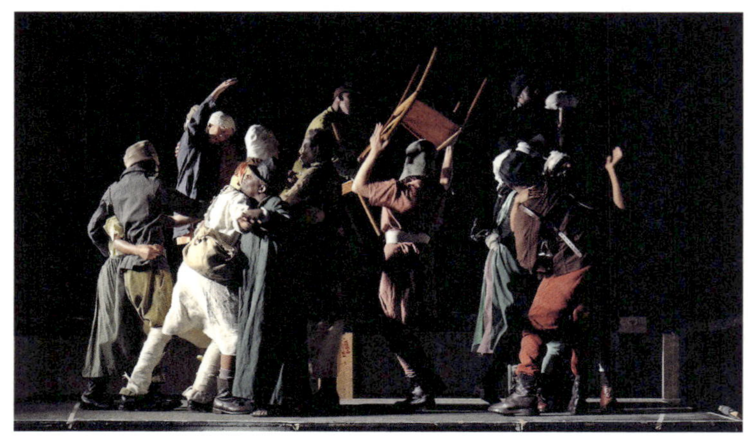

I did have just the thing. I had an eighty-metre processional performance, eighty-five minutes long – I pull the time out of thin air. Sixty performers; that was two bands, six principal actors, four dancers, chorus of thirty or so. Again, the numbers just invented on the spot – about Africa in World War I. Another performance of confidence to hide doubt.

More than that. It is as if the ideas, the images of the project were inside waiting to emerge. The project moved past me, over the cellphone towards the listeners. And I thought okay – this is what we are doing.

And now to give the substance. There is a willing a project into being. The list changes. Which collaborators will be part? The composer, the set designer, the light and costume designers and video collaborators, choreographer? A date for a workshop. The team from *Wozzeck*. The composer from the Rome *Triumphs and Laments*. Slowly, at the side, the project takes form. Except for the heart of it. What did I know of World War I and Africa?

Amnesia

Forty years ago, I had written an undergraduate essay on John Chilembwe and his doomed revolt in what is now Malawi, then Nyasaland, in 1915. When discussing the project on the phone and in writing a list of the components for a workshop to make the Armory piece, I had forgotten Chilembwe and his revolt. A productive amnesia – if Chilembwe's letter and revolt had been in my head I would never have arrived at a project suited for the spaces of the Armory – with its evocation of soldiers, orders called out, precise drilling – his revolt was by barely armed rural civilians. Coming to it later enabled it to find a space in the piece. The revolt was prompted by a letter Chilembwe wrote to a newspaper, about the presence of Africans in the present war, which the newspaper refused to publish. My remembering of the letter arrived halfway through our first week of work. A copy of the letter had sat in the drawer in the studio for forty years. I hunted through the papers and found it. We had a start in text.

Chilembwe was a Baptist minister who was trained in the United States. He had returned to Nyasaland and founded a church at the top of Chiradzulu Hill in the Shire Highlands. His letter to the *Nyasaland Times* was entitled "The Voice of the African Native in the Present War":

> "In time of peace, everything for Europeans only, and instead of honour, we suffer humiliation with names contemptible. But in time of war, it is found we are needed to share the hardships and shed our blood in equality . . . If this is a war for honour, government gain of riches, and so on, let the rich man, the bankers, titlemen, shopkeepers, go to war and get shot. Instead, the poor Africans who have nothing to own in this world, who in death leave only a long line of widows and orphans and utter want and dire distress, are invited to die for a cause which is not theirs . . ."

The letter ends:

> "We leave all for the consideration of the government. We hope in the mercy of Almighty God that someday things will turn out well, and justice will prevail."

> Signed John Chilembwe, on behalf of his countrymen.

Chilembwe's letter was suppressed. He led a revolt, which was suppressed. His church was dynamited. He was executed. Postcards of the dynamited church were sold in aid of the English war effort. This was part of the material presented to the participants when the workshop began.

As with the opera production *Wozzeck*, the workshop was a gathering of thirty or forty people in my studio, over ten days or so, in which we started with any possibility – all ideas, good material, bad material – in the hope that at the end of the ten days, nuggets of what would be in the final piece would have coalesced.

No good solution

I made a drawing based on a nineteenth-century engraving captioned *A Gang of Captives Met at Mbame's on Their Way to Tette*. It shows a group of people, already transformed into tradable commodities, on their way to the slave market at the coast. There is a question, not solved, not resolved: How to deal with images of historical violence, of the wounds of others, contemporary or historical? What is it to reproduce the image as it is?

I copied the engraving and then gradually erased the figures in the drawing, filming each stage of the erasure, leaving at the end an empty landscape with faint lines and smudges where the figures had been.

The question remains. Should such images not be seen? To not see the image is to be blind to a part of history. Are we simply reproducing historical horror? But to remove the figures, their presence from the landscape, also feels false. Do we go from an empty landscape which has forgotten or denies its history, to insist on the presence of these lives? Or do we remove the image

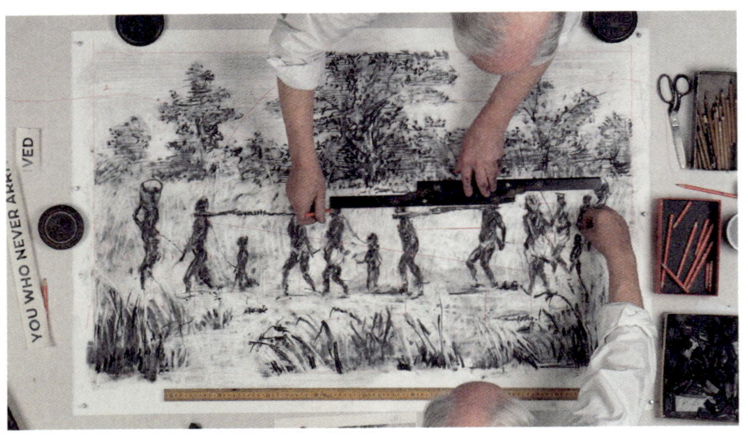
YOU WHO NEVER ARRI VED

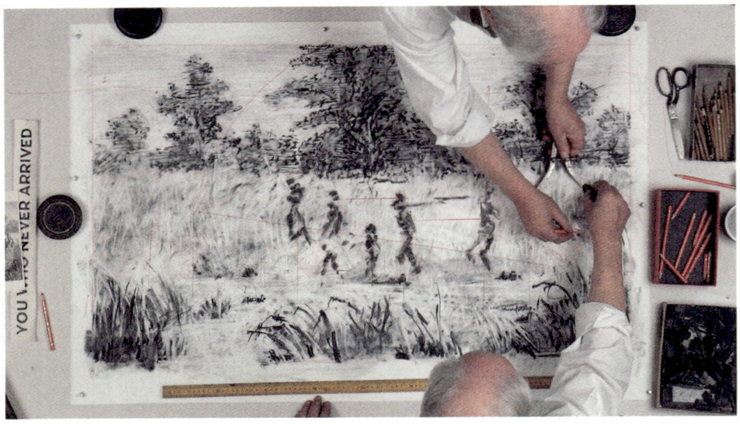
YOU WHO NEVER ARRIVED

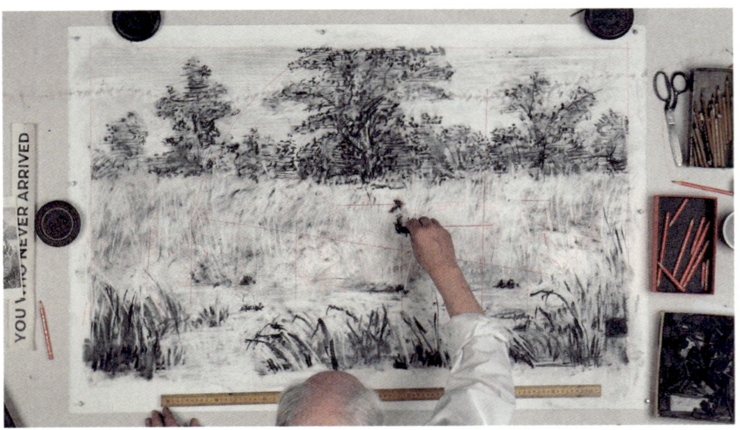
YOU WHO NEVER ARRIVED

of these lives, demonstrating the insubstantiality of historical memory? There is an impossible certainty in the labels one sees on museum walls that tell us so clearly which is the right way and which is the wrong way to look and think.

In the production we tried running this piece of footage forwards, making people disappear, and backwards, making the figures reappear. I cannot remember which way we used the projection in the end. This question is ongoing.

There is a quiet but important energy and comfort that comes from working alone in the studio, the solitary conversation with the drawing as it emerges. An encouragement from the paper. A sometimes critical look from the paper back to you. *Is this really the best you can do?* It is a particularly intimate conversation.

The energy of a workshop is utterly different. All is possible. Everything gets the benefit of the doubt. Is there a place for this performance of marching? And marching – as we discovered in a manual on training African soldiers – is simply exaggerated walking. Perhaps not the passionate absurd; rather the laconic absurd.

We started with the literal: walking round the room exaggerating styles of walking, as if there is a force pushing the small of your back, walking as if you are led by your knees, by the swing of the arms, led by your chin. An hour or so of walking and looking. In the end, the marching was abandoned and the awkwardness was restricted to saluting. I discovered that I was the only one of the forty of us in the room who had ever been drilled – first as a cadet at the government high school I attended (in the 1960s and early 1970s the school still based itself on English public schools), and then after school, when I did my national military service. After forty-five years, the "About turn!" was still somewhere in my muscles.

What if the military bugle calls are not made by a bugle but by a viola, and if a double bass makes the sound of a record needle stuck in its groove, and the sound of an air raid siren, and if drumsticks on the double bass become a machine gun? What if the strings playing the siren are doubled by a soprano?

There are many improvisations. Reading the Chilembwe letter straight through. Performing it. Interspersing it with a counter-text: "We demand the right to fight in the French army, as all good French citizens do. We offer a harvest of devotion." This from Blaise Diagne, the first African deputy in the French Chamber of Deputies. At first, the French wanted no African participation in this European war. But after 1915, when so many hundreds of thousands of French lives were lost, Clemenceau changed and welcomed this "harvest of devotion." We tried Chilembwe's letter with singing under it; we broke the text with the singing, trying to shatter the text so that it could be most clearly heard.

There is an energy from this excess, from saying this is not a lecture, not a lesson, but an open field, a *Tummelplatz,* in which we can discover what it is that we need to make. The cardboard hat is placed on a head, and a general is made. The actors are not given roles to play. From the actors, we discover who the characters are. An actor wears a skirt and a pith helmet and (from Karl Kraus) becomes a military reporter. We change the hat to a cap with a cardboard eagle attached. A black glove and a riding crop and the actor makes a Kaiser for us. An old trolley from an abandoned factory is found, and here we have a carriage for the Kaiser. Costumes are not just clothes, they suggest a way of moving, an energy, in this case a Kaiser with the range of voice from a guttural growl to the scream of a crow. The actor makes her role. She finds a text of the speech the Kaiser made at the outbreak of war and uses this to infuse and fill the Kaiser's grunts and bird cries. The performance is a mixture of costume and what the actor fills it with.

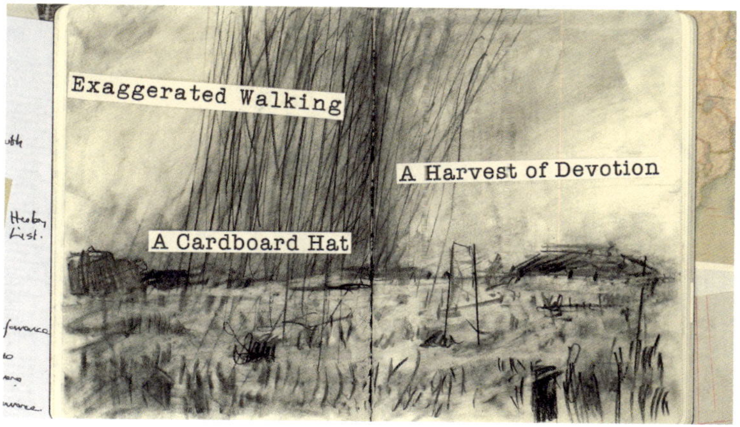

Carrying the boat

There is an invigorating chaos. Energising yes, but still chaos. How can the chaos hold? We had fragments of certainty. Fragments of text, of music. An image of a boat being carried across a continent.

The boat HMS *Mimi* was transported to Cape Town, dismantled and sent north by train. When the train line ran out, the boat in its components was put on the backs of oxen. When the oxen died of tsetse fly, it was put on the backs of men and carried to Lake Tanganyika. Our boat was made of cardboard, cut into two pieces, carried by two actors.

We had discovered that a procession could not be the sole form of the piece. However slowly our chorus moved, they would cover the eighty metres, or the sixty metres, as the stage now was, in a few minutes. It was not the five hundred metres we had in Rome. We had to fill our eighty minutes with more than a procession.

There were two obvious routes out of this chaos, which we tried to avoid. Was it possible to tell a story without telling it through the story of one individual – the girl, the soldier, the

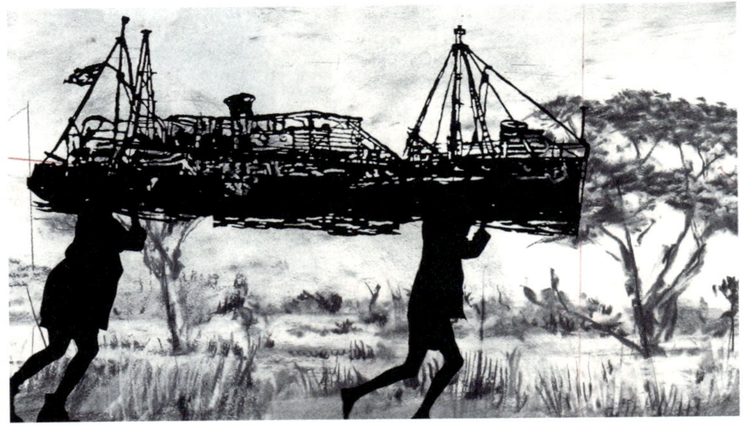

hero standing in for the whole war? To make not a tragedy, which is always constructed around one person; perhaps not even a comedy; but to work from the fragments. The studio fragments, certainly; but this seems more and more to correspond to history as a collage of fragments. To make the fragmentary form a central principle of the piece and to hope the final piece would be more than just a list, like a list of the songs on the programme of a musical. Could we make something with a trajectory, rather than a narrative? But also avoid an essay or a lecture.

I had a lecture prepared in my back pocket, ready to hand over to one of the actors to help the audience, if we felt that matters were getting out of control. I had it here. "Here it is. I mean, take it, take it. It will help." But the collaborators, the performers, held firm – no lecture. They had more faith in the process than I did.

The lecture we did not have

This is what we would have said in the lecture we did not have: The first shots in anger in World War I were fired in Togo, on

3 August 1914, and the war in Africa finished ten days after the armistice, when news from the end of the war in Europe reached East Africa. It would have talked of the campaigns in Togo, Cameroon, German South West Africa, German East Africa. It would have referred to the 30,000 soldiers killed. To the 300,000 African porters who died. Of the two million Africans dragooned into service as porters, carrying war material across the continent. The one million civilians dead. The chasing of the German General Paul von Lettow-Vorbeck in a cat and mouse campaign in East Africa. The carrying of the boat from Cape Town to Lake Tanganyika.

A brief history of colonialism. The lecture would have talked about the Conference of Berlin in 1884 – one could see the First World War as the completion of the Berlin Conference – and the arrangement of the map of Africa. All the colonies controlled by Germany at the start of the war – Togo, Cameroon, German South West Africa, German East Africa – becoming either French or British at the end of the war. The First World War as a colonial conflict. This was all in the lecture we did not have.

Which is not to say we did no research. Books were read. I spent time in the Imperial War Museum in London. A student scoured the archives in Dakar, hunting for words from Senegalese soldiers in the war. Very few firsthand African reports could be found.

We hoarded the fragments we found: words and songs, looking for a sideways illumination. We watched films of victims of shell shock, made in various English hospitals. We did not perform shell shock, but we watched closely the spasms of movement that took over the bodies of the victims. The "spasm of history" established itself as a phrase.

108 Coloured handkerchiefs

Now how to make the war itself? We had a machine gun's rapid rattle played with drumsticks on the body of a double bass; the artillery-induced tinnitus with words made with harmonicas. The idea of harmonicas to make tinnitus came from a list of items that were sent to African troops by the Committee of Welfare for African Troops in Europe. The objects sent to the troops included:

26 GRAMOPHONES
634 RECORDS
30 SETS OF DOMINOES
1 BAGATELLE BOARD
600 HYMN AND PRAYER BOOKS
600 PAIRS OF LEATHER GLOVES
1250 SCHOOL PRIMERS
120 PACKETS OF INK POWDER
600 MOUTH ORGANS.

We had no rifle in the production, but a spade was used for military drills, for shouldering and reversing arms.

Sometime before the project began, I had read a report of a man who kept a flock of pigeons in a dovecote on the roof of his building. They were his passion and delight. He had a daughter who contracted tuberculosis and died. He was told she might have caught the tuberculosis from the pigeons, so the man went to his roof and one by one wrung the neck of each of his birds. These birds became the displaced bearers of violence in the production. To emphasise, the story of the man and his pigeons is outside the studio, but when it comes into the studio it becomes the activity of drawing birds and of tearing up these

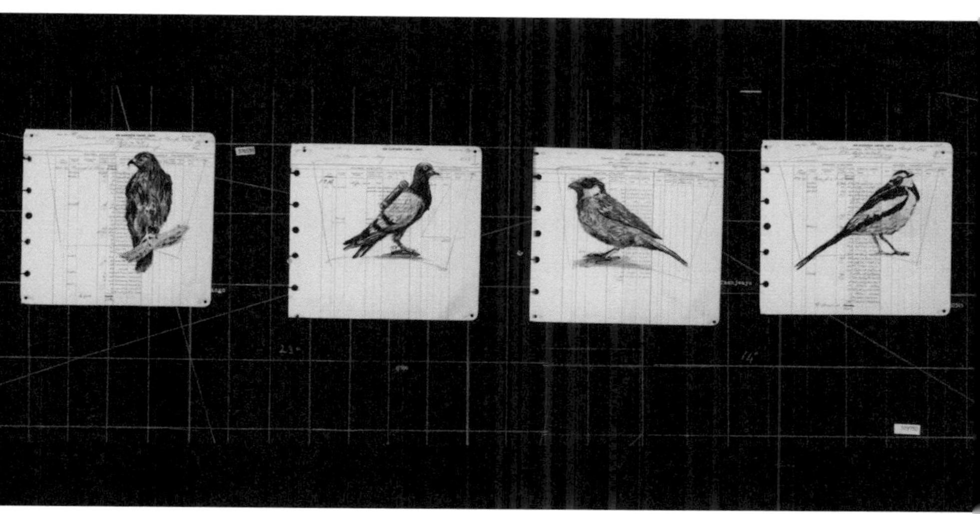

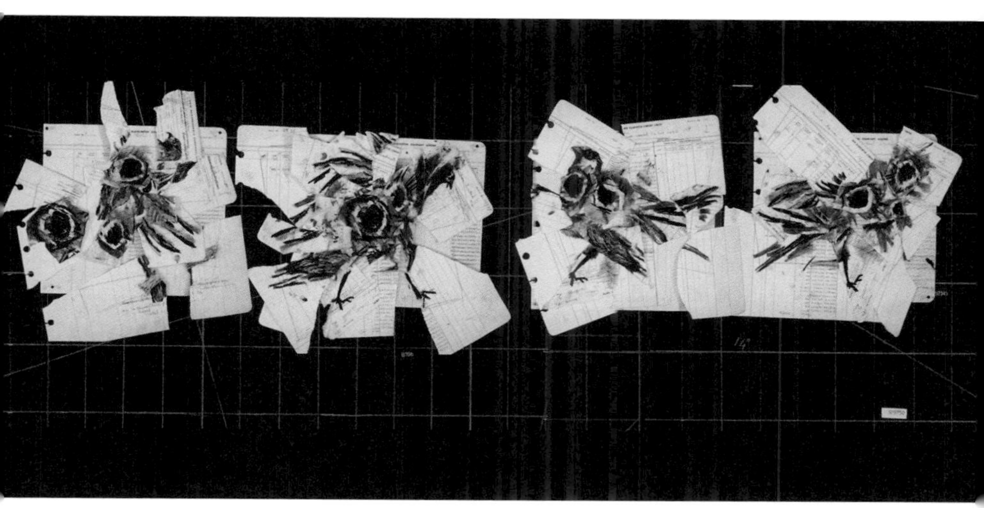

drawings. There is pleasure, not grief, in both of these activities. Particularly in this case, of tearing up the birds, not to make a new bird, but for the destruction of the image to be its meaning.

Comfort in the list

At the end of the first workshop, we had a list of possible fragments, which were arranged into a provisional structure.

ACT 1. Manifestos, orders, and commands. Cutting up the continent. Simple arithmetic (recruiting the carriers). The procession, too.

The procession, the starting point of the project, was reduced to one of fifteen sections. Our procession was cut from one hundred – these would have been volunteers from local community organisations, rehearsed into their parts in three days, and then costumed. How? What were we thinking? This was reduced to a chorus and a brass band of twenty.

ACT 2. Paradox. Eight things one must remember. The troubles of the body. Chilembwe's letter (in the centre of the piece). The man with a cat in his mouth (an African description of Kaiser Wilhelm and his moustache). Damaged heads. God Save the King.

ACT 3. Running. Running and falling. Wounded man dance. Procession from war. A list of the dead.

This was a list, sometimes just titles, some of them corresponding to real material we had already seen; some things existing only as a title or a name. We had an idea of what might be made to fill the list. There was a reassurance from this list. But more than that, it becomes an external, objective marker. We don't yet know what we are making, but the list does. Find comfort in the list.

Many of these items did correspond to shards discovered in the first workshop. Running and falling, a discovery of the scale change that a projected shadow allows – the actor stays the same,

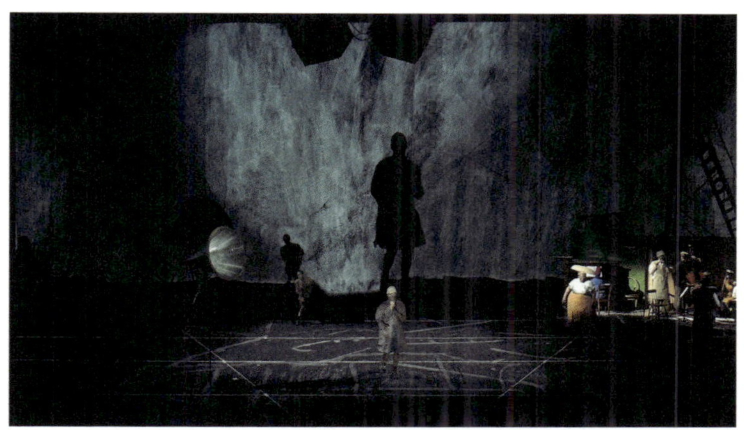

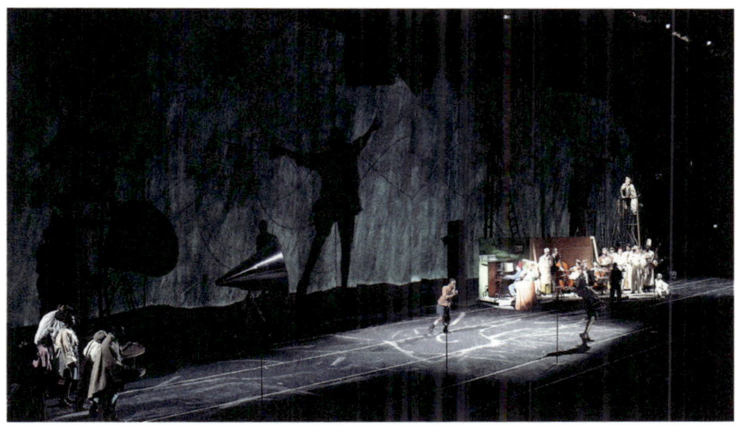

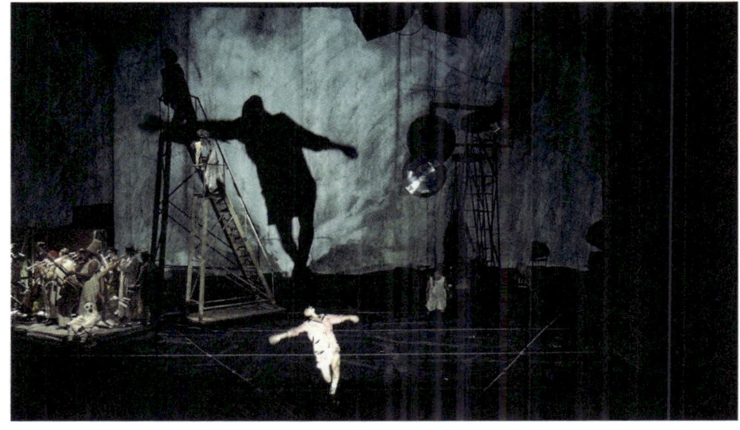

but his alter ego can fill the ten-metre height of our tarpaulin projection backdrop. Developing the grammar of shadows from Rome (the *Triumphs and Laments* project, described in lecture 3).

The map had been cut up – we would find a place for it. Simple arithmetic. The manifestos, the different texts cut up started setting an agenda for the libretto. Aimé Césaire, Frantz Fanon, Tristan Tzara.

After the workshop, we had five months to reflect or, to not reflect – there is so little reflection in the process. The work reflects and we follow – months to construct a text for performance, mainly from what we had used in the workshop; to continue with making drawings and animation. For the set designer, to focus on how to articulate our sixty-metre stage and how to move a fourteen-piece orchestra across. For the costume designer, to work on the costumes, cardboard and paper, thick felt. For the video editors to work on sewing the images for projection together. For the composers to gather the music developed in the workshop and start to write the score.

Let us try for once, not to be right

To get back to the start of this lecture, where we had a division of studio and history – the project developed a split axis. A horizontal spread: the sixty-metre stage and the history of African porters in the First World War.

The vertical division was given by the techniques of the studio; and by the rupture in Zurich in 1916 – a midpoint of the war – in the habits of artists made by the Dadaists, in whose shadow and in whose new illumination artists continue to work one hundred and ten years later. All of us, whose art is no longer restricted to oil paint on canvas. Even those painters are indebted to the Dadaists, for the world of possibilities they opened up: poem as a painting, found objects as a sculpture, simultaneous poetry performance, performances of objects. All things outside the traditional purview of the visual artist became possible. This is ironic of course, because the aim of the Dadaists, stated though not followed through, was to end art, and not reinvigorate it.

Today, my painting will be a poem.

Today, my drawing is a drawing is sixty metres wide, fifteen metres deep, ten metres high, with a duration of eighty minutes. A drawing in four dimensions, a performance, a projection, moving across the stage and through time.

Good logic leads to this: find the less good language

The lessons from the Dadaists, the text of Tristan Tzara, became a central element of the production. Tristan Tzara's manifesto joined the others' declamatory statements in the libretto:

– I SHOUT!
– THINK! THINK! THINK!
– THE FACT! THE FACT! THE FACT!
– KABOOM! KABOOM! KABOOM!
– THIS IS A FAIR IDEA OF PROGRESS!

From Fanon: "When the whites become too mechanised they turn to men of colour to provide a little humanity."

From Fanon, reading Aimé Césaire: "I can be dominated, but not domesticated."

Kurt Schwitters' *Ursonate*, our language reappraised.

Europe not hearing Africa – Chilembwe's unheard letter; and Africa making no sense of its evisceration by Europe.

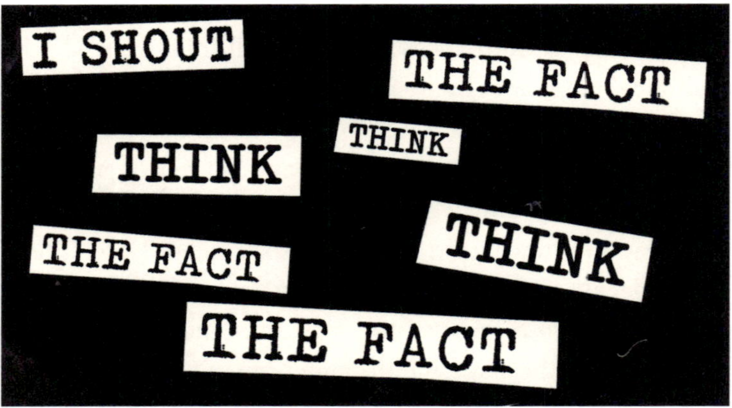

Language became like a drawing, only just hanging on to meaning. How far could we stretch it?

The pity of war

There was an existing corruption of language. The euphemisms hiding disaster and carnage. In the English writing of the period, the dead on the battlefield are the fallen. Bodies are ash or dust. Soldiers' blood becomes the sweet red wine of youth. We made a spoken Morse code in Swahili, in Hungarian, in English, messages sent from one end of the stage to the other, from Africa to Europe, hovering at the edge of comprehensibility. Making the familiar unfamiliar.

–   *Ash, ash, ash, dust.*

–   *Ni Ni Ni Sha. Lako. Ni Ni Lako.*

–   *Fi fi fi Lako. Ni. Lako.*

\-   *Ash dust naught save Ash Dust.*

\-   *Ni Ni Ko*
      Si Si Si pende
      Si Si Si taki

\-   *Di di dead die*
      Fall. Fall dead. Fallen dust. Ash.

\-   *Hai hai hai dhuru. Hai dhuru Ni Ni.*
      Ni Ni Ni Sha

\-   *Red sweat red Dust*

\-   *Sweet red wine Ash*
      Red youth red Dust

\-   *Hai dhuru Ni Ni*
      Nendo zugu sasa

\-   *Who who Dust Ash*
      Who's your lady friend
      Ash dust is the lady Dust Dust
      Your wife Dash
      Who who who's your lady friend
      Ash
      Is the lady
      Ash Ash
      Your wife
      Dust

Three kinds of ignorance

As the work proceeded, I realised that the principal goad I had was ignorance, my own ignorance. I thought I knew the history of the First World War and I started with the frustration of, "How could I not have known this history?" This was an ignorance I shared not only with the audience, but also with the other participants in the project.

A first ignorance: a deliberately constructed ignorance, a conscious effort by those in power, the colonial powers, to silence and hide history. The suppression of Chilembwe's letter can stand in for this. Also the absence of memorials to the Africans who died in the war. Every English church and railway station has its list of each man from the parish who died in the Great War. We made a list – a list of all the names not recorded. The absence of medals. Porters were seen as civilians, so they received no medals. The fact that they were not allowed to participate in the 1919 victory parades. Too expensive, they were told. "Lest their behaviour merit recognition, their deeds must not be recorded," wrote a colonial official.

The second ignorance I am complicit in. Every Remembrance Sunday in November – at my high school in Johannesburg – the headmaster would read out the names of former pupils and masters who had died in the war, while student cadets stood at the corners of the cenotaph with arms reversed. From English lessons filled with Siegfried Sassoon and Wilfred Owen, my mind was stuck with war solidified into those sounds. It was sufficient. Our conversation was with these English boys, not with the hundreds of thousands of African carriers. My head was filled with images of the mud and trenches. In other words, the most predictable images of history.

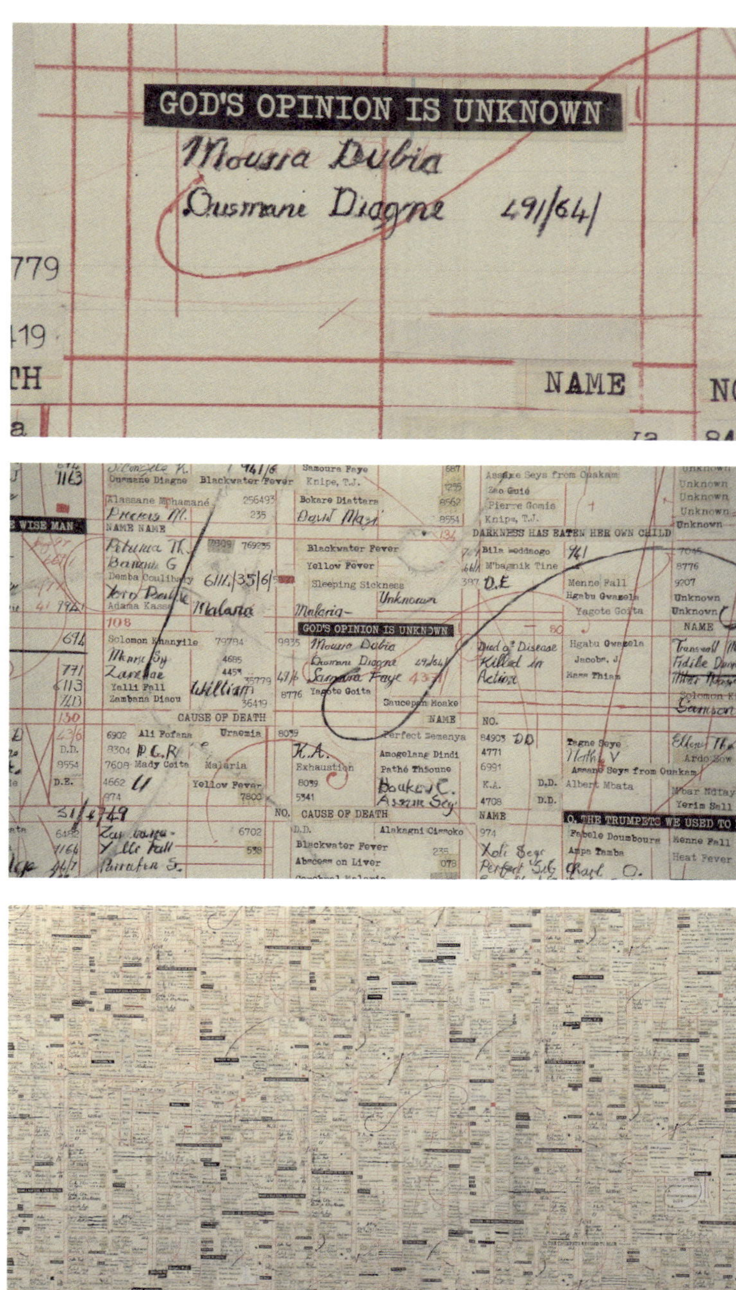

The third kind of ignorance was an inability or an unwillingness to put pieces together, even when I knew the pieces. I had Chilembwe's letter.

I knew of Lawrence of Arabia, of Gallipoli, of the Austrian–Italian campaign and Alto Adige, but they would not come together and displace Wilfred Owen. "What passing bells for these who die as cattle? Only the monstrous anger of the guns, only the stuttering rifles' rapid rattle can patter out their hasty orisons . . ." and so on.

Pa-Pa-Pa

How to acknowledge the weight these lines still carry, and attempt to shift that burden? We translated it. We dismantled it. First, we turned it into French. Then we turned it into half-remembered bad French. A French artillery officer trying to remember Wilfred Owen:

> *Quelles, quelles cloches sonnaient pour ceux qui,*
> *quelles cloches, quelles cloches, quelles cloches,*
> *qui meurent comme, comme, comme pa-pa-pa des bêtes*
> *sous la colère des canons,*
> *pa-pa-pa-pa-pa, mitraillettes, mitraillettes, ponctuaient*
> *pa-pa-pa-pa,*
> *ponctuaient leurs orisons.*

We translated it into dog barking, into the language of a crow.

We looked for other poems and songs, like this song from African porters from Malawi:

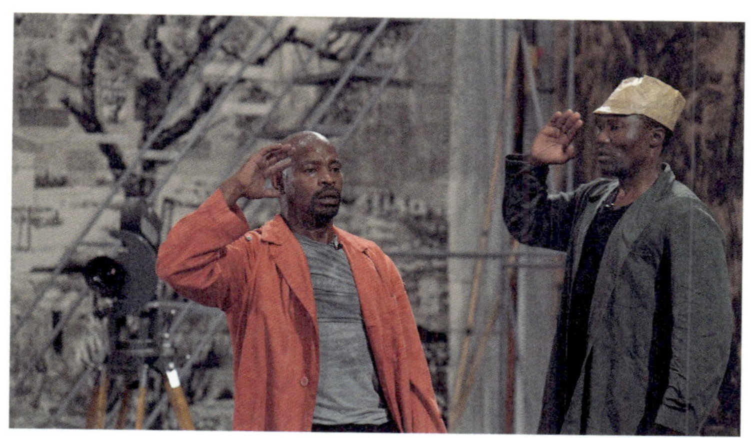

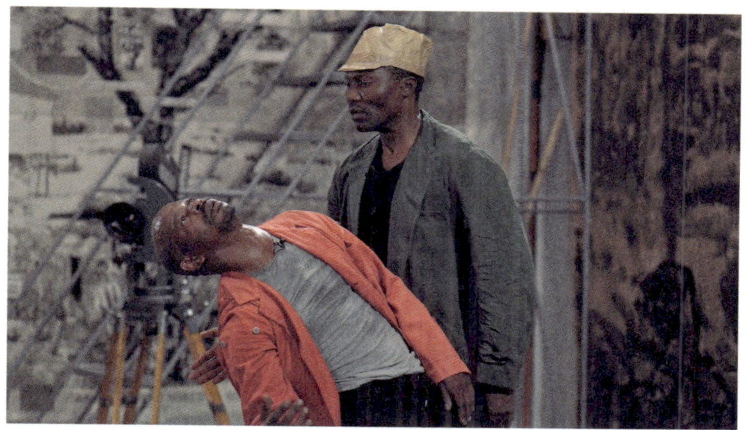

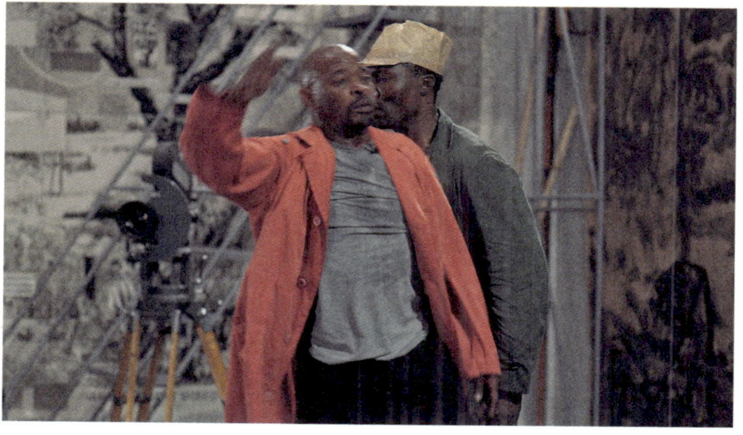

"They hope we will die and not return.
But that I will not do, but will return
home to enjoy the company of beautiful women."

African proverbs became text fragments finding their place.

OH, SLEEP; THE POOR MAN'S FAT.
THEY HAVE MILKED OUR GOATS DRY.
THE POOL DRIED UP WHILE I WAS LOOKING AT IT.
DARKNESS GOSSIPS ABOUT NO ONE.
HOPE CAUSES NO SHAME.
GOD'S OPINION IS UNKNOWN.
THE ROAD AHEAD IS NOT TO BE TRUSTED.

We made an attempt to think through non-language, to show the limits of language, and its role to hide and lie, as much as to clarify. In the same way we were using the body and its movements to find meaning. What were we waiting for in these actions? For something we recognise as it emerges. Perhaps recognition is not an adequate word.

In one improvisation, two dancers played with collapsing and starting it fresh. At first quite balletic, but in repeated iterations, pared down to an act of falling and recovery. We added a salute. It wasn't that we – the *we* being the whole workshop team of actors, musicians, designers, watching the improvisations – it wasn't that we recognised the themes of the piece in this repeated action, but there was an energy, a power of this performance, that we all felt.

Here was an emotional centre, not a performance of emotion.

The performance was deadpan, two of the greatest dancers working at the edge of strength and technique, and trust between each other.

The emotion was ours, not theirs.

From this, again, emotion is the wrong word. We did not have tears.

A much more primitive feeling in the pectoral muscles, in the salivary glands. An apprehension, a meeting of what the improvisation was sending out, from which many associations spread. Here was the spasm of history. The passionate absurd.

To join the army and offer the harvest of devotion; or to resist, like Chilembwe. To want to join the European project, to be taken as French and English citizens; or to resist. To understand and proclaim the bad faith, the disingenuousness of all colonial invitations to the colonial project. To expand the project from a consideration of the First World War in Africa, to allow examination of the broader paradoxes of colonialism.

THE PROCLAMATION OF UNIVERSAL VALUES.
THE LONG-DISTANCE CONTEMPT.
THE PROMISED BOUNTY OF GLOBALISATION.
THE CLOSED BORDERS OF EUROPE.

Then came, of course, the work. The making of the set, the consolidation of musical ideas, the writing of the score and the libretto, the editing of video for projection across the sixty-metre backdrop. The rehearsals, then the eighty-minute performance.

The Head and The Load
2018
Composers: Philip Miller with Thuthuka Sibisi
Projection design: Catherine Meyburgh
Choreography: Gregory Maqoma
Costumes: Greta Goiris
Sets: Sabine Theunissen
Lighting: Urs Schönebaum

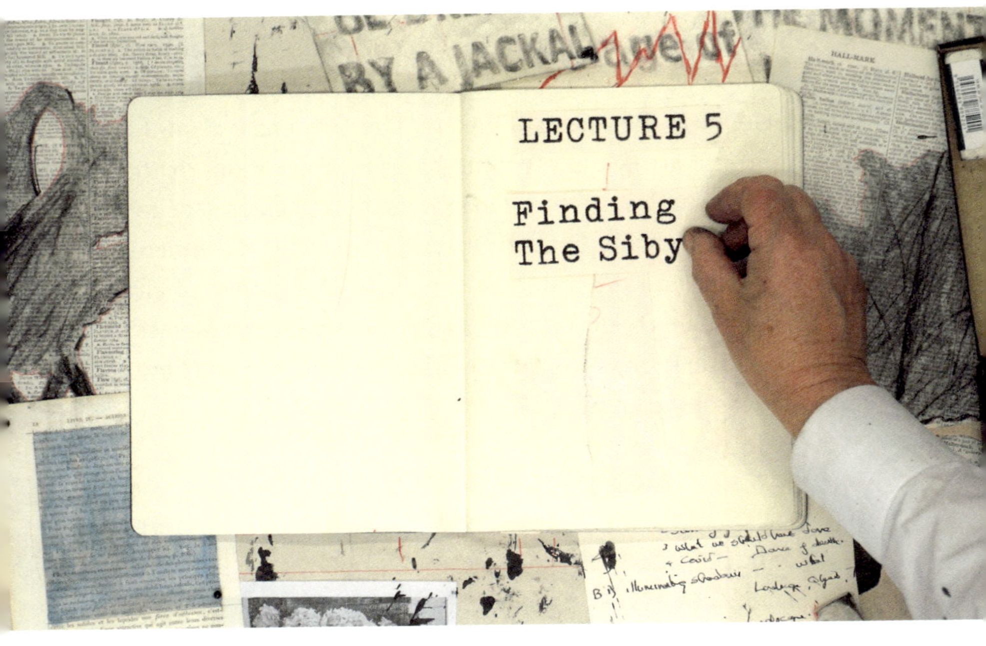
LECTURE 5

Finding
The Siby

FINDING THE SIBYL

There is a story my father used to tell, of a merchant from Baghdad who sent his servant into the marketplace. The servant returned to the merchant empty-handed, and explained to him that, while he was in the market, he had seen, at a distance, the figure of Death. The figure of Death had looked from under his hood, and, with his finger, had beckoned towards the servant. The servant, terrified, had run straight home. And the merchant, understanding his terror, told him at once to head off for Samara. The servant set off.

Later that morning, the merchant himself went to the market. There, he now saw the figure of Death. The merchant approached him, and he said to him, "Why did you frighten my servant so terribly?" Death said to him, "You know, I was very surprised to see him in the market this morning, because I have an appointment with him this afternoon, in Samara."

The story sent chills down my spine as a child. It still does.

Work in progress

This lecture will be the third case study of a particular work. *Waiting for the Sibyl* is a one-act opera. It was commissioned by

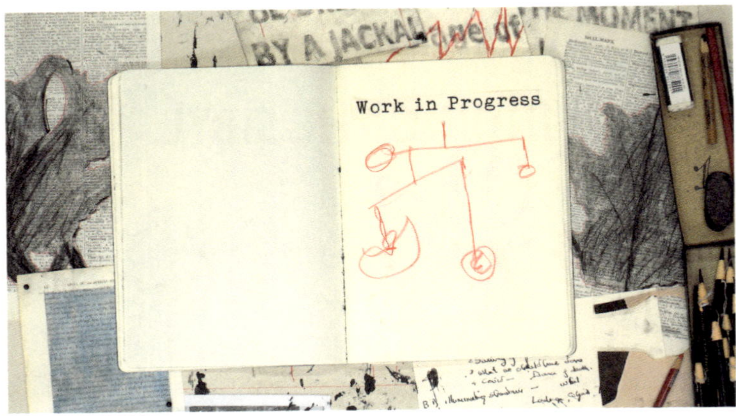

the Teatro dell'Opera di Roma in 2016 in Rome. In 1968 they had presented a performance by the American artist Alexander Calder called *Work in Progress*. The performance ran nineteen minutes long. It uses Calder's familiar *mobiles* and *stabiles*; some descend from the flies, others emerge from the trap doors in the stage. Stagehands on bicycles ride figure eights on the stage. It consists of a series of short images, more than episodes, the front curtain falling and rising between each scene. The front curtain and the backdrops were paintings by Calder. There was recorded music for this by Niccolò Castiglioni, Aldo Clementi, and Bruno Maderna.

In 1968 I was thirteen years old. I cannot remember having seen Calder's mobiles, but I was very aware of the atmosphere of the era (secondhand of course). There were also images and reports of the student revolts in France and in the United States. Fewer reports of the Cultural Revolution in China. South Africa was far from the Beatles, the hippies, and the Summer of Love in San Francisco. But news of this other world came through the newspapers, through the photos in a *Life* magazine – images of a blessed innocence. At any rate the Calder mobiles with their

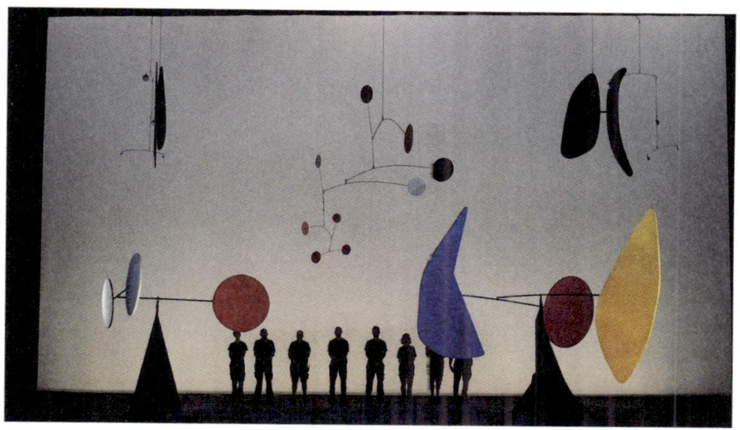

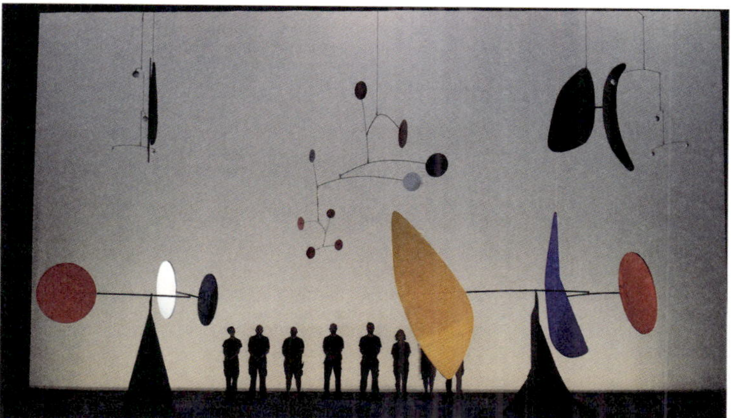

bright primary colours, their weightless movement following the vagaries of air currents, seemed to me an echo of the images of freedom and innocence.

The Calder piece is extremely beautiful, bright colours, clear shapes. The colours and shapes don't have to mean anything – it has no argument to make. The innocence of the piece now feels impossible.

Rome wished to revive this performance. The invitation to me was to make a second part of the evening.

Return

Some years earlier, I had made a series of sculptures that could revolve. They were a form of anti-sculpture – three-dimensional objects that only make sense as two-dimensional images. I would start with a flat image, a silhouette or drawing. I would fragment the image and then extrude the drawing forwards and backwards (usually the torn paper components stuck to wire that came from a central post). So that from only one exact position all the components would make up the original image. But from all other positions, or as the construction turned, the coherence would disintegrate. The image was chaotic. There was only one moment of cohesion. But having once seen the coherent moment, all the other views change. They are abstract chaos, but we know that inside them, there is a provisional momentary sense.

I filmed these turning sculptures and showed them on the fire curtain of the La Fenice opera house in Venice, while the audience was coming in and the orchestra was tuning. The coherent and chaotic sculptures corresponded to the fragmented cacophony as each musician played tunes independently, and the moment of harmony when the oboe gives the orchestra an A (usually followed by more chaos as the instruments go off on their own afterwards).

The pleasure was in the making of the sculptures, finding a way to arrive at the placing of the fragments so they made the single image – a drawing on the walk, a camera facing the sculpture as it was constructed, connected to a projector, projecting the sculpture-in-construction over the drawing of the image on the wall.

We have gone from the turning of the Calder mobile where the elements of the mobile hold on to their abstract formal selves (they are at ease wherever they are, whatever their relative positions) to objects which turn but have a moment of coherence built

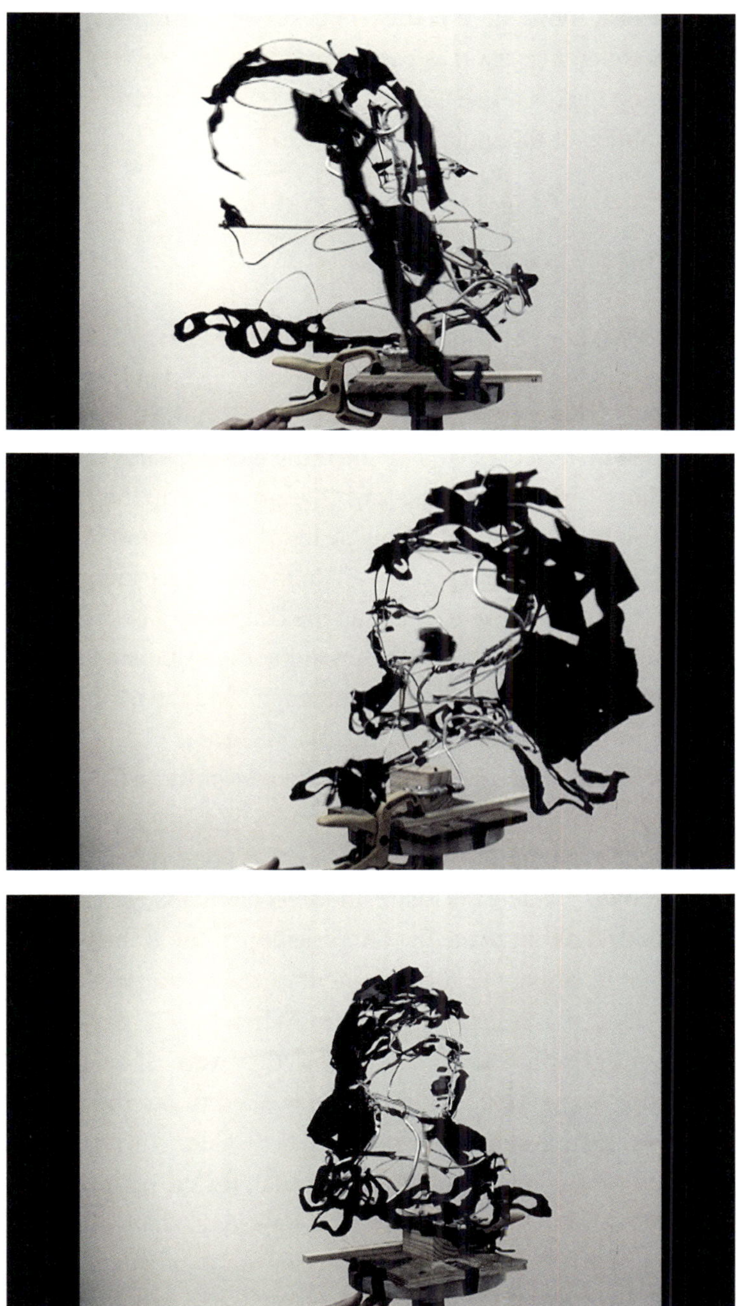

into them, a moment of clarity, a possibility of understanding. Then incoherence again as they pass this point. Neither saying everything makes sense nor saying, "Let us be content with the inscrutability of the mobile of the world."

A billy goat is an overcoat

Within Cockney rhyming slang, a "billy goat" is an "overcoat"; "feet" are "plates of meat"; "apples and pears" stand in for "stairs." Very often, when the rhyming phrase is used, only the first term is used. So instead of having the rhyming part – "pears" to rhyme with "stairs" – you will simply say, "I've got to go up the apples." When you say, "I must get off my plates of meat," sometimes the last part is dropped, and you say – "Ah, my plates are killing me." So, you somehow have to imagine the connection between the plates and the heavy flat-footedness of some exhausted waiter, or the apples bouncing down the stairs, to find the connection. But the immediate point of connection is lost.

And as it turned out, the Calder nineteen-minute piece is no longer performed with the one-act opera *Waiting for the Sibyl*. The connection that explained our work is gone.

When the Calder was made, the steel elements, which were Calder's design but made by the workshop of the Rome Opera, were kept in storage in the basement of the opera house, with all the other sets, where they still are. When they re-performed it, as they did with *Waiting for the Sibyl*, they were taken out and handled as stage props and sets. We wanted to put the performance on tour, to show our opera and the Calder, further afield.

Then we ran into the conundrum that, for the opera house, they were simply props, but for the *Belle Arti*, the controllers of fine arts in Italy, these were seen as works of fine art. The insurance on these steel components became impossible for us to pay. And even though the originals are owned by the Rome Opera, the right to make a copy that we could tour with was held by the Calder Foundation in the United States. The Calder Foundation refused any permission to make copies to tour with. We couldn't take the original. We couldn't make a copy. *Waiting for the Sibyl* became separated from its Calder first half.

Waiting for the Sibyl was made in 2018, two years before the pandemic. But of course, its meaning was affected retroactively. The present always influences and changes the past. Dead artists are influenced by living artists. So many certainties were and still are shaken by the pandemic. Our confidence in science to tell us what is going on and what we should do was badly shaken. People still don't know how COVID started, bats or in the laboratory. Which of us and how many of us would get COVID and who would die? We scrubbed our vegetables with bleach. Washed our hands like a world of demented Lady Macbeths. There were more unnatural actions taken than in the fourteenth- and seventeenth-century great plagues. In the West – Europe, the United States, and Britain – the expectation of a safe, comfortable old age was blown up, the sense that a life of seventy-six years was a human right together with liberty and the pursuit of happiness. Fear, doubt, and uncertainty were daily bread, which they always have been in the Global South. For many there the feeling was, "Welcome to the world, what were you thinking?"

This is not a polemic we started with, nor indeed a polemic we held at any stage. The idea of imminent premature mortality, of what deaths we grow inside us, emerged in the process of making. These themes have always been the material for artists, singers, and poets. Obscure anxieties come centre stage.

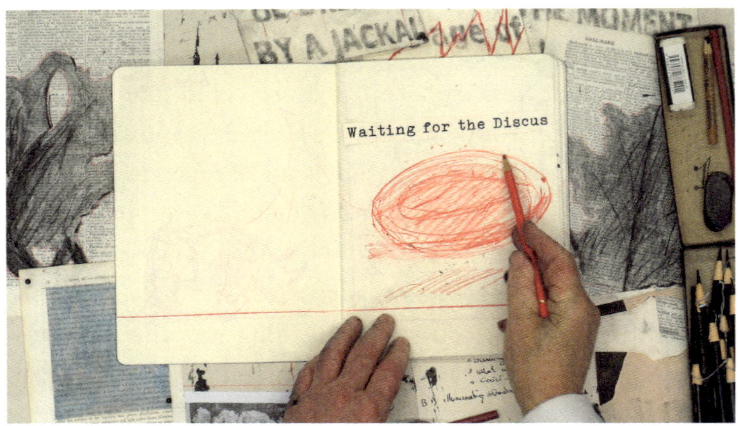

Avoiding the discus

There are other stories of fate. One is an extension of the story of the merchant of Baghdad. This is the story of Perseus. Again, as with many of the stories which stick so closely to me, this was a story first heard in childhood, in which the emotional power is so strong. One of the demands, I suppose, as one grows older, is to try to recapture the strength with which those first, clear emotions – as either questions of injustice, of violence, or in this case of fate – are experienced.

King Acrisius of Argos asked the Oracle how long he would live. The Oracle didn't give him an age but told him he would be killed by his grandson.

So, King Acrisius has his daughter Danaë locked up. But Zeus, the king of the gods, sees her through a crack in the wall of the tower she is walled into, and enters as a shower of gold, impregnates her, and Perseus is born. King Acrisius is terrified now that he has a grandson and tries to drown the child. But the grandson survives, as does Danaë, and he becomes a hero. The story of Perseus who kills the Gorgon is familiar. He has heard about the prediction of the Oracle that he will kill his grandfather, and what his grandfather tried to do, but he decides he has no ill will towards his grandfather, and he will come back to the island of Argos and tell his grandfather that he has forgiven him, there is no need for any anxiety. And he sets off towards Argos.

King Acrisius hears that Perseus, who has slain the Gorgon, is on his way to Argos. He knows – he knows in this moment – that Perseus is on his way to kill him. So, he flees, disguised as a beggar, in ashes and sackcloth. Perseus, on his way to Argos, decides to stop at the town of Larissa, to take part in an athletics competition. If he wins the laurel wreath, he says, he will give it to his grandfather as a sign of goodwill. He takes part in the discus competition. He bends back. He allows the weight of the discus to stretch his arm, to allow the strength to grow, and he launches the discus. It flies across the field, past the markers of his rivals, and up into the stands. And there, in the back row, it strikes and kills an old man, a beggar in ashes and sackcloth.

Now, as a seven-year-old, this was intolerable. Why did the grandfather have to run away? Why did he have to sit in that seat? If he had sat one seat to the left or to the right, he would have been safe. How could the discus know where to go? Surely this could all have been avoided.

Why did the grandson have to be such a show-off?

That's one story of fate.

A leaf storm

There is another, the story of the Sibyl, in this case the Sibyl of Cumae. Apollo promised the Sibyl eternal life if she would sleep with him. In the end, she refused. So, in a fit of spite, Apollo told her, well, she could still have her eternal life, but not eternal youth. So, the Sibyl grew older and older, and shrank more and

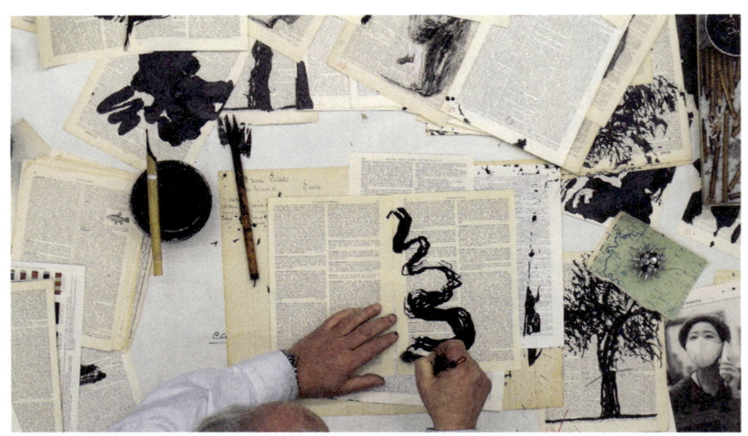

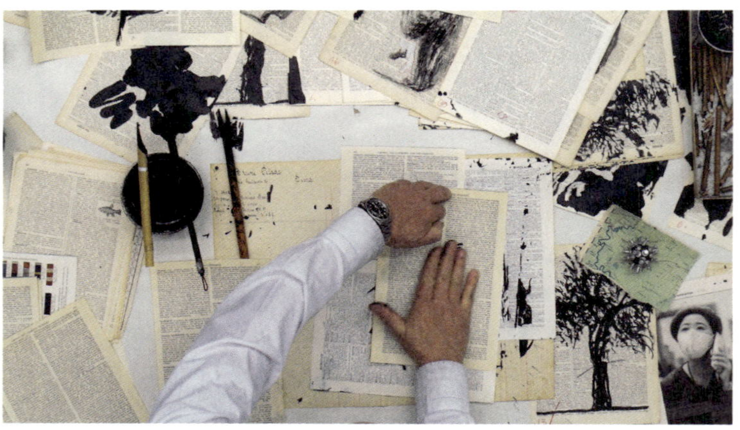

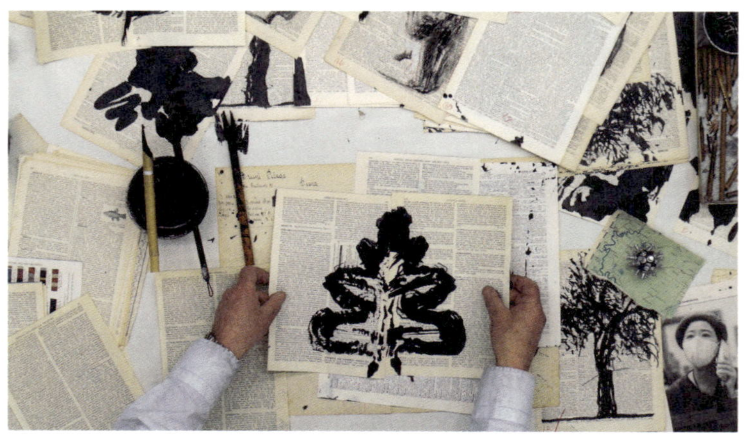

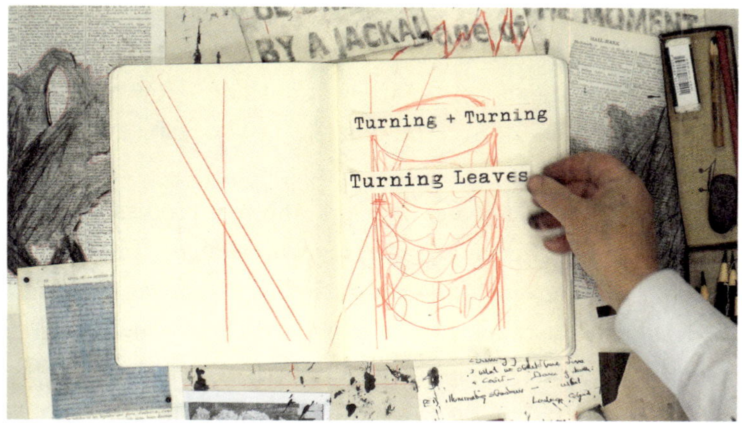

more, until in the end, the boys of Cumae put her into a little amphora and suspended that from a tree. If you put your ear to the bottle, to the amphora, it is said you could still hear her voice, calling out, "Let me die. Let me die. Let me die."

But the story of the Sibyl that I'm most interested in is that of her predictions. She lived in a cave outside Naples. You would take your question to the cave, write your question on a leaf, and leave it at the mouth of the cave. She would take your question – "How long will I live?" "Will I survive this pandemic?" – and she would write the answer on an oak leaf and put that too at the mouth of the cave. There would be a pile of leaves of all the answers. You would go to collect your fate, your leaf. But as you reached the mouth of the cave, there would always be a wind. The wind would blow and stir the leaves, so that you could never tell if the leaf you were picking up was your fate, or someone else's fate.

These turning leaves became a central element in thinking about what to do with the Calder, or what to do with the opera. It became a question of turning, not mobiles, but turning leaves, spinning, tumbling. But also transforming turning leaves into pages. In English, French, and Italian this is very easy: *"feuille"* is both from a tree and a book. From the wind moving the leaves it became clear we were also dealing with questions of instability and uncertainty. The answer is there, but as you reach for it, it shifts. How much can we know of our fate? How much can we anticipate the future? You don't know your fate, even if the leaf does.

The process of making the work, the very process itself, often leads to a theme. When working with charcoal animation – drawing, filming, erasing part of the image, redrawing, filming – the erasure of the charcoal is never perfect. There is always a grey trace of the image left on the paper however conscientious the erasure. This trace (a product of the technique itself) prompts a theme of the animation – a trace of time – and the evocation of questions of memory. The thinking is in the charcoal. With the leaves and the mobiles, a theme of uncertainty emerged.

Finding the less good idea

The Centre for the Less Good Idea is a physical space – a series of rooms and studios in downtown Johannesburg. Spaces for rehearsal and performance. The name comes from a Setswana proverb: "If the good doctor can't cure you, find the less good doctor." Its principle is to bring people together from different fields: dancers, writers, musicians, visual artists, and to be open to the discoveries that may arise when they work together. Many of the participants in the making of the chamber opera *Waiting for the Sibyl* came from the Centre.

One starts with an idea; one doesn't start from nowhere, but very often as one starts to work, in a rehearsal, in a studio, something that felt so clear in its impulse starts to show its cracks. Arguments don't quite hold. An image which was so clear in your head becomes feeble as it is drawn. One can do one of two things; one can hang on to this first idea, draw the lines

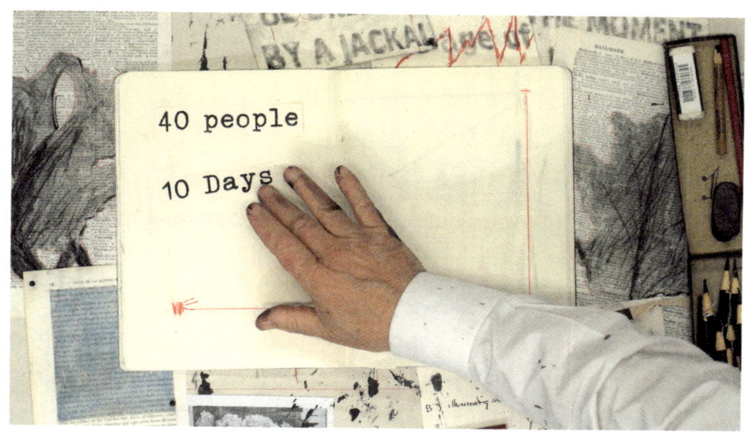

40 people
10 Days

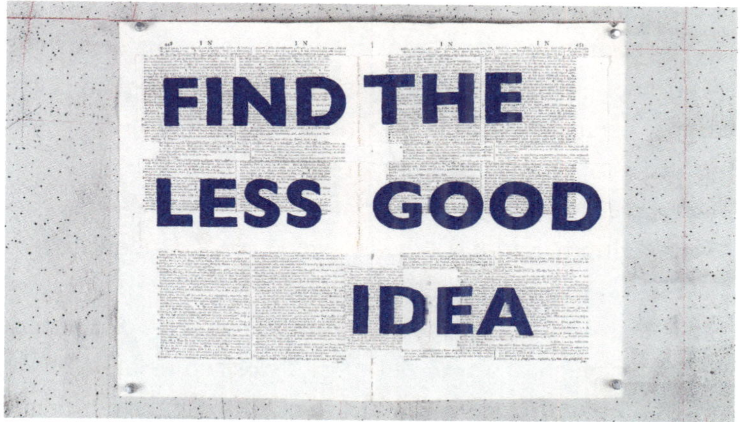

FIND THE
LESS GOOD
IDEA

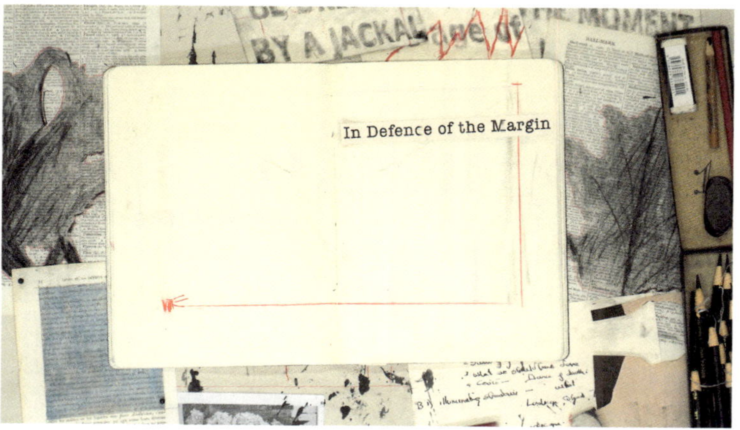

In Defence of the Margin

with thicker and darker ink, with the hopes that the cracks will disappear. Speak more loudly, shout the lines in the hope that volume will be convincing. One can bring in an army to support the idea that has lost stability. The loudness of the shouting is as much to convince the maker as the audience.

Or one can give the cracks their space, to allow these ideas from the *lacunae*, the interstices, to have their say and shape the thought. These are the less good ideas.

This obviously is both about a practical strategy of working in the studio, but also has implications of how we move through the world, looking for particular local solutions and being sceptical of the grand ideas.

The calamitous histories of the twentieth century make one sceptical of all the grand projects, of theorists and politicians, who are certain they know best for everyone, who need to beat humanity into happiness with an iron club.

We need to be attentive to what arises at the edges of performances, improvisations – the less good ideas. Understanding that these sideways recognitions can often shift the first idea and lead to discoveries that a more measured, logical process resists. It is both a practical way of working – a close observation of improvisation – and a polemic of the importance of the periphery, the margins. Artistically and even politically. The great ideas have failed us. Let us look at the more local, partial solutions. The Centre is an ongoing test of this proposition.

There are two public seasons a year at the Centre (interrupted of course by COVID); in each of which there have been several remarkable presentations. And of course failures. The Centre is both a safe space for doubt, giving the impulse the benefit of the doubt, but also a safe space for failure, when the less good ideas are just that.

Practical Epistemology

To return to the workshop in my studio: I gathered together dancers, singers, actors, set and costume designers. I showed the participants the Calder Rome performance. I showed them the turning sculptures made for the fire curtain. But after this there was an openness for improvisation. For thinking about what the sound could be that would accompany the Sibyl. Testing movement, song, text. I arrived at the workshop with a notebook of different lines, culled from many different poets. These as a provocation for the singers, for the composers. There is an accretion of energy. There is an openness, and together with this openness, an openness to recognise things as they appear. It is a recognition, not necessarily of something being right, but something exciting, an energy in the activity of seeing. In other words, something that you may not be able to name exactly, but which sparks associations and memories.

We know that when we look at a picture, or we look at any object, there are two things happening. The world is coming towards us – what is outside of us – in most cases, into our retina or into our ears. At the same instance, onto this image flood hundreds of associations – of other thoughts, of objects that are turning, of other Calder mobiles, of Calder making his work for the Spanish Pavilion where Picasso had his *Guernica*; of the excitement of seeing a particular improvisation between two dancers; between the shape of a costume which starts off as a Calder mobile, but in the end becomes an Oskar Schlemmer–type circular spiral inside which someone gyrates.

There is both this openness for activity in the studio, and an openness for recognition. It's felt as almost a physical quickening of the pulse as something takes off in front of your eyes as it is being made.

My first idea was to have only one dancer: one dancer turning, somewhat like the Calder. The brief from the Rome Opera was to only work with recordings. But of course, within three days, or two days, or four minutes of working with singers and musicians in the workshop, in the rehearsal room, it became clear that to work simply with recordings would be a great diminution of what the audience hears.

We had a dancer who would perform the Sibyl – her movements referring both to the wind blowing the pile of leaves, but also to the shaking and trembling of someone in a trance.

The voice of the Sibyl

What is the voice of the Sibyl? If she is making her prophecies, what could her voice be? We worked with a throat singer, a person who can sing two notes at a time – a particular style of singing, not just in Tibet, but also in parts of South Africa. That became the voice of the Sibyl.

The music expanded from this possibility of the throat singing, outwards. One of the improvisations we did was to listen to Stockhausen's *Stimmung*, which is a series of very tightly controlled choral pieces, all based on the chord of B-flat. We would start off with our group of singers copying the Stockhausen very closely, singing over the recording, and then we would fade out the Stockhausen, and they would continue.

It slowly developed particular local inflections of rhythm, of timing, new rhythms, and different solo improvisations started taking over. The music, having had its origin in part of the Stockhausen, found its own register.

In many religious sects and different groups, particularly of African Christian churches, there is a form of ecstatic singing and praying which involves turning on your own axis in a group

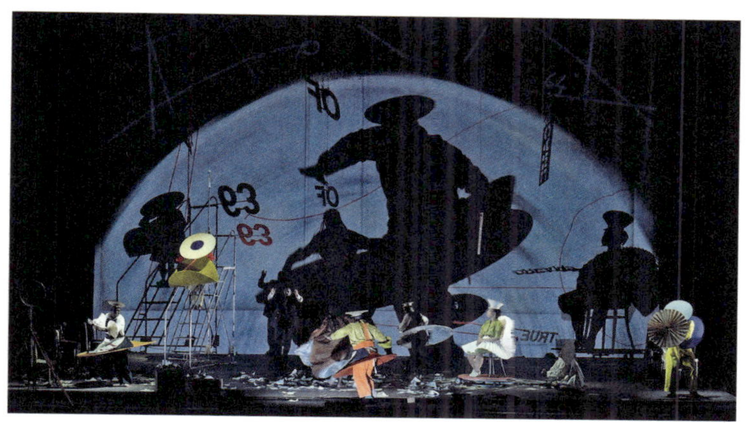

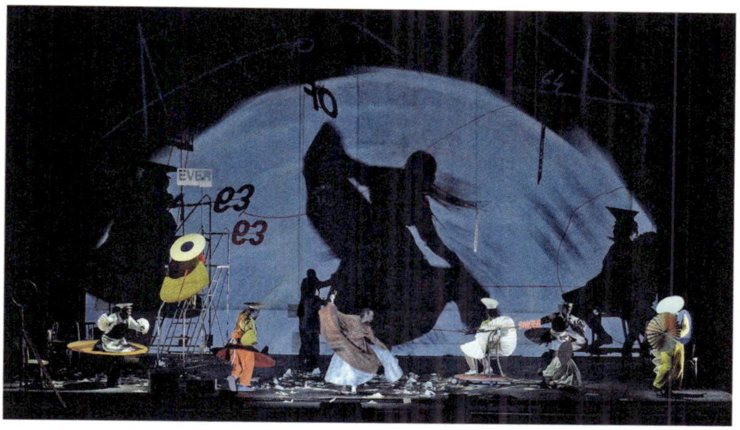

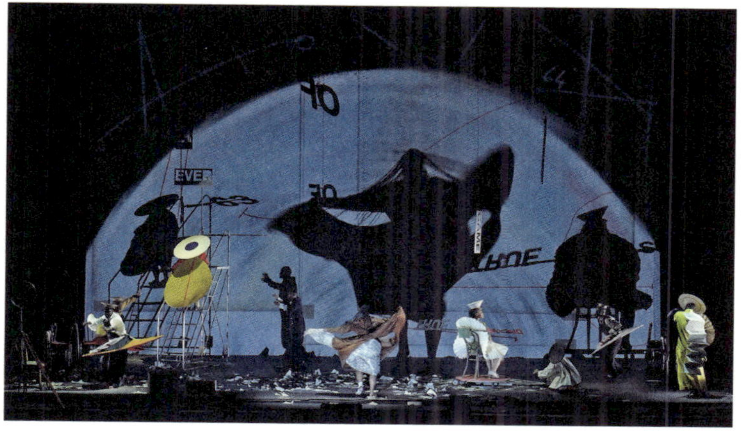

of people, and the whole group of people turning, like a kind of bicycle wheel. Wheels within wheels. We could make a human mobile, the singers and dancers gyrating on the spot and around the stage. Nothing is too stupid not to test it out. To give the idea the benefit of the doubt. We tried many different pieces of music, from fast dance music to African hymns. Different movements, fast, advancing and retreating swoops, large circular cardboard skirts. Not so much testing our ideas as seeing what ideas are prompted by the improvisation unfolding.

At this point we had several elements.

WE HAD THE ELEMENT OF VOICE.
WE HAD THE ELEMENT OF CIRCLING.
WE HAD THE ELEMENT OF DANCE.
AND WE HAD THE IDEA OF PAGES.

Lff

At the end of *Paradiso* of Dante's *Divine Comedy*, Dante writes about the connection of leaves and pages. Dante writes in Canto 33: "So in the wind that stirred the light leaves, were lost the oracles the Sibyl wrote." So, the leaves spin around. Dante writes later on: "But within the depths, I saw gathered together, bound in a single volume, leaves that lie scattered through the universe." So, we have here both an image of the leaves scattering into the wind, but then coming back together to be bound in the single volume, which gave an idea of both these leaves as loose pages, but also of the bound book of the Sibyl.

This idea of these pages and book continues, of course. James Joyce, at the very end, the very last page of *Finnegans Wake* talks again: "My leaves have drifted from me. All. But one clings still. [I'll bear it on me.] To remind me of. Lff!" I am sure there is a

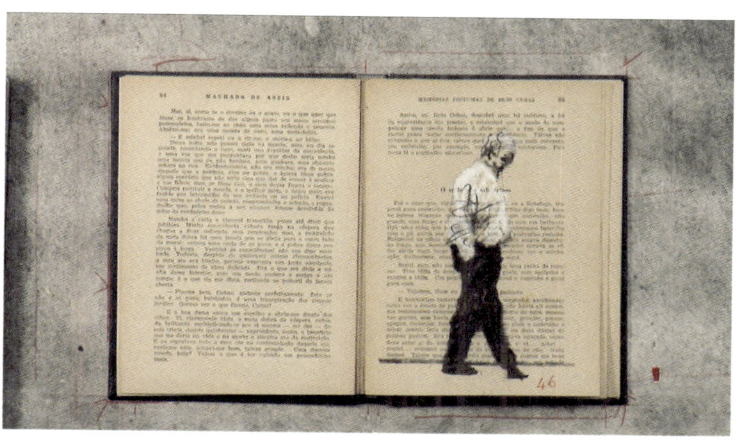

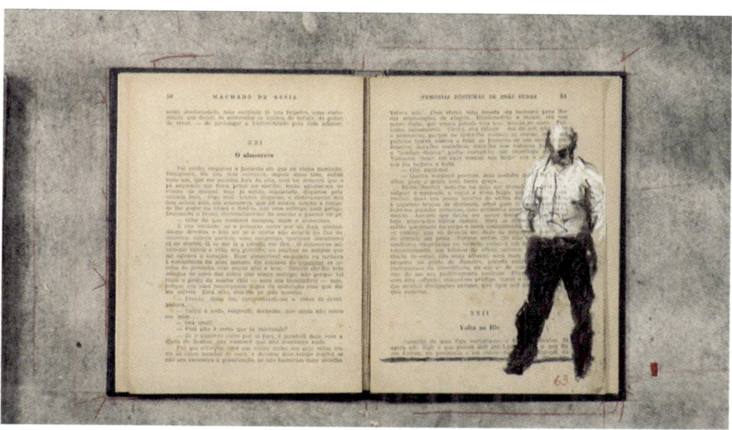

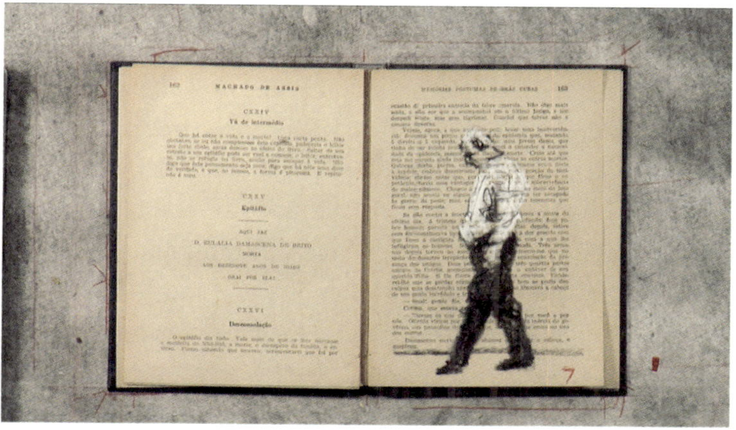

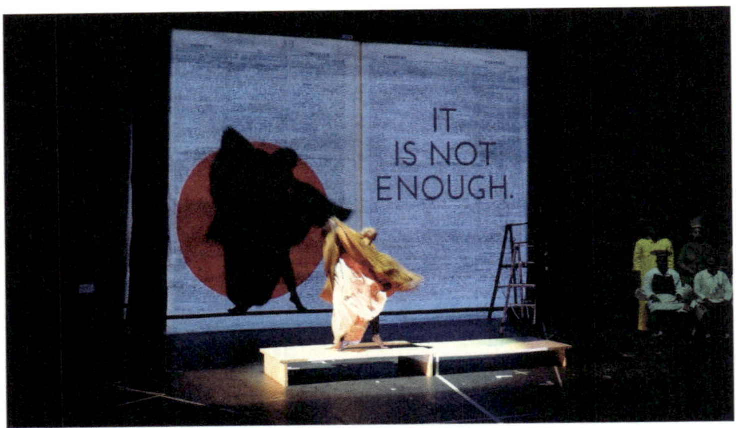

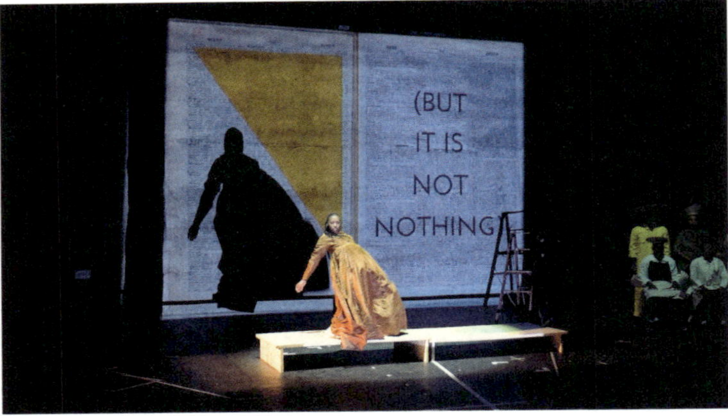

connection between that and the Dante. Of course, from Joyce one has to go down to Beckett, with his tree in *Waiting for Godot*: one leaf on the tree in Act 1 and no leaves on the tree in Act 2. So, we had an idea of the leaves and pages of the book of the Sibyl.

Pages I had worked with. I had made several films which were extensions of flip books, where you flip through a series of pages, and you have the illusion of a one-and-a-half-second movement. Eighty pages with small alterations from page to page.

Two steps to cross the book. We see a man pacing on a page, unable to escape the book.

This is unlike the technique of animation which I have used, in which one drawing gets altered and erased and filmed and redrawn many, many dozens of times. Here each page would be its own drawing.

If one had someone circling, instead of fifty alterations to a single drawing – as in the technique of charcoal animation in which a single drawing is altered and re-photographed many times – it would be fifty different drawings on fifty pages. Many shelves full of pages, some with scribbles, some with careful drawings, some with texts which stand like the pile of leaves that can be at the mouth of the Sibyl's cave.

How does one learn the grammar of this book? Are there singers to the side of the projections of the book, or incorporated into the projection? How do we put the performance into the book?

This we tested by having the dancer, our Sibyl, perform on a platform in front of the book, with her shadow thrown onto the screen with the projection of the book. This was a question of adjusting the particular projector, the distance the dancer was from the projector, the scale of the projection of the book, and then, of course, finding the rhythm between what the dancer, our Sibyl, was doing and the turning of the pages. Do we show one page at a time? Two frames? Do we show a page for three frames?

Much of the work comes into this sphere where meaning disappears. One is not thinking of meaning. We are learning the grammar of what we are making. This is the slow work of the studio. Meaning is lost in the flying paper, in the counting and turning of pages, in the understanding that if you attend carefully to the demands of the medium that you've chosen for yourself, a meaning will emerge, and a coherence may yet arrive.

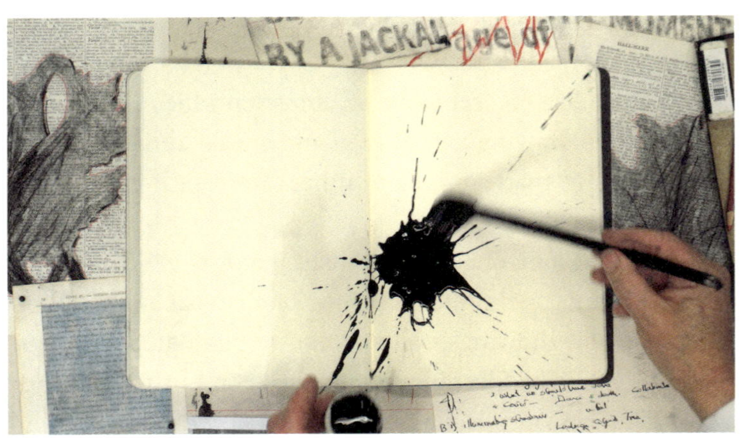

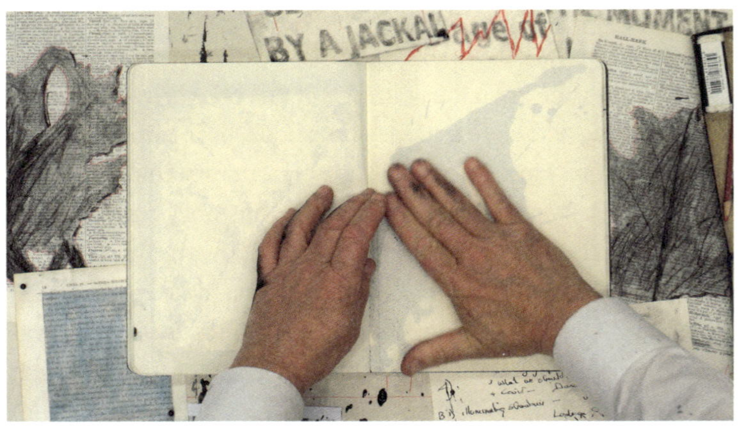

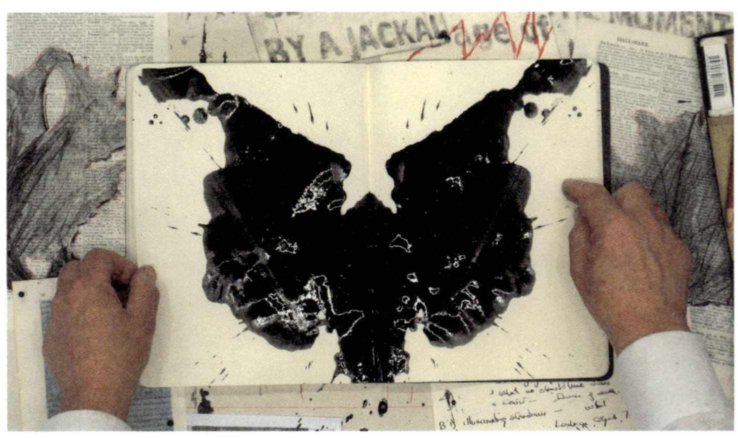

Enantiomorphs

We also asked: What are the other kinds of prediction that happen in books? A splash on a page. We thought then of Rorschach tests; of inkblots; of ink pages. A splash on the page. You'd blot the page, smooth down the top sheet, and open it up. You paint one hand, and the image reveals a pair of hands. You blot the page, and you see a pelvic- or bat- or flower-like shape. Psychological tests are done using these images. Corporations used to use them to assess prospective employees. Depending on what the applicant saw in the shape – pelvis, skull, flower – they would be judged reliable or unemployable. A primitive algorithm.

I am sure this is not an accurate description of the process. The images in a Rorschach test are not randomly generated inkblots, but carefully considered mirror images. But fidelity to Rorschach technique is not the point. The ideas of the inkblot test are enough to set in motion many possibilities: a mirror dance, the symmetry of leaves (painting half a leaf on a single page and blotting with another page on top to make a double-spread leaf). To make a random brush mark turn into a specific image. A splash of ink on a page, blotted, the sheet opened up: a telephone, or a tree, or a megaphone is revealed.

The idea of a Rorschach test became one of the components of the piece.

You say: How does one dance a Rorschach test? If people are covered in cloth, can they be a moving Rorschach blot themselves? What kind of music do we need? Is it still going to be late European modernism, like the Stockhausen, which has a connection to the music that was used in the Calder? Or do we allow other things from different trajectories and traditions in South Africa to come into it?

In the workshop, we test movement, we test shadows, we list possible scenes. We were trying to find the evasive action that meets the decisive strike.

In the story of Perseus and of the merchant of Baghdad, it is the action of avoiding an anticipated goal that provokes that goal. What is it that eats into us here? Not just the injustice of fate, but that the world can operate that way. There is an element of this that goes through these lectures, through the studio practices of the past three decades. How far can you move your aim from the target and still hit it? Or in reverse, why (here again in the studio) does it not work to aim at the target? One arrives at an argument about the First World War by trying to work with a sixty-metre stage. An opera about fate comes not from thinking about fate, but by trying to copy a Calder mobile.

This is not necessarily good thinking, it is not a conclusion I am certain of, but it is perversely the argument the studio makes again and again. It is the central argument of these lectures. It is not a proposition I am inclined to believe. The artist in me says: "But that is how it is. You have seen it yourself." The rationalist, the lecturer, says: "I want further, better proof." Does he not understand that the story of the merchant, of Perseus, may be invented, but still hold a truth we cannot escape?

Thinking of the story of Perseus and the grandfather in his seat: that whichever seat he chose would be the wrong seat. Every chair would be the wrong chair, the wrong chair, the wrong chair.

We made a game of musical chairs, in which there are not quite enough chairs for the performers. It then became a question of different ways of falling off a chair. It turns into: What happens if you have an unreliable chair?

A subsection of the workshop became making a collapsing chair. We made one first with the legs simply hinged with elastic bands, so that as you sat on the chair, the force of your sitting would splay the legs out and the chair would collapse. Then we became more sophisticated, and put servo motors inside a chair, and used an aeroplane radio control box to collapse the chair in different ways. In the end, the image of Perseus and the right chair and the wrong chair is gone, like the rhyming slang, but we are left with a scene of trying to choose a safe chair to sit in.

A Programme

We were gathering ideas, phrases, possible scenes. This is what we had:

WE HAD SIBYL IN THE BOOK.
WE MADE A WAITING ROOM FOR THE SIBYL, THE SIBYL'S OFFICE.
WE HAD THE VOICE OF THE SIBYL.
CIRCLING AND TURNING
A *BALLET MÉCANIQUE*
STOCKHAUSEN'S *STIMMUNG*
READING THE LEAVES
READING THE INKBLOTS
OBJECTS THAT TURN
THE WRONG CHAIR
PROVISIONAL COHERENCE
THE JOURNEY OF THE DISCUS
SIBYL'S PAGES
WHAT OF THESE LEAVES, OF THESE PAGES?

And what of our desperate wish to undo fate? For us to UNSAY, UNDO, UNREMEMBER, UNHAPPEN? Wishing we could run time backwards and make another decision. There is a German

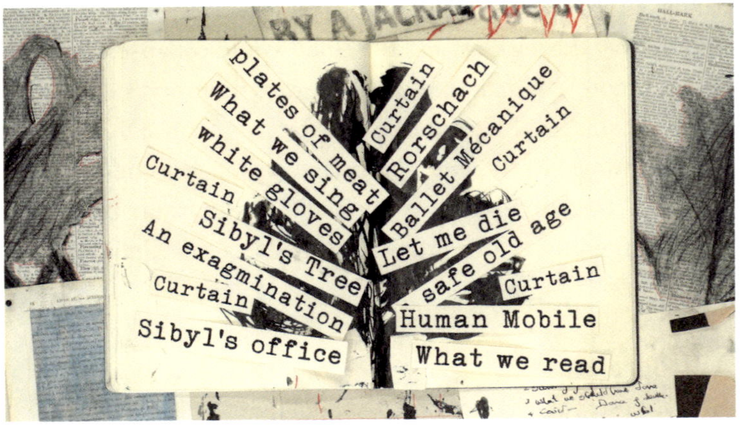

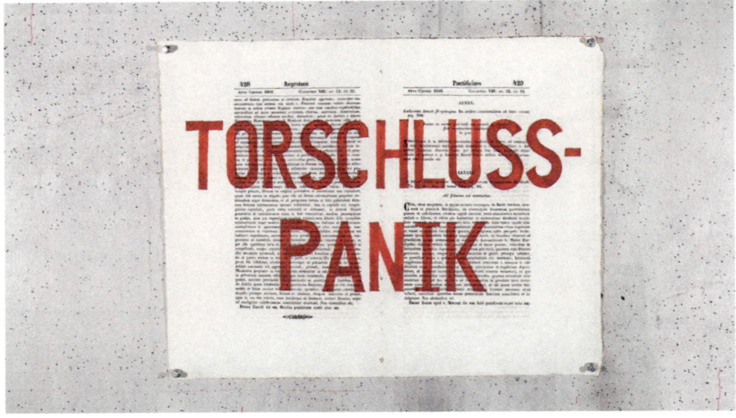

word for this: *Torschlusspanik*. The panic of the closing door. The closing down of possibilities as one decision is made, leaving others behind.

We have a sheaf of papers arranged on the table, a text, or a drawing. We blow or throw these pages into the air, and we know that it is highly unlikely they will land again in the exact same configuration. This unlikeliness is the basis for our confidence in entropy, in the growth of disorder in the universe. In the studio we can resist this. We can learn the grammar of the paper and train it to land well every time. Though we know that outside the studio, this is so much wishful thinking. A wish for unhappen, but we know the weight of happen, happen, happen.

In the studio we can run time backwards. Run the film backwards, and the jar shattered on the floor reconstitutes itself. There is utopia in the perfect repair. Tear a sheet of paper, run the film backwards and it repairs itself perfectly every time. We start with an image (a tree) drawn across many pages of the dictionary (new secondhand copies of the Shorter Oxford English Dictionary were bought from the secondhand bookshop near my studio). We blow the pages into the air – several of us flapping cardboard sheets. Then we run the film in reverse. The leaves fly through the air and settle into the image. A simple technique, but always a jolt of pleasure as the pages find their coherence.

In the studio we can hold on to time, make it material. Four minutes of time becomes four hundred feet of film, eight hundred grams in your hand. Time can become distance, the length of the successive frames in the film. This is the length of a Hollywood kiss, and this is the length of a long Hollywood kiss. But from the shards we can also make something new. We can't resist time, but we can resist entropy.

We had to make the libretto. What is the text that is either being read or being sung, a book that we would see projected behind our dancing Sibyl? I keep a notebook simply labelled *WORDS* in which I write down odd phrases or texts that strike me as being interesting or intriguing. Whenever a project begins, there is a raid of these phrases. Sentences or lines of poetry are printed out, cut up, put on the drawing table, and rearranged.

My grandmothers

My father's mother, who I knew when she was a chain-smoking bridge player, was the first woman in Johannesburg to get a driver's license (in the 1920s). When she took her test, as she was a woman, she was not required to reverse. My mother's mother was the first woman barrister in South Africa, the second in the British empire (also in the 1920s). But when I knew her in my childhood and adolescence, she had long left law behind her and was engrossed in writing a book. Her table was filled with pages she had typed, spread across its surface. Or rather, fragments of pages she had typed, some half a page, some just a sentence. A big pair of tailor's shears, a sticky tape dispenser and fragments of text taped together, recut, rearranged, recorrected. There was no end to this work. The book was unfinished when she died.

Words, ah yes, words

I think of myself with these fragments of text repeating her, the neurotic symptoms ongoing, with the fragments of text rearranged on my drawing table. There were phrases like:

THE COMIC ROUTINES OF POVERTY.
ALL THINGS ARE FILLED WITH LABOUR.
THERE IS NO REMEMBRANCE OF FORMER THINGS.
ALL IS VANITY AND VEXATION OF THE SPIRIT
(this is of course from Ecclesiastes).
OPPRESSION MAKES A WISE MAN MAD.
I'M NOT AFRAID.
I DANCE A MINUET WITH FEAR.
FRESH GRAVES WILL BE EVERYWHERE.
BLOOD SMELLS ONLY OF BLOOD (this from Anna
Akhmatova).
I KNOW THE LIST OF CRIMES I AM DESTINED
TO COMMIT.

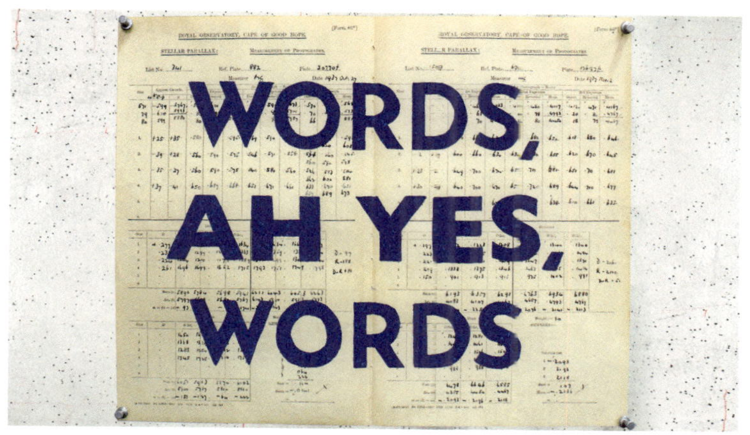

A GIGANTIC GRIEF LAY OVER THE TOWN AND A
HUNDRED TINY GRIEFS (this is Mayakovsky).
THE HUGE SUMMER HAS GONE BY (that's Rilke).
THE GREAT YES, THE GREAT NO. (Cavafy).
WHAT NEEDLESS, FUTILE REGRET.
MY RESOLUTIONS LASTED TWO WEEKS AT MOST.
HALF-OPEN CLOTHES, A QUICK BARING OF FLESH
(this is Cavafy).
LET MY BODY REIGN.
LET ME TRAVEL, SOJOURN, SNATCH, PLOT, HAVE, FORGET
(John Donne).
NOW WHEN I AM DEAD AND NEED TENDERNESS.
I DID NOT KNOW THIS TODAY. I KNEW IT BEFORE
YESTERDAY (that's Zbigniew Herbert).
THE PULL OF GRAVITY, DEATH. A BRIEF
WEIGHTLESSNESS, LIFE (that's Ted Hughes).
LOVE, MAKING A GOD FROM A GROCERY CLERK
(that's Victor Hugo, but Victor Hugo quoted by Freud).
ONE HALF OF YOU IS ME, THE OTHER HALF IS MINE.
I HAVE DONE THAT, SAYS MY MEMORY.

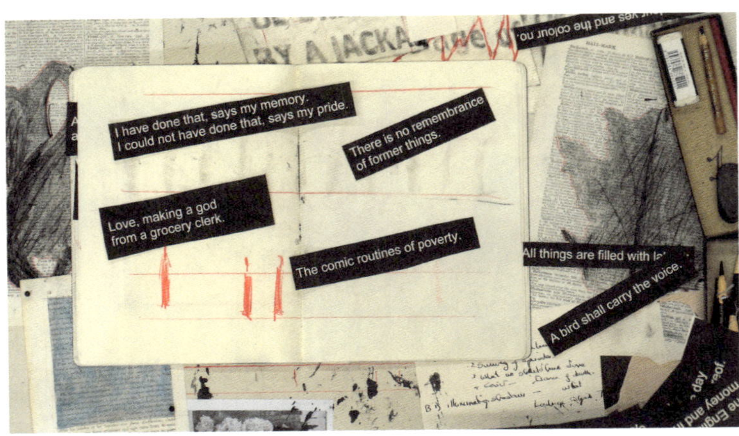
I have done that, says my memory.
I could not have done that, says my pride.
There is no remembrance
of former things.
Love, making a god
from a grocery clerk.
The comic routines of poverty.
All things are filled with la
A bird shall carry the voice.

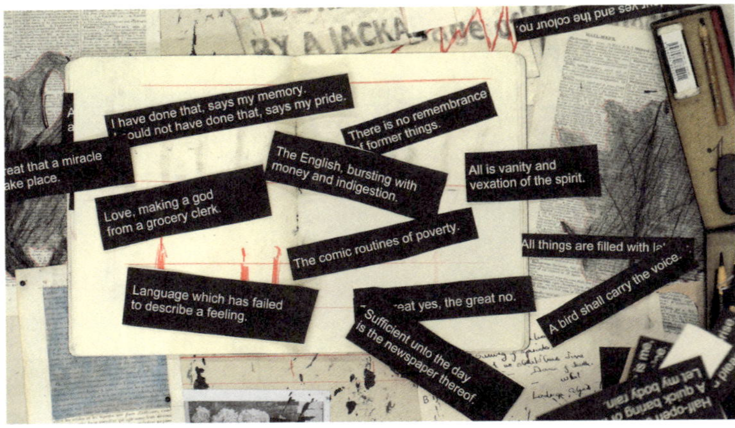
I have done that, says my memory.
ould not have done that, says my pride.
There is no remembrance
f former things.
eat that a miracle
ake place.
The English, bursting with
money and indigestion.
All is vanity and
vexation of the spirit.
Love, making a god
from a grocery clerk.
The comic routines of poverty.
All things are filled with la
A bird shall carry the voice.
Language which has failed
to describe a feeling.
eat yes, the great no.
Sufficient unto the day
is the newspaper thereof.

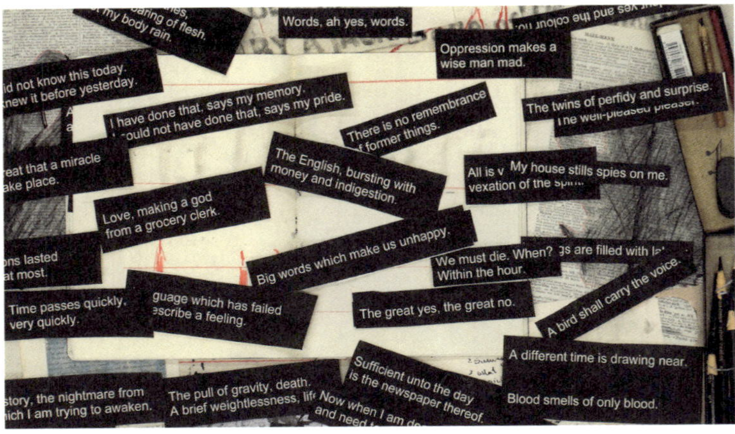
aring of flesh.
my body rain.
Words, ah yes, words.
Oppression makes a
wise man mad.
id not know this today.
new it before yesterday.
I have done that, says my memory.
ould not have done that, says my pride.
There is no remembrance
f former things.
The twins of perfidy and surprise.
The well-pleased pleaser.
eat that a miracle
ake place.
The English, bursting with
money and indigestion.
All is v My house stills spies on me.
vexation of the spir
Love, making a god
from a grocery clerk.
ns lasted
t most.
Big words which make us unhappy.
We must die. When? gs are filled with la
Within the hour.
Time passes quickly.
very quickly.
guage which has failed
escribe a feeling.
The great yes, the great no.
A bird shall carry the voice.
A different time is drawing near.
tory, the nightmare from
ich I am trying to awaken.
The pull of gravity, death.
A brief weightlessness, lif
Now when I am d
and need
Sufficient unto the day
is the newspaper thereof.
Blood smells of only blood.

(this is all from Freud's *The Psychopathology of Everyday Life*).

These texts would be transcribed, cut up, all the texts put on the table. Then rearranged, finding connections, allowing a whim to make the connection. Once they were assembled, perhaps ten pages of text, then began a process of rough editing. This is not aleatoric, it is not the automatic writing of the Surrealists. It is not chance at work, either in the choice of text, or in the fragments of the libretto, but neither is it planned. The construction comes from a place between.

The fat pig

There is one section of the chamber opera about the Sibyl of today. The algorithm has become our contemporary oracle. We rely on it all the time. To know what the weather will be tomorrow, we look at our phones. We understand our conundrum. On the one hand, we wish to starve the algorithm, not to be simply sources of data, to try to resist machine thinking.

It is said, for example, that when you apply for a bank loan, if you use the words "God," "promise," or "family" in your application, statistically it has been shown that the chances are you will not repay the loan, and so the bank will refuse your loan, or the computer will refuse your loan. The computer says NO. But if you use the word "university," and three other four-syllable words, the chances are you will repay your loan. So, the computer says YES. There is always an authoritarian element, subsuming the vagaries of the individual into the mass determinations of the data of the many.

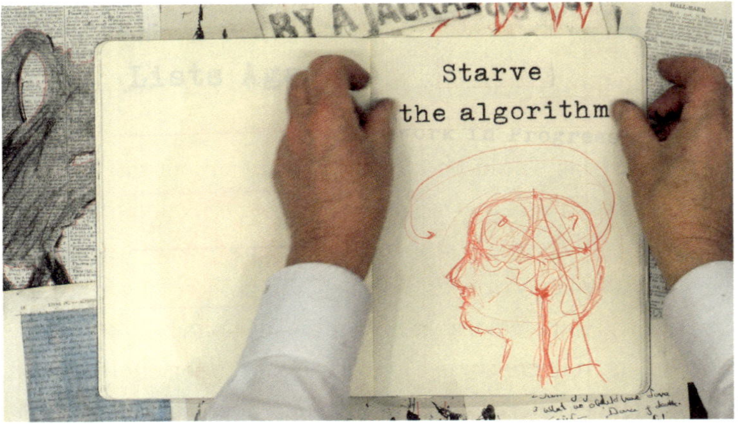

But one has to make a space for that which does not com-pute, that which cannot be owned by the algorithm. One needs to find a space for stupidity in the face of artificial intelligence, for understanding, at least in the studio, the role of stupidity, of doubt, of uncertainty.

One can think of the algorithm that surrounds us as this huge, fat sow with a teat for everyone to suck on. But instead of us getting fatter from what we draw from the sow, in fact, the teat is sucking us in. The sow gets fatter and fatter, more and more bloated, until, as Yeats would have said, who knows what fattened "beast, its hour come [round] at last, slouches towards Bethlehem to be born."

When I was nine, two trees were planted in our garden. My childhood was spent waiting for them to grow big enough to put a hammock between them. A few years ago, one of them was struck by lightning and died. This was shocking. A tree is meant to outlive us. If the tree would only survive sixty years, where did that leave us?

We grow our deaths inside us. From the moment we are born we are also growing our death; like a shoot or sapling, we grow our death inside us. The shock of a premature death is that the sapling inside us has not had a chance to grow to its fullness. We do not expect to outlive the tree, but that we should give the tree a chance to grow magnificently.

We know evasive action will meet the decisive strike. We have to take our chances against this. We know through indolence and elegance, we will do the work of fate. This is the terrain we live in. We know the ending, certainly. But in the space before the ending, we have to work as if that ending was not there.

Waiting for the Sibyl
2019
World premiere: September 11, 2019 at the Teatro dell'Opera di Roma, Rome
Composers: Kyle Shepherd and Nhlanhla Mahlangu
Costumes: Greta Goiris
Sets: Sabine Theunissen
Lighting: Urs Schönebaum
Video editor: Žana Marović

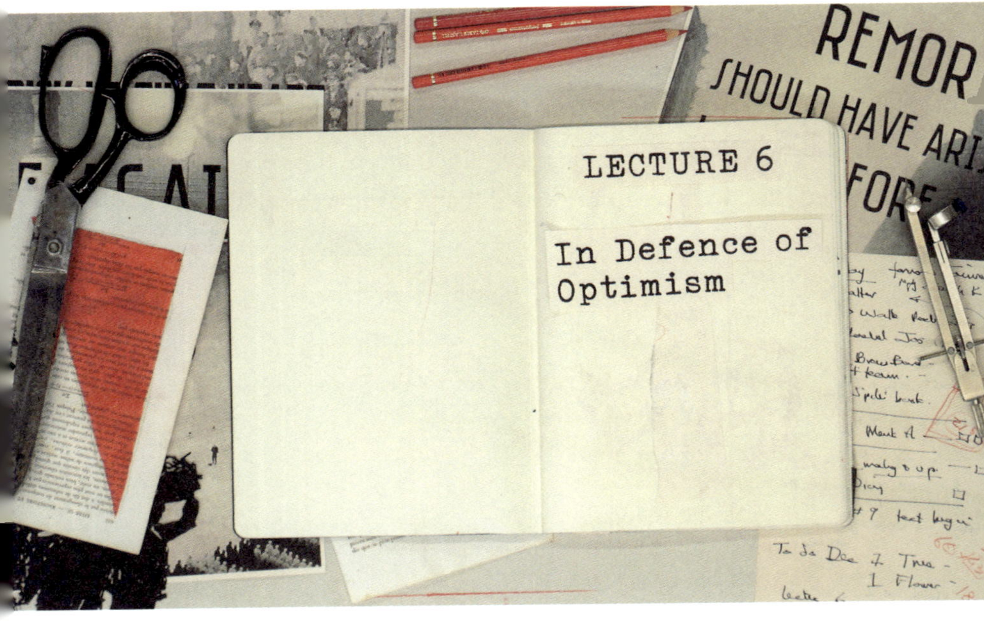
LECTURE 6

In Defence of
Optimism

A DEFENCE OF OPTIMISM

My notebook of 25 November 2021:

COVID NOTE.
INFECTIONS ALMOST AT ZERO.
THE MOUNTAIN RANGE OF INFECTIONS IS FLAT,
ALMOST AT SEA LEVEL.
TUESDAY: BRASS BAND IN THE STUDIO.
TOUR GROUP FOR SFMOMA ARRIVING.
START WRITING NOTES FOR LECTURE 6.

After the usual circling of the studio, I began. These were my notes:

A FINISHED DRAWING. IT IS MINE, BUT MORE THAN ME.

I leave the room, the drawing remains – the optimism is in that moment when the charcoal touches the paper. A movement from potential (all the drawings possible in the stick of charcoal), to a commitment, the work even if it is provisional and can be altered, erased and altered again. These were the first notes.

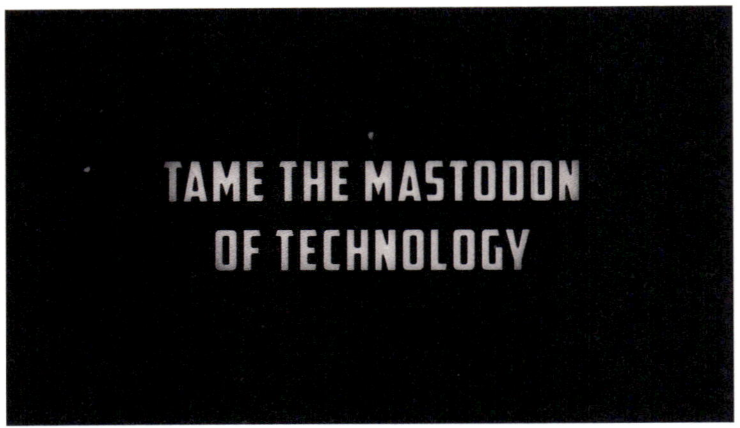

Ophelia

In 1927, the Soviet author Yuri Olesha published the novel *Envy*. It tells the story of the vicissitudes of a manufacturer of sausages. But what held me in the novel was a section (a subplot) about the invention of a perfect machine.

This is the era, the Soviet Union in the 1920s, when the hope for the future of mankind was seen in industry and technology, more production, more electricity, more subjugation of nature. Communism as Soviets plus electricity. Another novel of the period anticipated ChatGPT and recent advances in artificial intelligence. In *We* by Yevgeny Zamyatin (set unrealistically three hundred years in the future, rather than just the one hundred years in the future we now inhabit), there is technology that can write a lecture in five minutes, three sonatas in half an hour.

In *Envy* Olesha writes of Ophelia, the perfect machine that can do anything. It can blow up mountains, it can crush ore, it can replace the kitchen stove, it can make a new artillery weapon, it can solve differential calculus. A perfect machine. It can blow up the Eiffel Tower. The question of labour is solved. An anticipation of the current robotic and drone warfare.

But then the writer goes on:

"The bitch! The slut," here he is writing about Ophelia, "gets all sentimental, starts singing love songs of the last century!" and all collapses. This was half the work of the Soviet project – making machines do what humans did.

The corollary to this was again the idea of an industrialised world, but in this case making humans worthy of it. Leon Trotsky writes in 1926: "If only we could solve that part of the human machine known as psychology, we could make a person worthy of the new world being built." Humans and machines, circling each other like wrestlers trying to get a handhold.

To recall our history. Leon Trotsky, the righthand man to Vladimir Lenin in the Revolution of 1917 (this is a year after the Cabaret Voltaire of the Zurich Dadaists), was head of the Red Army in the civil war after the revolution and a rival of Stalin after Lenin's death in 1924. Stalin wins this battle. Trotsky and his faction in the Bolshevik party lose out. Trotsky is driven from power and in 1929 he is sent into exile.

These were the thoughts circling the studio. The optimism of making, questions of emancipation – the Russian Revolution ending the centuries of Czarist repression (with its echoes in

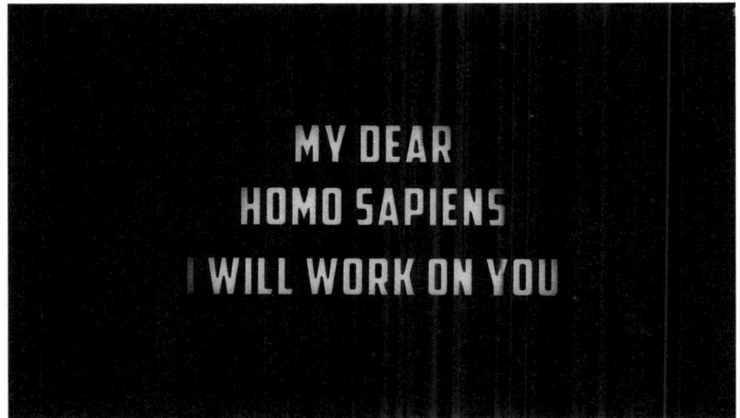

the South African apartheid era). Utopia – the wish, the need for an image of a less calamitous world. What does one do if optimism in the project of emancipation is no longer possible? The ideas by themselves give no answers. They need a material in which to manifest themselves. Grand questions in the world retreat into the studio.

Buyukada Island

Some years ago, I was invited to take part in the Istanbul Biennial, and hunted for some connection to this place, or to Byzantium or to Constantinople. What did I know of Istanbul? What line of connection did I have? Only a child's song came to me (my father used to sing it to us): "Constantinople – C-O-N-S-T-A-N-T-I-N-O-P-L-E – Constantinople. It's as easy to say as to sing your ABC."

That didn't get me very far. But then I was told that in Trotsky's exile, he spent three years on Buyukada Island outside Istanbul. And so the project, *O Sentimental Machine*, made for the Istanbul Biennial in 2015, began.

Trotsky, 1933, Istanbul. Revolution but also experiments in human psychology. The absurd pokes its head out at this prospect. I started thinking of Trotsky, goatee beard, declaiming his politics, emphatic gestures, rousing the crowds. I made a paper beard and cardboard glasses, found an old doctor's coat (similar to Trotsky's civil war jacket, buttoned to the neck). How little did one need to describe the specifics of the man? I filmed myself striding around the studio, standing on top of the studio ladder, addressing the drawings on the wall. Playing while working for an idea to emerge.

And then a gift: finding archival footage of Trotsky in a Dutch film museum. Trotsky making a speech in French, which was filmed in Istanbul, to be projected for French comrades. (He could not get a visa for France.)

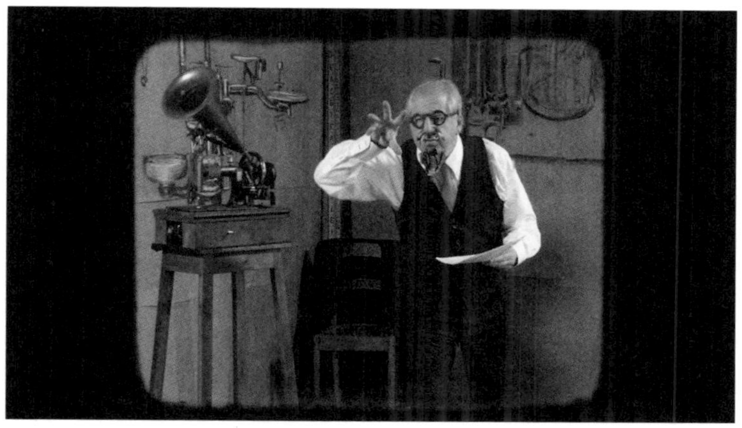

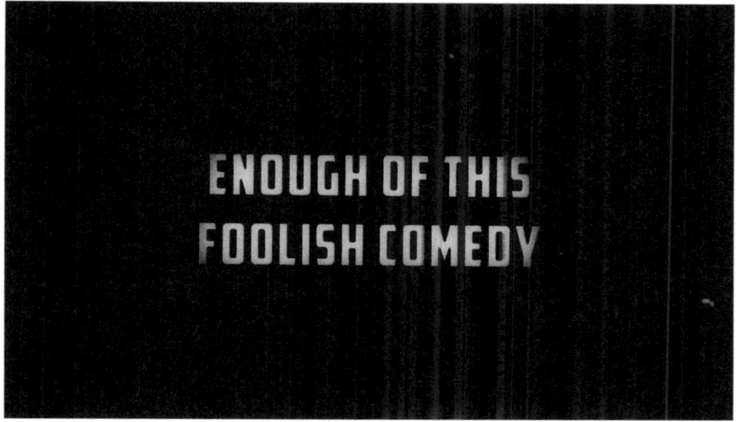

Duck Soup

Two further prompts. Firstly, *Swallows and Amazons*. I spoke in
Lecture 1 about children's books. This is a 1930 novel by Arthur
Ransome. Set in the English Lake District, Lake Windermere, and
Coniston Water. Children sailing their boats in these benevolent
waters. These books were published in my mother's childhood,
and she loved them. I read them and tried to love them on her
behalf. At any rate, my surprise to learn that Arthur Ransome had
married Trotsky's secretary. No imagination could have predicted

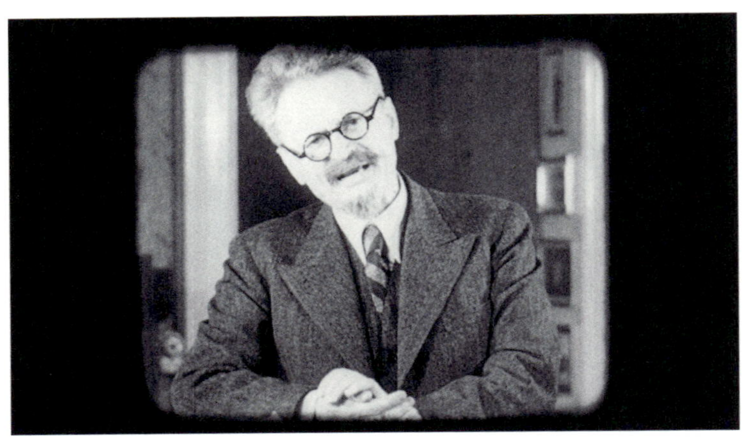

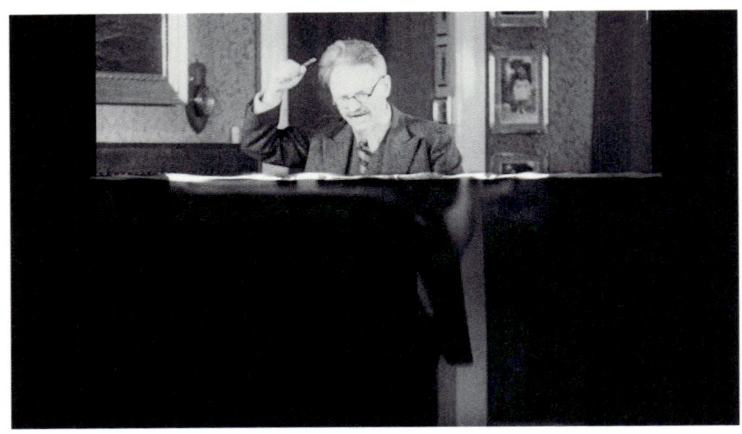

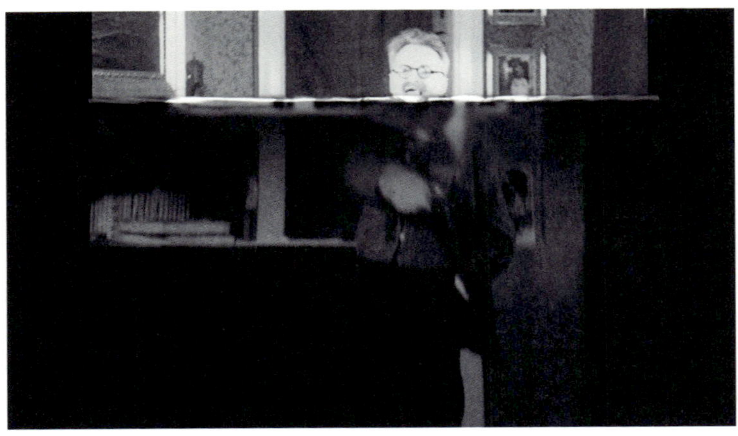

this, the paradox of the English childhood and the civil war in Russia – one latches on to such moments. We had machines falling in love. A megaphone stands in for the machines. We had a motorised megaphone in the studio, which had been made for a project on the history of time. It stood unused in the corner of the studio for some years. It was dusted off and brought in to perform the role of the lover. One project's detritus feeds the next. Trotsky. His secretary. A love affair with a megaphone and his secretary.

1933.
TROTSKY ON BUYUKADA ISLAND.
HITLER IN BERLIN.

And the Marx brothers masterpiece *Duck Soup*; in particular the famous mirror scene, in which two brothers play their mirror images. In our production we used an imagined mirror, but performed the same actions twice: first in front of and then behind the imaginary mirror. Essentially following the "Is it a mirror or isn't it a mirror?" game of *Duck Soup*.

Here were components enough and more than enough to set the project rolling. Often, there is an overdetermination of starting points, different branches coming together to make a blaze. The mirror scene from *Duck Soup*, the precise absurdity of the Marx brothers, the barely controllable megaphone, Trotsky's mechanical hand gesture while giving a speech.

Trusting the impulse

This lecture is about the optimism inherent in working in the studio. An optimism present in the very act of making a work.

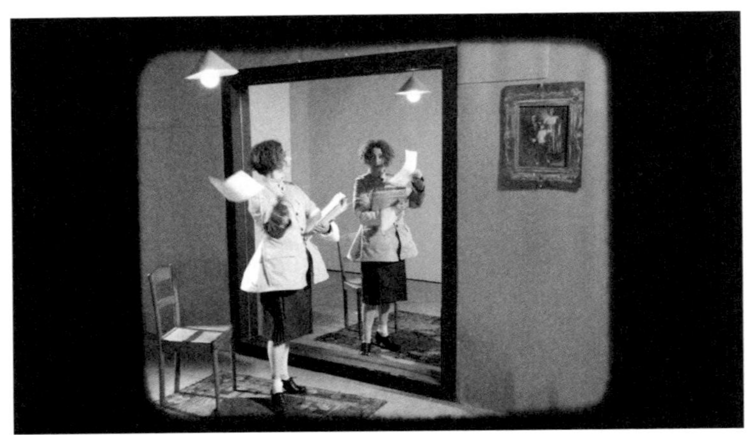

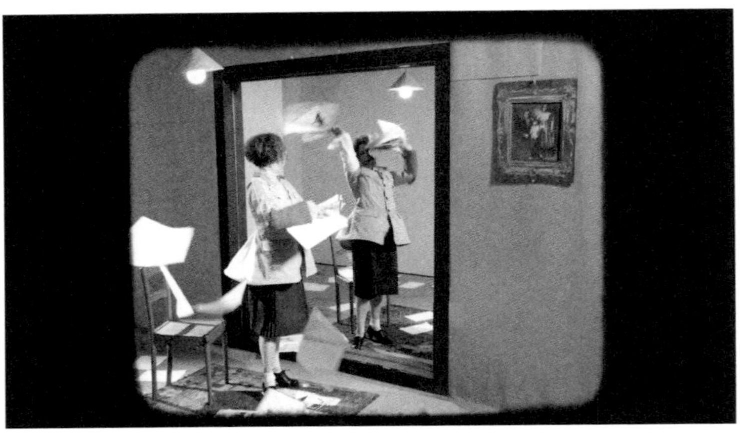

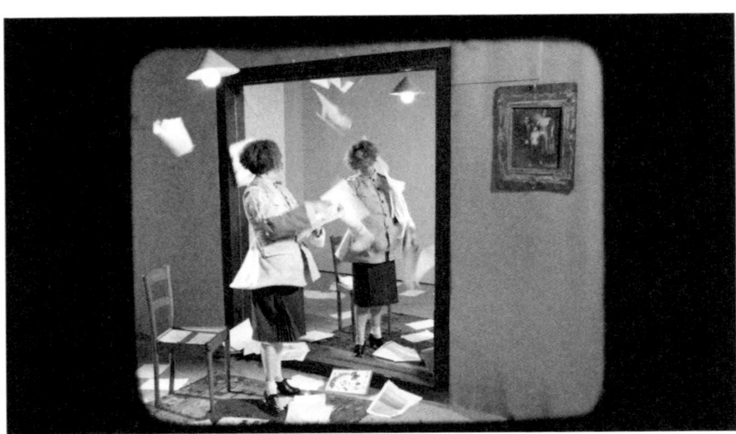

An optimism of agency in the arm moving across the paper (the notebooks in which I write). Whether the drawing is a jar of peonies or a bleak landscape, the very act of making something rather than leaving the paper blank implies (amongst many other things to be sure) a confidence in some future. The drawing finished – of looking at something now there that before was only potential (even if the viewer is only the artist himself). The utopia of reversals: what happens when you unmake something.

We look at film shown in reverse. The chaos of a table with its pot of ink overturned and brushes and pencils strewn across the studio, returned to a perfect order (a prelapsarian state). The delight in this reversal; this resistance to entropy – a performance of agency in itself; a demonstration of an impossible perfectibility. Again, the subject of the film is secondary. The outside world dissolves into the materials of the studio. How dark should the ink be? What is the kind of brush? How precise, or how loose should the work be? The fact of making it, the heat and energy of anticipation of making it, having in that an optimism (the excitement of the first glimmer of what the drawing or film might be, the sweat – I feel it in the pectoral muscles under the armpit, in the back of my tongue).

When what you are doing is not fast enough for the idea – the speeding up of the walk across the studio; when sentences can't finish themselves because the urgency of thought is too fast; not to miss the idea as it rushes out to be displaced by the next one, although one has to go back to find where the first impulse was abandoned, even if the excitement is misplaced and the final film, drawing, or sentence ends up so much more prosaic than intended. It often does.

Excitement and sweat do not on their own produce radiance. But in all these actions, there is a moving outward, a desire for the pen or charcoal to meet the paper that feels like an optimism.

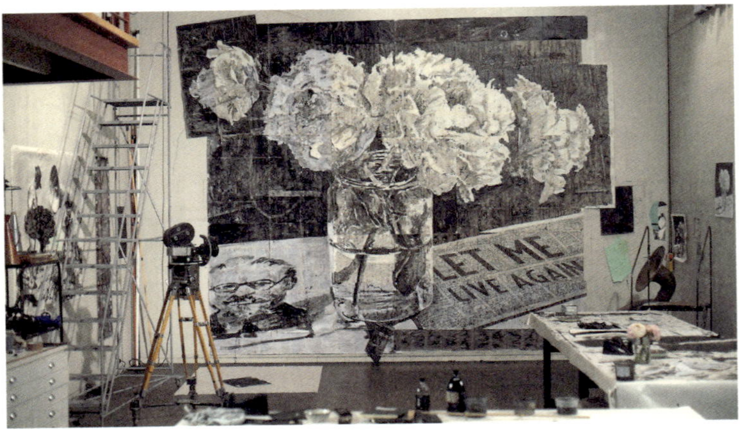

Symphony No. 10 in E minor

In 2020 I received an invitation from the Luzerner Sinfonieorchester to make a film to accompany a performance of a Shostakovich symphony. An orchestra with ninety-five musicians and their conductor, and behind them a screen on which the film will be projected. The broad task: how to make a film that is neither a background wallpaper to the music, nor a film that turns the symphony into a film score. Hoping the music will illuminate the images and that the images will enlarge how we hear the music.

Shostakovich's tenth symphony was first performed in 1953, a few months after the death of Stalin. Some critics have claimed the symphony as a portrait of Stalin. This specific question is not one which interests me, but I thought it would provide a lens through which to look at the Revolution of 1917 and the paradoxical position of artists during the time of the Revolution and the decades following.

Many different projects are swirling around in this lecture. I try to push it into shape, cutting and pasting, but it won't be pushed into a comfortable shape. Too straight a line misses the chaos of different projects overlapping and intersecting. The migration of different thoughts and images migrating across from one project into another.

October 1917

Here we are again, back in the years of the First World War and its aftermath. Not to look at it as a historical curiosity or historical calamity, but as a current question (as the looking at African troops as carriers in the First World War was not a study in history, but a way of circling the paradoxes of colonialism, in whose mire we still wade). The questions of the Russian Revolution are both inside and outside the studio. Questions of power and transformation that are the basis of the news daily in South Africa, but further afield, too.

Why Russia and the Bolshevik Revolution? There has been racial oppression in South Africa since the first white settlers arrived in 1652. But the codification and rigid enforcement reached its height after 1948 with the introduction of apartheid as state policy. So, through my childhood, adolescence, and adulthood, until I was thirty-five, the question of the ending of apartheid was inescapable. When? What? How? Would emancipation be achieved? This is not an abstract question, rather an immediate question of political rights, health, housing, education. There were movements of civil disobedience, nonviolent protests and in the end, an underground armed struggle.

My parents were both committed liberals and sceptical of all Marxist ideas and political movements. But they had many friends and colleagues who (in their commitment to ending apartheid oppression in South Africa) were communists – openly, until the law "The Suppression of Communism Act" made that illegal. Many continued in the underground. My sister, a stamp collector, would get the large, colourful CCCP stamps from friends of my parents who had regular communication with Moscow. I would help with floating the stamps off the envelopes. I was impatient and the Soviet glue was strong. I ruined many of her stamps of Anna Pavlova as the dying swan. Yuri Gagarin – this was in the 1960s.

Viva freedom, viva!

What different emancipatory paths should be followed? Maoism? Swedish social democracy? African socialism? Marxism? So, the example of Russia or the Russian Revolution was not an abstract historical nicety. The failure of the revolutionary project was evident not just in 1898 when the Soviet Union collapsed, but decades earlier. The contradiction between the promise of emancipation and the violence needed to enforce the promise became too evident to be willed away. But this did not remove the question of hope for a new society.

How did a project that started as emancipatory (from each according to their ability, to each according to their needs) go so wrong? A push towards both justice and equality (a naivety to think they were the same); a desire, a need, and urgency in that direction. We know the dangers of utopian thinking. The dangers of thinking one knows what is best for humanity.

From Plato, with the benevolent dictatorship of his Republic, to Robespierre and the apotheosis of its citizen, to Marx's certainty that the proletariat understood the world. To Lenin's Bolshevik party as the sole holders of the truth. And so on . . . All great ideas, which became a nightmare. Emphatic social certainty. All of them with the idea of forcing humanity into happiness by whatever means necessary.

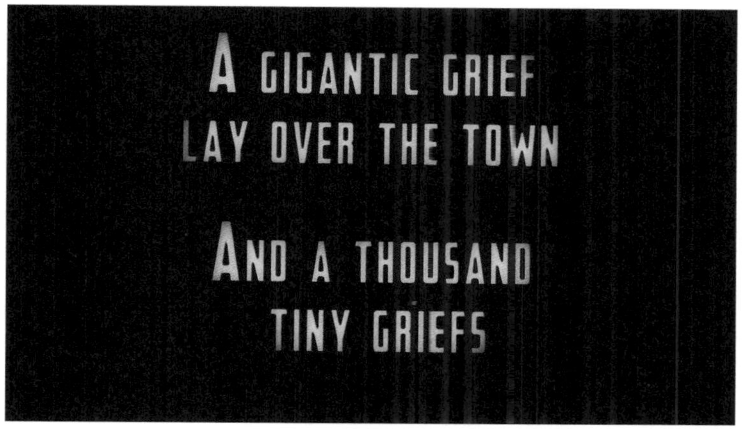

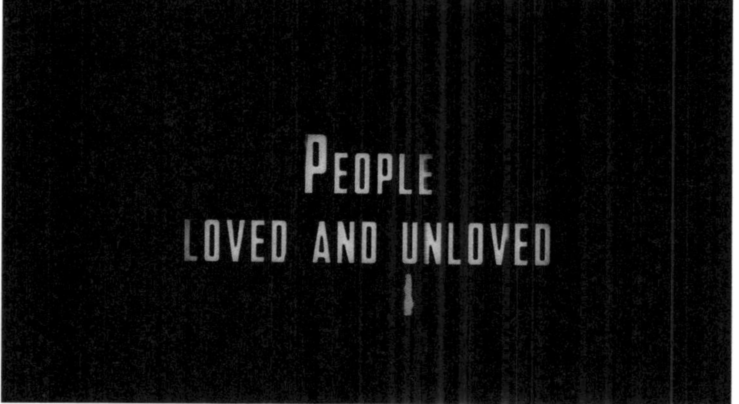

Save us from the grand ideas

But without utopia, without a wish in that direction, there is a gap, a lack. A lack both outside and, in the end, inside the studio. A hopelessness. How to fill this gap? Golf, Netflix, and conspicuous cuisine are not enough.

In the 1970s when I was a student there was a dominant understanding of the trajectory of the *avant-garde* in the visual arts. Its lineage was traced from the Impressionists to the

Post-Impressionists, Expressionists, and Fauves through to Matisse; and from him, around the time of World War II, across the Atlantic to artists in New York, the Abstract Expressionists and later to the New York colour field artists and a Greenbergian formalism which was dominant when I was a student. All of which seemed impossible to me, in its blindness to the political world, so inescapable in South Africa. But also impossible in the studio: oil paint and colour. My hands felt paralysed.

I needed to find a strand of modernism that kept a connection to the world, which I did in looking at expressionism, at the artists of the German *Neue Sachlichkeit* and the Russian Constructivists and Max Beckmann. The figurative was to be allowed in without it being either academic or reactionary. There were also abstract images. The work of El Lissitzky and other Constructivists was irresistible. The red wedge divides the white circle was an emblem for me of one kind of commitment. A commitment to the emancipatory impulse of the revolution made with great formal clarity. Still, 108 years later, the energy and formal inventiveness of that era is astonishing. I still look at the designs of books, of theatre sets from that period and am amazed. The early poems of Mayakovsky do not lose their power.

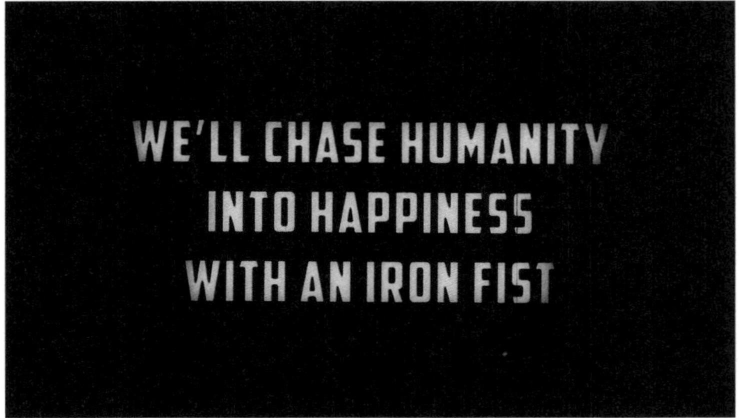

Of course, we read them now knowing the limits of that energy and enthusiasm. We know of the firing squads, the constructed famines, the gulag, the purges, the assassinations – their shadows continue to this day. Mayakovsky, the great poet of the revolution, who committed suicide at the age of thirty-six, can stand in for this disillusion: "My beloved boat is broken on the rocks of daily life. I have paid my debts, and no longer need to count the pains I have suffered at the hands of others. The misfortunes, the insults. As they say, 'The incident is closed.'"

To remember our history

Dmitri Shostakovich, Symphony No. 10 written in 1953. Four decades of death, four movements of the symphony. We try this as a structure but the music refuses to be constrained.

LENIN DEAD IN 1924 OF A STROKE.
MAYAKOVSKY SHOOTS HIMSELF IN 1930.
TROTSKY IS ASSASSINATED IN 1940.
STALIN DIES IN 1953.
SHOSTAKOVICH DIES IN 1975.

What remains? His symphonies are still played, now more than ever. He is the survivor.

I am not so much interested in the debate as to whether Shostakovich was a state artist, producing triumphant music for the state, or a secret dissident. Both are there, across all the music and all the decades. His survival during the years of Stalin doesn't tell us one way or the other. Many devoted Stalinists were shot, some nonbelievers survived. What I am interested in, particularly in his early years, as with Mayakovsky, is how

PEOPLE'S ARTIST
OF THE USSR

HERO OF
SOCIALIST LABOUR

the belief in the Revolution and the utopian transformation it promised, acted as a source of energy for his music.

Was the opening a breaking up or down of old social constraints, the traditional boundaries of art forms themselves – between music, sculpture, and film; or of writing, in the case of Mayakovsky?

This energy sustained him, even after the dangerous world he had moved into was clear (at the height of the purges, he would spend nights at the top of the stairs, a packed suitcase at his side, in expectation of the KGB).

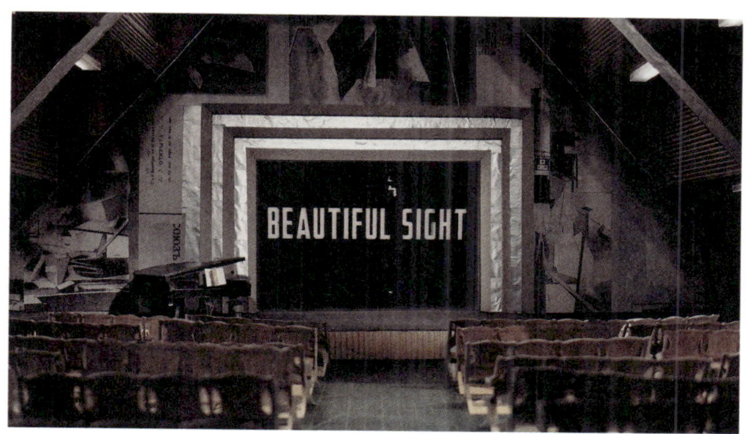
BEAUTIFUL SIGHT

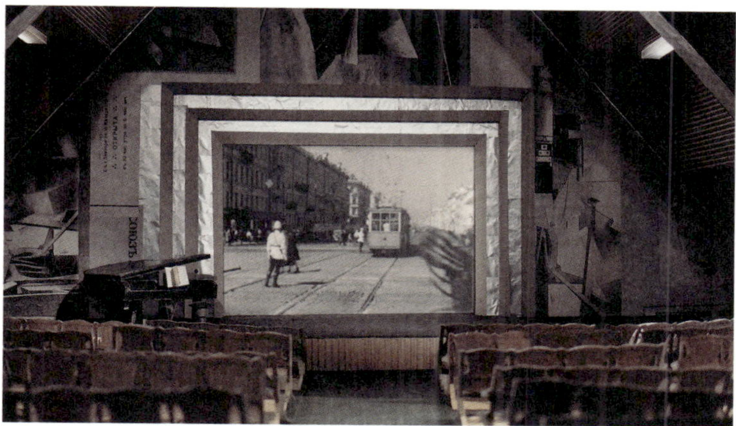

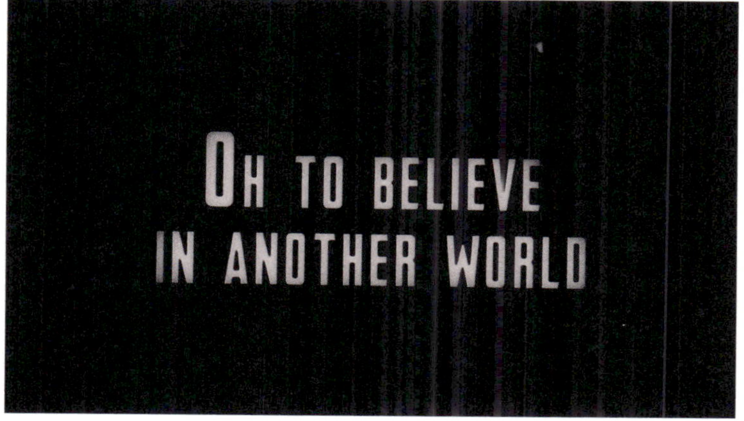
OH TO BELIEVE
IN ANOTHER WORLD

At the moment of the revolution all seemed possible. A new world waiting to be made. How did this feed into the studio? What is the connection between the extraordinary art made at this time and a belief in what the revolution offered?

Poetry, stage design, typography, photography, film – we are still digesting this. We have not yet caught up to 1929. How did the possibilities the revolution opened up (however short-lived) feed the studios, writing rooms, editing rooms, to yield such a flowering of inventiveness? And if this heady belief is no longer possible, where is that energy to come from?

It is impossible to think of utopia without invoking its underbelly of violence, as you cannot think of the Enlightenment without calling up its shadow of colonial conquest. The point is not to defend Utopian thinking, but to acknowledge the gap, the void we feel when its possibility is removed. The regret that such a belief is no longer possible, along with the energy and inventiveness that comes with the confidence in the transformation of the world.

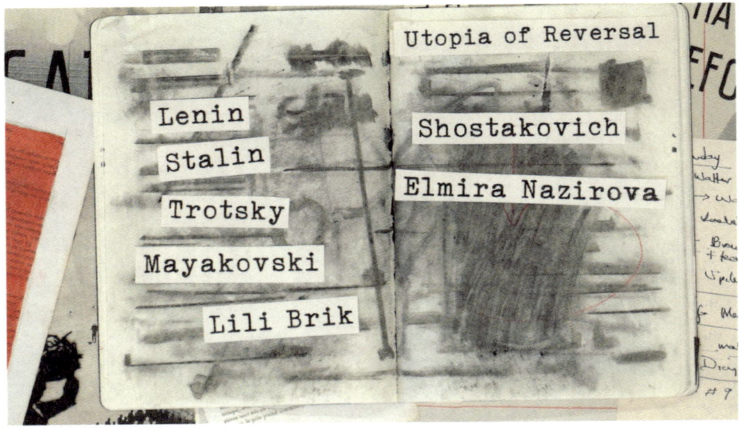

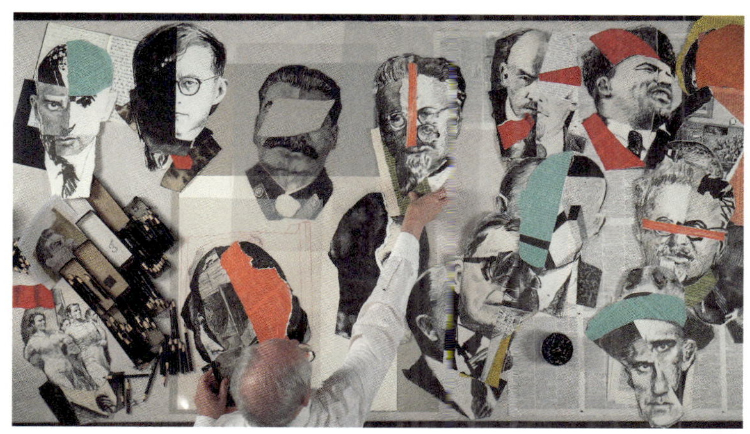

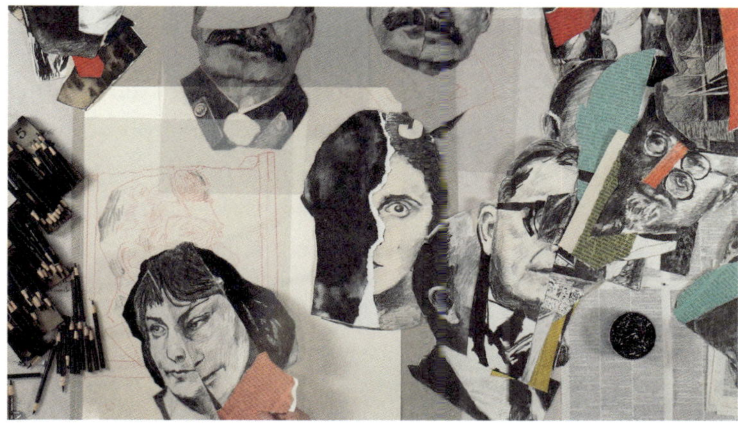

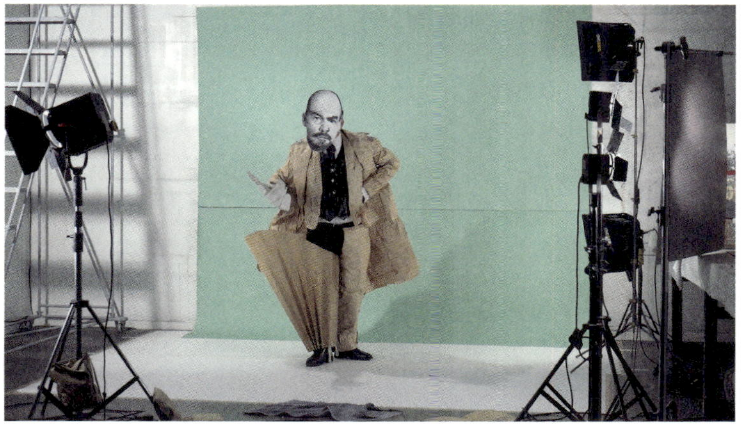

A gigantic grief and a thousand tiny griefs

Back to Shostakovich's tenth symphony.

    We assemble a cast of characters for the film.

THE POLITICIANS – LENIN, TROTSKY, AND STALIN.
THE POETS – VLADIMIR MAYAKOVSKY AND LILYA BRIK,
HIS LOVER AND MUSE.
SHOSTAKOVICH HIMSELF, OF COURSE.

And the composer ELMIRA NAZIROVA, with whom Shostakovich was in love, though apparently this was not reciprocated.

    I make cardboard portraits to be used as masks. Photographs retouched with Indian ink, to emphasise the eyes – the unblinking stare of the masks – looking back at us. The cardboard faces to be held in front of the actors, making them halfway between puppets and actors, a new language we have to learn.

    We gather in the studio: dancers, actors, editors, cameramen, costume and set designers.

All together now

The collaboration in the studio is deeply rooted. In the 1970s I was part of the Junction Avenue Theatre Company, a troupe of actors made up of students (white – the university was whites only) and librarians, cleaners and other staff at the university (black). The plays we made were dependent on the coming together in the rehearsal room. We all knew too well, that after each rehearsal, the white students would go home to the leafy suburbs and the black actors would go home to the township, some twenty kilometres from the city. The separations were huge (and in many ways remain even thirty years after the end of apartheid). But in the working space, the rehearsal room, there was a moment of how things could be, of an equality in contribution to the project – of a human contact away from the hierarchies within which all life outside the rehearsal room was lived. A glimpse of utopia.

One of the tasks of the studio is to make visible processes usually invisible in the world outside. To make time physical and visible in animation; to reveal that the meaning is constructed, not found – as in collage.

What is the tone of the Shostakovich film? If we are dealing with these calamitous histories, how are they to be approached? Through collage, not as the tragedy of the individual, not simple comedy, but trying to track the breakdown in logic, in language, through the absurd, even the comic grotesque? Depicting the events, but also showing the disjunctions and paradoxes we have to make sense of.

In the 1930s, Stalin has defeated Trotsky. Trotsky is sent into exile, first in Turkey, then in Mexico, where Stalin has him killed. Stalin is in control of the Soviet Union. One by one, his comrades in the Central Committee of the Communist Party are purged.

In the 1930s, the party is eating itself, divided against itself, and Bukharin, its most loyal member, is accused of treason. He has his back against the wall.

Finding the absurd

The transcript of Bukharin's trial by the plenum of the Central Committee of the Communist Party of the Soviet Union, February 1937 (an internal trial inside the Central Committee, before the public show trials that followed) is terrifying. Language games and banter (and much laughter) that we know (and they knew) would end with a man's execution (a bullet in the back of the head) in Lubyanka prison.

What tone is adequate to this contradiction? Laughter, not of defiance (though Bukharin does use humour to try to keep at bay the dogs circling for the kill) – laughter of complicity. The absurd emerges, not as a joke, but as a form of naturalism following the grotesque comedy of the trial.

Bukharin:	Whatever they are testifying against me is not true. (Laughter, noise in the room.) Why are you laughing? There is nothing funny in all this. But I cannot admit, either today or tomorrow or the day after tomorrow, anything which I am not guilty of. (Noise in the room.) I feel compelled to recall a certain ditty, which was published in its time in the now defunct *Russian Gazette*: "They may beat me, they may beat me senseless, they may beat me to a pulp. But nobody's gonna kill this kid, not with a stick, a bat, or a stone." (Laughter breaks out throughout the room.) I cannot say, however, that "nobody is gonna kill me."
Kaganovich:	Who, may I ask, is the kid here, and who the person wielding a stone?
Bukharin:	Obviously it was I who was struck and beaten with a stone. And now not a single member of the plenum, I dare say, thinks that I am concealing some sort of "stone" of resentment, not even the stone-faced Kamenev. (Laughter.)

Shkiriatov:	But they are all testifying against themselves.
Bukharin:	If I know who believed what in connection with this, why they were testifying against themselves, I would have told you. But I don't know . . .
Molotov:	And is their testimony plausible?
Bukharin:	Yes, it's plausible.
A voice:	You're lying! (Uproar in the room.)
Bukharin:	You can say "You're lying!" all you want.
Mikoyan:	And when Rykov, speaking about your note, says that where there is smoke, there is fire – is he telling the truth?
Bukharin:	Generally speaking, it seems there can be no smoke without fire. (Laughter.)
Mikoyan:	Well, that's precisely what we are talking about. (Laughter.)
Bukharin:	Why are you laughing? There is absolutely nothing funny about any of this . . . Please permit me to finish and explain this whole business to the best of my ability.
Kaganovich:	You are not very good at explaining it – that's the whole point.
Bukharin:	Whether I explain it well or poorly, I am speaking sincerely, my thoughts are sincere.
Kaganovich:	Not every act of sincerity is correct.
Bukharin:	In any case, I am speaking sincerely.
Molotov:	And we too are criticising you sincerely. (Laughter. Uproar in the room.)

I write this addendum on 11 December 2021. Round four or five of COVID-19 – still here – minus the anxiety. Rather with a changed anxiety – which of the panoply of long-term effects of COVID is coming towards us?

My father, ninety-eight when I started writing the lectures, is now 102 (and still sceptical of how I spend my days). The Shostakovich project, interrupted by the COVID lockdowns, has been completed.

When my children were young, I would make a puppet show for their birthday parties. The puppets were all made on the day of the party, assembled from objects in the house – a coffeepot in a doll's dress, a corkscrew, a bread roll as its head. This practice of assemblage continues in the studio, decades after the last puppet show.

During COVID, I was working long-distance with the costume designer, thinking about Mayakovsky. We made a series of puppets. Some in paper, some out of old tools. A thinking in garden shears, in cardboard, being led by the objects around us.

The puppets became a cast of characters looking for a home. Twenty-seven characters in search of a production or a stage. When the invitation came from the orchestra in Lucerne to make a film, these figures were already under construction. Some already made, some as collages, but a beginning. Could we make the film just using these puppets? How much affect could be generated by these almost inert objects?

We needed to expand the range of movement of the puppets. The puppets were very simple and had usually only one or two points of articulation. So, we thought of making the puppets as full-size human-scale costumes and having actors inside the structures of puppets.

Thinking in cardboard

We make a world to the scale of the puppets. We imagined the setting for the symphony as an abandoned Soviet museum. A tabletop world in cardboard. For once a model that was not

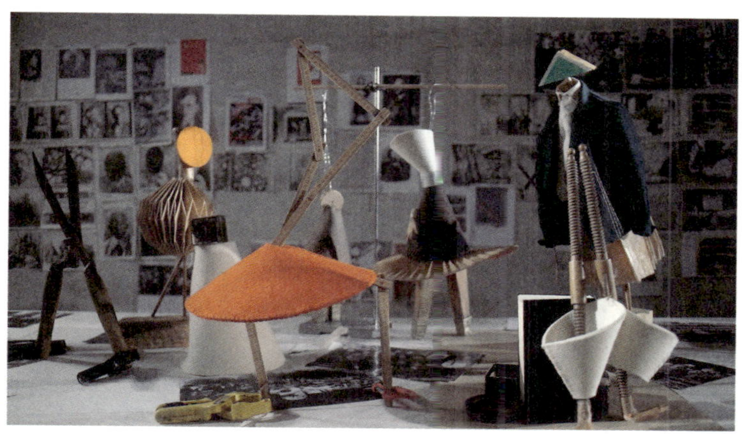

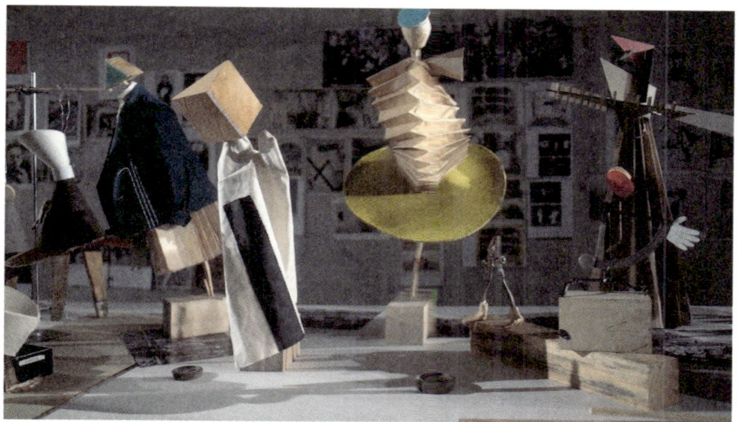

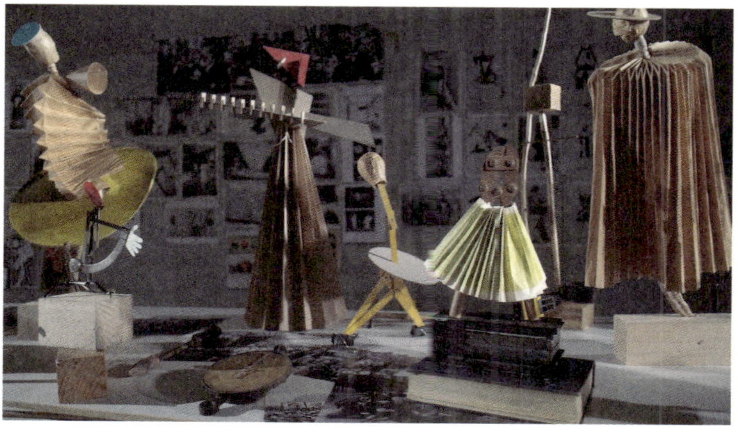

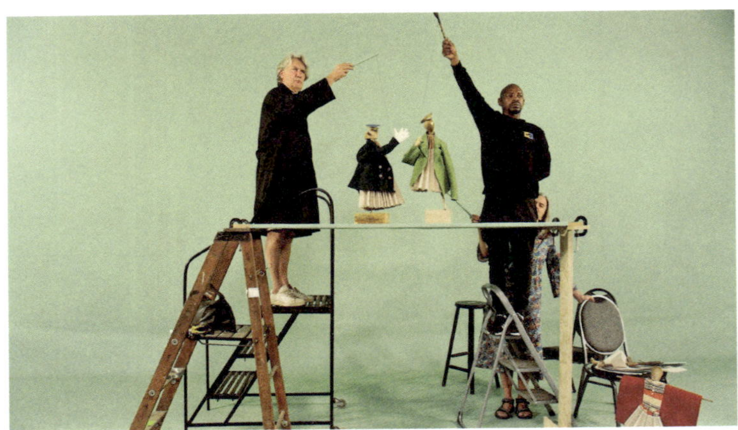

there to be enlarged to the size of a stage. Using a phone or a miniature camera, we filmed and pushed the camera through the cardboard rooms. The scale could be altered in the editing and in the projection. A twenty-centimetre wall can become fifteen metres on the screen behind the orchestra.

CARDBOARD
SANDPAPER
COPIES OF PHOTOGRAPHS
MASKING TAPE

There was a free-form accumulation of fragments. Walls and rooms could be rearranged on the studio table. We made archways, colonnades of corrugated cardboard, corridors with display cases and dioramas, large empty halls. An endlessly flexible space, a labyrinth of a museum. We gave the Soviet museum a public swimming pool, each tile cut out of insulation tape. We made a community theatre, chairs of cutout photographs, and a sliding cardboard curtain.

There was a whole grammar to learn of the performance of the cardboard heads and cardboard costumes, the speed of the gesture. What feels comfortable as an actor, became illegible when performed behind a mask. We discovered we needed a far more deliberate movement, a stillness between movements. Each on its own quite simple and learnable. Together, they transform the mask and character from a familiar body behind a piece of cardboard to an irresistible presence of the character on the mask. A double vision of seeing the performer at work but being unable to resist the sense of agency of the cardboard character. The mask and the costume make their own demands.

The project, the film for the symphony, starts to find a form. In the first movement we move through the corridors of an abandoned museum (a cardboard museum about fifteen inches high, a miniature camera pushed through on a stick). We film the characters (politicians, poets) against a green screen, shrink them and composite them into the film of the museum. Photographs from the 1920s are exhibited in the corridors of the museum (where shiny wooden floors are made with masking tape and shoe polish) and there are also characters visiting the museum. The puppets made from tools – a yellow pleated skirt on a pair of pliers – are placed in the vitrines that line the corridor. A public swimming pool is lined with ceramic tiles made from fingernail squares of plastic insulation tape. The corrugated cardboard Doric columns are both cardboard and stone. We learn the transparency of the technique as we go – even the masks can at times be removed.

Archival films from the Soviet Union in the 1920s are used for the driving, raucous second movement – tractors, printing presses, Shostakovich at his piano. A romantic interlude in the third movement for Shostakovich and Elmira Nazirova (with text from a 1920s love poem of Mayakovsky). We film Stalin in his cardboard costume on top of the diving board, gun in hand. We spin a disc with portraits of the members of the Central Committee and black their faces out with ink (to intercut with

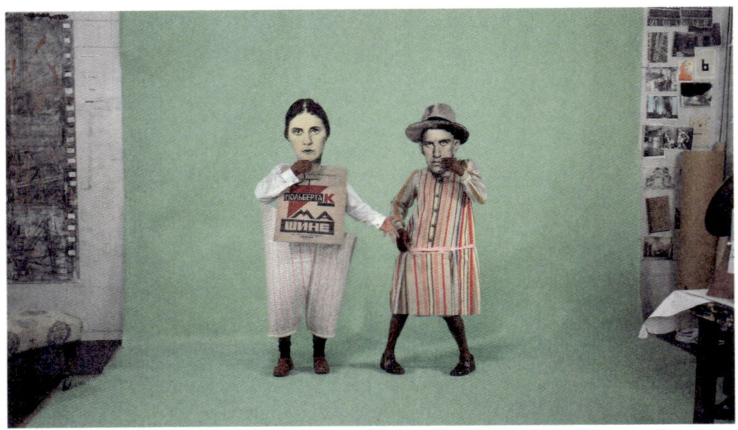

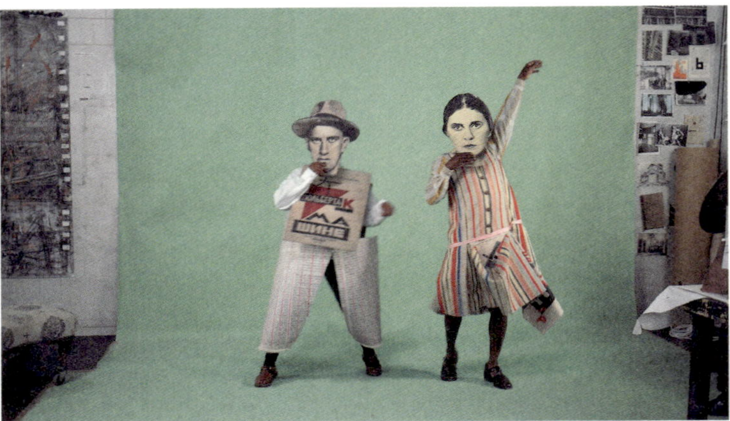

Stalin firing his revolver). This for the heart of the fourth movement. The final blaze of the coda shows all the protagonists dancing in the empty cardboard swimming pool. We wait to see the film with the orchestra in front of it, at its first performance.

There is no answer

This is an obvious question. How can we let the material, the vagaries and inessential nature of the material, be the basis for a meaning? Cardboard heads push one meaning forward. But if ink or charcoal had been used, would we arrive at a completely different shape, a different meaning? Here we have cardboard, not ink. One path taken, not another. We live with what we have. We work with material as assiduously and sincerely as possible.

The place we have reached, a cardboard understanding of where we are, arrived at by a mixture of habit, observation – and there is a polemic here – the belief in uncertain endings. We are in the realm of the absurd, but not comedy or tragedy. But with a confidence in this as a way of both describing and understanding the world.

This confidence does not in any way reduce the 4 a.m. panic, when it is clear that the project can only be a failure. The cardboard museum and cardboard heads cannot sustain the fifty-three minutes of the symphony, nor match up to the orchestral music in front of the projection. The only hope is that the panic can be productive – throwing all the elements into doubt (that had seemed in place during the rehearsal) in the hope that in the morning, they will have landed in a better place. Usually a vain hope.

The optimism I think of is not a confidence in the project finding a form that can hold its different impulses together. It is not a question of temperament, or of having a sunny disposition. I have a more than cautious pessimism over the future of my country and further afield. Optimistic and pessimistic futures both unfold. To hold on to only one or the other is a distortion. One needs to contain both.

The optimism at work is stronger than doubt, anxiety, or rational assessment of conditions. It sits in the space between the hand and the paper, the mask and the actor. It sits in the dark carbon of the stick of charcoal, in the ink-filled barrel of the fountain pen. It proclaims itself as the first mark is made.

Oh To Believe in Another World
2022
A film to accompany the performance of Shostakovich's
Symphony No. 10 in E Minor
World premiere: KKL, Lucerne, 15 June, 2022 with the
Luzerner Sinfonieorchester
Video editors: Janus Fouché, Žana Marović
Costumes and puppets: Greta Goiris
Sets and models: Sabine Theunissen
Cinematography: Duško Marović

IT IS FINISHED

IT IS FINISHED
BRAVO

BRA A A VO
BRA A A A A VO

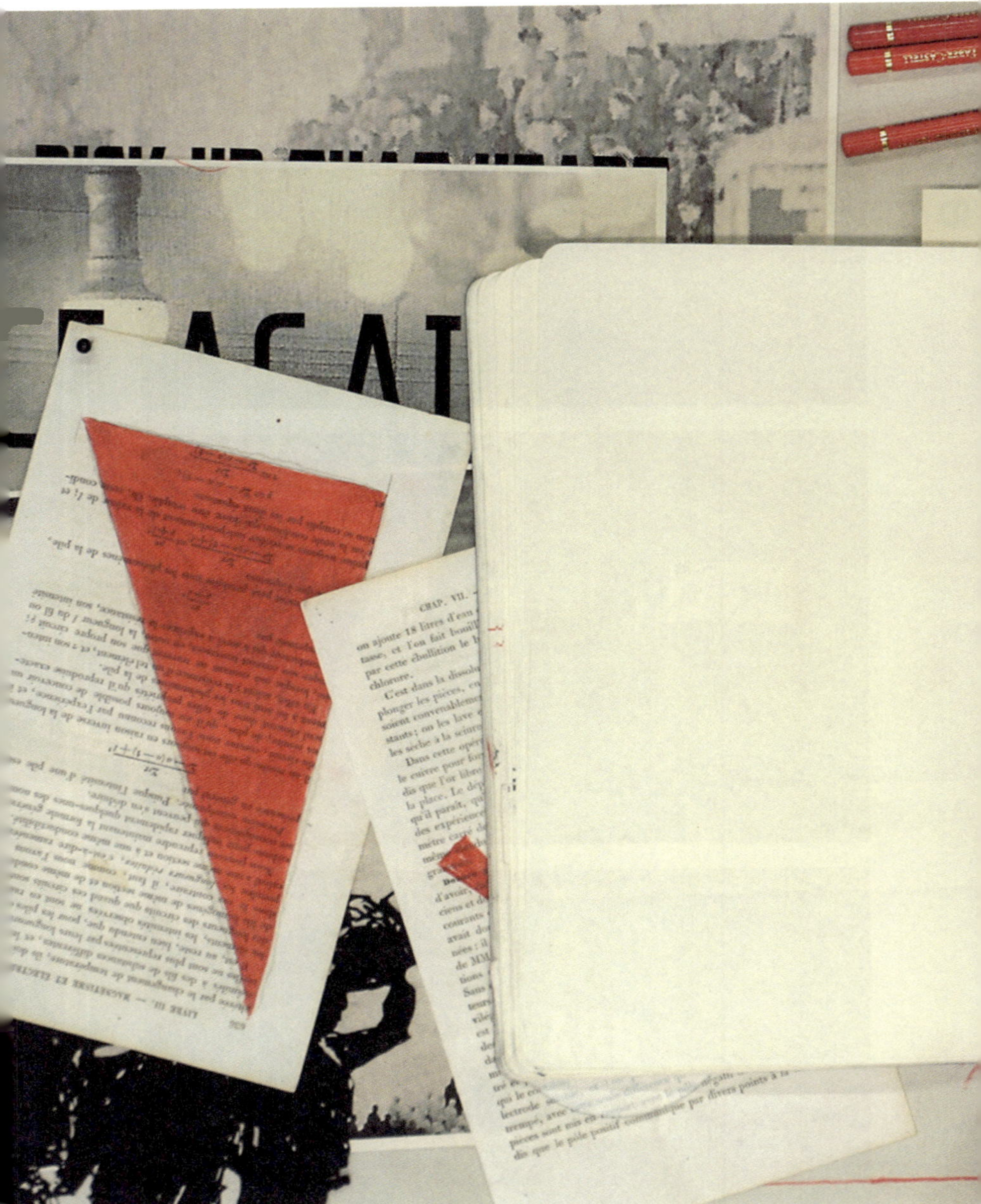

End Here

REMORSE SHOULD HAVE ARISEN BEFORE